# Bumper Book of
# Baby Names

Georgina Wintersgill

## foulsham
LONDON • NEW YORK • TORONTO • SYDNEY

# foulsham

The Publishing House, Bennetts Close, Cippenham,
Slough, Berkshire, SL1 5AP, England

Foulsham books can be found in all good bookshops and direct from
www.foulsham.com

ISBN: 978-0-572-03338-5

A CIP record for this book is available from the British Library

Georgina Wintersgill has asserted her moral right to be identified as the
author of this work

Printed in Dubai

# Contents

# Choosing Your Baby's Name

Congratulations – you are expecting a baby! And now for one of the most exciting and enjoyable parts of the preparation … choosing a name. Of course you want something you love the sound of (after all, you may be yelling it for the next 18 or so years!) but you are probably looking for something with a good, positive meaning too. You may be after something that will make your child stand out – in a good way, of course – or looking for a name that will reflect your heritage, whether that's African, Asian, Cornish or Irish.

But choosing a name isn't just fun – it will have a huge impact on your child's whole life, not only in the playground but also in the workplace and beyond. So you'll want to look for names that could help your child get on in life, while avoiding ones that could potentially embarrass or define him or her. And then there's the difficulty of finding something that works with your surname.

If it sounds like a minefield – well, maybe it is. But don't worry; our tips will guide you through how to make the right choice without slipping up. And with a selection of 5,000 names to consider, we're sure you'll find 'the one' in this book. The names listed here are mostly from English-speaking countries, but we've also included some with Asian, African, Oriental and European influences. Happy hunting!

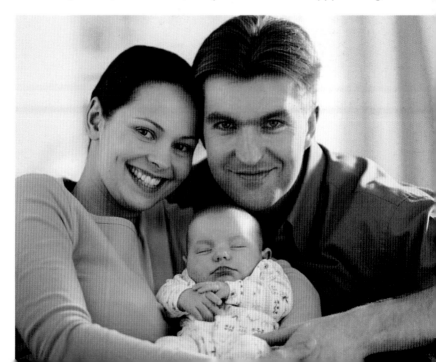

# Things to Think About

There are many elements to choosing a name, some of which are listed below. It's a good idea to go through each, one at a time, jotting down thoughts and ideas as you go.

Your notes don't only have to comprise names you like the sound of. You can make a note of any reminders that might be useful in your decision-making process, so put down things you don't like as well as things you do. Surprisingly, it can help to guide you in the right direction.

## What kind of name do you want?

Firstly, ask yourself what you are looking for – whether you'd like something traditional, modern, religious, exotic or unique. Do you want to find a name that reflects your heritage – perhaps a first name that harks back to your partner's Asian roots and a second name that honours your Scottish granny?

If you are thinking about using a family name, consider whether the other side of the family will feel left out or snubbed – if so, you may have to promise to name your next child after your in-laws' side! And if you'd love to honour your grandad but don't fancy his first name, consider using his surname instead. Using surnames as first names is currently very fashionable but also has a long heritage – for example, we may think of Grant, Dean and Keith as first names, but actually they all started life as surnames. Many surnames work well for girls, too – what about Taylor, Harley or Cassidy?

## Are you going to use a middle name?

Of course, you don't have to, but it's a particularly good idea to choose more than one name if you have a common surname. It is also useful in this world of modern global communication; fifty years ago, you would never have met up virtually with hundreds of people through e-mail! It also gives your child the option of using it if (heaven forbid!) they hate their first name, without having to change their name by deed poll.

As a rule of thumb, if you wouldn't even consider giving your choice of middle name as a first name, think twice. You may think the school bullies will never find out your child's middle name but – don't kid yourself – they will!

# Do the names sound good together?

Say the complete name – first name, middle name and surname – out loud, over and over again. You may find that the first and middle names you spent so long choosing simply don't sound right together, or don't go with your surname. A short first name may sound better with a long surname (Max Bickerstaff rather than Maximilian Bickerstaff), or an unusual first name may work better with a common surname, and vice versa. Also beware of names that rhyme (Michaela Taylor) or sound too similar (Joseph Jarvis).

# Check the initials don't spell anything embarrassing

If Oscar Douglas Downes is considered a bit, well, ODD… then you have only yourselves to blame. Watch out for acronyms, too: TBC (to be confirmed), DOA (dead on arrival) and LBW (leg before wicket) will all raise a snigger when they're written on your child's lunch box or gym bag. Finally, check how the initials work with your surname. IM Batty, RU Shaw, B Hynde and R Sole are all best avoided.

# Look out for teasing opportunities

Does the name rhyme with anything unfortunate (Silly Billy, Charlotte the Harlot)? Or are there obvious jokes that will be made about it (Nelly the Elephant, Ten-Ton Tessie)? Look at the short forms in this context, too: Richard may be called Dick. Yes, children will always find something to tease their peers about, but try not to make it easy for them!

# Check out the meaning and associations

Don't choose a name just because you like the sound – it's wise to know what it means, too. Will baby Cameron really thank you for 'bent nose' or Rachel for 'ewe'? Other meanings are distinctly underwhelming. Fabian means 'bean' while Brogan means 'shoe' – hardly names to aspire to!

And how about the associations? Ophelia is a beautiful Shakespearean name, so it's unfortunate that the character went mad and committed suicide. And remember that associations change over time. To you, the name Hannibal may only bring to mind the outstanding general who led his army across the Alps, but for most people the name is now unavoidably connected with Dr Hannibal Lecter, the fictional serial killer in the book and film *The Silence of the Lambs*.

# Look at the short forms

If you love the name Lily but hate Lil, how will you feel when that's what her friends end up calling her? Because sooner or later, it will happen. Also, check that any shortened versions of the name still work with the surname. Nathalie West and Benjamin Dover sound fine, but Nat West and Ben Dover are in for a lifetime of tiresome quips.

Alternatively, if you love the short form of a name but aren't that bothered about the longer version, are you happy just to register your child as Katie, say, rather than Katherine? Short forms are very fashionable at present, with names such as Jack, Harry, Alfie, Evie and Ellie proving much more common than the formal versions. But be aware that giving your child the formal version – Eleanor, say, rather than Ellie – will increase her options as it will allow her to choose which name she prefers at different stages of her life. She may go with Ellie as a child, Elle as a teenager and Eleanor when she starts training to be a lawyer!

# Will the name always be appropriate?

It's all too easy to forget that you are choosing a name for life, not just for a baby. Mimi might be adorable for a tiny newborn, but will it still suit her when she's trying to make a name for herself as a forensic scientist – or a wrestler? Try to come up with a name that will suit her through all her life stages and whatever she decides to do or be. Imagine her using it as a surly teenager, when she's applying for university, when she wants to be taken seriously in a high-flying career, when she's a middle-aged mum and when she's a pensioner.

# Avoid names that define your child

If you call your newborn Tiger, what if he prefers collecting stamps to schoolyard scraps? If you call her Bella, what if she's plain? And if you call him Romeo, what if he's the shyest boy in school who never gets a date? It's great to give your child an inspiring name, but try to avoid monikers that could make them feel that, through no fault of their own, they've failed to come up to your personal standards. After all, they should feel free to be the person *they* want to be, not who you want them to be.

It's also wise to think twice about names that might stereotype your child. It's only natural that people will expect Brutus to be a little tyrant and Lolita a teen temptress. It can be hard to break out of these kinds of stereotypes – and they may even end up shaping your child's character.

# Think carefully about stand-out names

Wouldn't it be great if celebrities started calling their babies John and Sarah? Instead, most of them seem to be looking for a unique name that will express their child's 'individuality' (or at least give the parents a bit of extra publicity).

Think twice before giving your child a thoroughly wacky name. Of course, she may love constantly being in the limelight – or she may just be embarrassed every time she introduces herself. It's all very well being called Fifi Trixibelle if you hang out with the stars – but what if you hang out at the local park? And what about when your child's trying to be taken seriously as an accountant – will her name open doors or close them?

So, if you love the name Fifi, there's nothing to stop you calling her that for short – but in years to come she may be grateful if her birth certificate says Fiona.

# Will the name date?

Beware of choosing a name that seems very modern as, chances are, it will seem equally dated in a few years' time.

For the same reason, think twice about naming your child after a current celebrity. At the very least it will date her in years to come (you can't get away with knocking ten years off your age if you were named after Shirley Temple, Marilyn Monroe or Kylie Minogue!) The worst case scenario is that in ten years' time the formerly A-list celebrity namesake will be a washed-up alcoholic reduced to occasional appearances on reality TV shows.

# Is the name gender-specific?

These days, it's increasingly popular to use traditionally male names for girls (Jordan, Ashley, Cameron). If you are considering one of these, remember your daughter may have to spend the rest of her life correcting people who assume she's a Mr not a Ms. Using a more obviously female spelling may help clear up any confusion: for example, Darcy for a boy but Darcey or Darcie for a girl. Also, try to give her an unambiguously female middle name (Ashley Kate, for example, rather than Ashley Rowan).

# Is the name easy to pronounce and spell?

It's tempting to make a commonplace name unique by deliberately choosing an unusual spelling – Melaney rather than Melanie, for example. But the truth is, your child is unlikely to thank you when people misspell their name for the rest of their lives.

Similarly, be wary about names that are difficult to pronounce. Niamh (pronounced 'Neve') may have to get used to being constantly addressed as 'Nyam'. One solution is to spell the name phonetically, like the actress Neve Campbell – or prepare your child for a lifetime of correcting people.

And what about very complicated names? Zephanaiah is an unusual Biblical name and will certainly stand out at nursery (and at school … and in the workplace …) But he'll rarely get a birthday card with the correct name on the envelope and will have to get used to being introduced to people by the wrong name – if at all. So don't be surprised if he's calling himself 'Z' by the time he's a teenager. Or Bob.

# Is the name sufficiently different from other family members?

It may sound very cute to call your three sons Jake, Josh and Joe – but three lots of Mr J Jones in a family will lead to lots of confusion, especially when they start opening each other's exam results and cashing each other's cheques!

Think twice about using 'matching' names, too – especially with twins. It's very tempting to go for Cleo and Coco, or Billy and Bobby, but it's bound to lead to mix-ups. And there will come a time when your children are desperate to be seen as individuals, not one of a pair.

# Check the name's popularity

Before making your final decision, make sure your child isn't going to share his first name with half the nursery. After all, you probably remember having five classmates at school with the same first name – and the fact that they all ended up being known by their surnames or unflattering nicknames.

Check out this year's most popular baby names at the following websites:

UK names: www.statistics.gov.uk
Irish names: www.cso.ie
US names: www.ssa.gov
Canadian (British Columbia) names: www.vs.gov.bc.ca
Australian (New South Wales) names: www.bdm.nsw.gov.au

If you are still keen to use a name in the top five, consider choosing a more unusual middle name.

# Being Imaginative

There's never been a more exciting time to choose a name, as unusual celebrity choices mean it's now quite acceptable to call your child after a fruit, flower or place, or even an emotion or concept. Or, of course, you can just make up a name!

If you are looking for something a little out of the ordinary, literature, films and television, folklore and myth will all provide lots of suggestions. We've also compiled six themed lists that may help you give rein to your imagination. Those expecting girls are likely to find more scope for choosing something really unusual, but there are still plenty of options for the boys.

# Fruits, flowers and plants

Naming baby girls after flowers became popular in Victorian times, and pretty, old-fashioned names such as Rose, Daisy and Lily are once again extremely fashionable. However, celebrities have pushed the boat out with names such as Apple and Bluebell, and it's now quite acceptable to choose more unusual botanical names. Check out gardening books for inspiration (but make sure you don't choose a weed – or anything poisonous!).

Some of the most popular ideas for girls are: Cherry, Holly, Iris, Jasmine, Poppy and Willow.

Boys are less well represented but you may like to think about: Aspen, Bracken, Moss, Rowan and Sage.

**Girls**
Acacia
Anemone
Anise
Apple
Aspen
Azalea
Bay
Begonia
Berry
Betony, Bettony
Blossom

Bluebell
Briar
Briar-Rose
Bryony, Bryonie,
Briony
Camellia
Cherry, Cherrie
Chrysanthemum
Cinnamon
Clematis
Clove
Clover

Cypress
Daffodil
Dahlia, Dalia
Daisy
Fern, Fearne
Flax
Flower
Hazel
Heather
Holly, Hollie
Hyacinth
Iris

Ivy
Jasmine, Jasmin
Jonquil
Juniper
Laurel
Lavender
Lilac
Lily, Lili, Lilly, Lillie
Lotus
Magnolia
Marigold
Mimosa
Myrtle
Olive
Orchid
Pansy, Pansie
Peach, Peaches

Peony
Pepper
Petal
Petunia
Plum
Poppy
Posey, Posie, Posy
Primrose
Primula
Rose
Rosemary
Rowan
Saffron
Sage
Sorrel
Sugar
Sweetpea

Tansy
Tigerlily
Violet
Willow, Wyllow
Zinnia

**Boys**
Ash
Aspen
Bay
Birch
Bracken
Cedar
Leaf, Leafe
Moss
Rowan
Sage

# Precious things

Parents have been naming their children after gemstones for thousands of years, and it's once again very fashionable. If you are looking for a precious stone with a special meaning for your baby, why not check out their birth stone? Alternatively, look at stones with a special meaning for you and your partner – perhaps the stones in your engagement ring.

Some of these girls' names are popular: Amber, Ebony, Jade, Pearl, Ruby and Sapphire.

Ideas for boys might include: Garnet and Jet.

| **Girls** | Garnet | Silver |
|-----------|--------|--------|
| Amber | Goldie | Topaz |
| Amethyst | Ivory | |
| Beryl | Jade | **Boys** |
| Coral | Jewel | Bronze |
| Crystal, Chrystal | Opal | Garnet |
| Diamond | Pearl | Jade |
| Ebony | Ruby | Jet, Jett |
| Emerald | Sapphire | Silver |

# Colours

Novelist Margaret Mitchell started the trend for giving colours as names when she chose the name Scarlett O'Hara for her feisty Southern belle heroine in her 1936 novel *Gone with the Wind*. But there have always been names with meanings that refer to hair or skin colour – Melanie, for example, means black, while Rufus means red or ruddy. There is also a long tradition of giving people nicknames based on their hair colour: how about Sandy, Goldie and Ginger?

Scarlett, which has had a recent popularity boost thanks to actress Scarlett Johansson, remains the most popular colour name, but there are plenty of others to consider. Check out colour charts and artists' paint names for inspiration.

Girls' names that you may consider are: Blue, Cerise, Magenta and Sienna.

You are less likely to find boys named in this way but you might want to set a trend with: Gray, Indigo or Teal.

| Girls | | Boys |
|---|---|---|
| Aqua | Magenta | Auburn |
| Auburn | Mahogany | Azure |
| Azure | Pink, Pinkie | Blue |
| Blue | Rustie, Rusty | Crimson |
| Cerise | Scarlet, Scarlett | Cyan |
| Crimson | Sienna | Gray, Grey |
| Cyan | Tawny | Indigo |
| Indigo | Teal, Teale | Rust, Rusty |
| | Turquoise | Teal |

# Qualities, virtues, emotions and concepts

The Victorians loved using virtues as names – and although names such as Chastity and Prudence have yet to come back into fashion, the idea of naming your baby after a quality, characteristic, emotion or concept (Grace, Bliss, Harmony) is once again very popular. It's certainly a good way to give your child a name with a strong, positive, aspirational meaning – rather than just one that sounds nice! In the US, one of the fastest-climbing names of recent years is Nevaeh – which is 'Heaven' spelled backwards.

For inspiration, try writing down a list of the qualities you value most.

For girls' names, you might think about: Charisma, Destiny, Faith and Liberty.

For boys' names, perhaps you could try: Maverick or Rebel.

**Girls**
Bliss
Blythe
Candour
Caprice
Charisma
Charity
Chastity
Clarity
Clemency
Comfort
Constance
Destiny
Diva
Faith
Fidelity
Fortune
Gentle
Glory
Grace
Harmony
Heaven
Heavenly
Honesty
Honor, Honour
Hope

Infinity
Innocence
Integrity
Joy
Joyous
Justice
Liberty
Love
Loyalty
Mercy
Merry
Modesty
Mystique
Nirvana
Patience
Peace
Precious
Promise
Prudence
Purity
Sassy
Serendipity
Serenity
Spirit
True
Truly

Truth
Unique
Unity
Utopia
Verity

**Boys**
Candour
Justice
Kingdom
Maverick
Rebel

# Place names

Naming your child after a country or town is currently very fashionable, but the tradition goes way back; in fact, many of our surnames come from place names.

One advantage of a place name is that there are so many to choose from, your child shouldn't end up with half a dozen namesakes in their class. What's more, there's unlikely to be a problem with spelling or pronunciation as the name should still sound familiar (depending on the place you choose, of course!).

Another advantage is that you can choose somewhere that has a special meaning for you. It might be the place where your partner proposed or where your family comes from (whether Devon or Africa). However, if you decide to name your baby after the place in which he or she was conceived, best keep the reason for your choice quiet – or it could become a lifelong source of embarrassment for your child!

For inspiration, check out a map book or atlas – you'll find the choices are almost limitless.

Girls' names you might already know include: Asia, Egypt, India, Iona, Lourdes and Paris.

This is one theme that favours boys and girls equally, so you may know of: Arran, Brooklyn, Preston and Tyrone.

| **Girls** | China | Jordan |
|---|---|---|
| Africa, Afrika | Cuba | Kendal, Kendall |
| Alabama | Dakota | Kenya |
| Arizona | Dallas | Lourdes |
| Asia | Delphi | Montana |
| Atlanta | Devon | Montserrat |
| Beverley, Beverly | Egypt | Nairobi |
| Britney, Brittany | Florida | Nebraska |
| Cairo | Geneva | Nevada |
| Camden | Georgia | Odessa |
| Capri | Havana | Olympia |
| Carolina | India | Paisley |
| Catalina | Indiana | Paris |
| Chelsea, Chelsey, | Iona | Persia |
| Chelsie, Chelsy | Jamaica | Philadelphia |

| | | |
|---|---|---|
| Phoenix | Dallas | Nebraska |
| Riga | Damascus | Nevada |
| Sahara | Denver | Oslo |
| Savannah | Derby | Panama |
| Senegal | Devon | Paris |
| Siena | Dublin | Pembroke |
| Skye | Dudley | Perth |
| Tobago | Fife | Phoenix |
| Trinidad | Hamilton | Preston |
| Valencia | Hampton | Rhodes |
| Venice | Harlem | Richmond |
| Verona | Harlow | Rio |
| Vienna | Hastings | Royston |
| Zaire | Henley | Scafell |
| | Houston | Senegal |
| **Boys** | Hull | Sherwood |
| Arran | Indiana | Stafford |
| Austin | Israel | Stanford |
| Bexley | Jericho | Stanton |
| Boston | Jordan | Sutherland |
| Brooklyn | Kendal, Kendall | Tennessee |
| Buxton | Kent | Tobago |
| Cairo | Lagos | Toledo |
| Camden | Leicester, Lester | Troy |
| Carlisle, Carlile, Carlyle | Lewis | Tyrone |
| Caspian | Lincoln | Utah |
| Cayman | Livingston | Vegas |
| Chester | Ludlow | Warwick |
| China | Memphis | Wellington |
| Cuba | Milan | York |
| Dakota | Montana | Zaire |

# Nature

Using the natural world as a source of inspiration became fairly common in the 1960s and 1970s – and names such as Meadow, River and Sky are increasingly popular again. Animals have always been a huge source of inspiration: Orson means 'bear cub', for example, while Everard means 'strong as a wild boar'.

If you are looking for a name with a meaning that's special for your baby, consider their star sign – such as Leo or Gemini; the time of year at which they'll be born – Summer, Autumn; or the month – April, May.

If you are still undecided about names by the time of the birth, you can also consider the day of the week – Wednesday, the daughter from *The Addams Family* cartoon, TV series and films, springs to mind; the time of day or night – Dawn or Star; and even the weather – Storm or Misty.

Examples of girls' names include: Brooke, Echo and Honey.

Popular boys' names might be: Forest, Glen and Heath.

| Girls | | |
|---|---|---|
| April | Friday | Panther |
| August | Frost | Pony |
| Autumn | Gemini | Rain, Raine, Rayne |
| Beck | Haze | Rainbow |
| Bird, Birdie | Honey | Raven |
| Breeze, Breezy | Jaguar | River |
| Brooke | January | Robin, Robyn |
| Bunny | July | Saturday |
| Dawn | June | September |
| December | Kitten | Shadow |
| Dell | Lake | Sierra |
| Delta | Lamb | Sky |
| Dove | Lark | Smokey, Smokie |
| Dusk | Libra | Snow, Snowy |
| Echo | May, Mae | Spring |
| Ember | Meadow | Star, Starr |
| Falcon | Misty, Mistie, Mysty | Storm |
| Fawn | Monday | Summer |
| February | Moon | Sunday |
| Fen, Fenn | November | Sunny |
| Flame | Ocean | Swift |
| | October | Tempest |

Thursday
Tuesday
Vale
Wednesday
Winter
Wren

**Boys**
Aries
Beck
Bird, Byrd
Brook
Conch
Dale
Eagle
Falcon
Fen, Fenn

Flint
Ford
Forest, Forrest
Fox, Foxx
Frost
Glen, Glenn
Granite
Hail
Hawk, Hawke
Haze
Heath
Ice
Jaguar
Lake
Marsh
North
Ocean

Peat
Pisces
Raven
River
Robin
Rock, Rocky
Scorpio
Shade
Shadow
Storm
Stone, Stoney
Swift
Taurus
Tempest
Wolf, Wolfe

# Registering Your Baby's Birth

You've made your choice and you're happy with it. Now for the official part!

You are legally required to register your baby's birth. If you live in England, Wales or Northern Ireland, you have to do this within 42 days of the birth. If you live in Scotland, you have just 21 days.

If you gave birth in hospital, it's often possible to register the birth there. If not, look in the *Yellow Pages* to find your nearest register office. It's best to go to the office in the district where your baby was born, but if this isn't possible you can go to any register office and they will forward the details to the appropriate district office. A birth certificate will then be posted to you from there, so it will take a day or two longer. Most offices require you to book an appointment, though some offer a drop-in service.

If you and your partner were married at the time of your baby's birth, then either of you can go to the register office (you don't have to bring your baby). If you live in Scotland, you will need to take your marriage certificate. If you weren't married but you want the father's details entered in the register, it's easiest if both parents go together. However, if this isn't possible, contact your local office for advice on what to do.

If you gave birth in hospital, it's useful to bring your hospital discharge summary, if you have one.

You'll be interviewed by a registrar who will need the following information:

## About the baby

- Full name. Make sure you and your partner have agreed on the exact spelling of first and other names and which surname the baby will use.
- Gender.
- Date of birth.
- Place of birth.
- Time of birth if you are registering twins, triplets or more, or if you live or are registering the birth in Scotland.

# About the mother

- Name, and maiden name, if applicable.
- Address.
- Date of birth.
- Place of birth.
- Occupation or last occupation.
- Date of marriage, if applicable, and place of marriage, if you live or are registering the birth in Scotland.
- Number of other children, if applicable.

# About the father

If you wish, you can choose not to include the father's details.

- Name.
- Address, if you live or are registering the birth in Northern Ireland.
- Date of birth.
- Place of birth.
- Occupation or last occupation.
- Date of marriage, if applicable, and place of marriage, if you live or are registering the birth in Scotland.
- Number of other children, if applicable.

# Checking the record

After the registrar has taken all the information, you'll be asked to check the record and sign it. You'll then be given one free, short birth certificate – just showing your baby's name, gender, place of birth and date of birth – and a registration card. You'll need the card to register your baby with a doctor and the birth certificate for a number of reasons, such as applying for Child Benefit.

If you want more copies or a full birth certificate, showing all the information you've given to the registrar, you'll have to pay a small fee. If you don't have to wait, the process should take about half an hour.

For more information, visit www.direct.gov.uk.

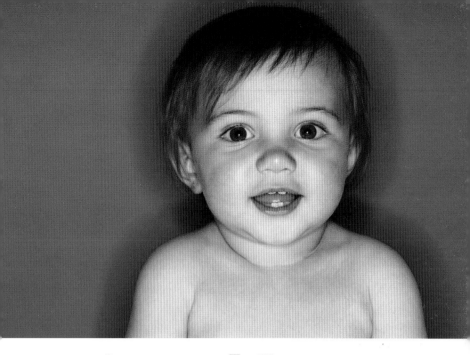

# Girls' Names
## A–Z

My Notes

# A

| Name | Definition | Short forms/ Variations |
|------|-----------|------------------------|
| **Aaliya** | Dignified (Arabic) | *Aaliyah, Aliyah* |
| **Aarini** | Brave, daring (Sanskrit) | |
| **Abbie** | Short for Abigail or Abilene | *Abbey, Abby, Abi* |
| **Abelone** | Danish form of Apollonia: from the Greek sun god, Apollo | |
| **Abi** | See **Abbie** | *Abbey, Abby* |
| **Abielle** | Female form of Abiel: my father is God | |
| **Abigail** | Source of joy (Hebrew) Once a common name for a lady's maid | *Abbey, Abbie, Abby, Abi, Gail* |
| **Abilene** | Grass (Hebrew) | *Abbey, Abbie, Abby, Abi* |
| **Abir** | Fragrance (Arabic) | |
| **Abital** | Dewy (Hebrew) | *Avital* |
| **Aboli** | Flower (Sanskrit) | |
| **Ada** | Noble (Germanic) | |
| **Adah** | Adornment (Hebrew) | |
| **Adair** | Negotiator (Scottish) Traditionally a boy's name | |
| **Addie** | Short for Adelaide, Adele, Adeline or Audrey | *Addy, Adi* |

| Name | Definition | Short forms/ Variations |
|---|---|---|
| **Addison** | Originally a surname, meaning Addie's son. Also a boy's name | |
| **Adeela** | To act justly (Arabic) | |
| **Adela** | See **Adele** | Adèle, Adélie, Adeline, Della |
| **Adelaide** | Noble kind (Germanic) | Ada, Addie, Addy, Adi, Alida |
| **Adele** | [A-dell] Noble (Germanic) | Addie, Addy, Adi, Alette, Della / Adela, Adèle, Adélie, Adeline |
| **Adelheid** | German form of Adelaide: noble kind | Heidi |
| **Adélie** | See **Adele** | Adela, Adèle, Adeline |
| **Adeline** | French pet form of Adele: noble | Addie, Addy Adelina, Adi |
| **Adelita** | Spanish form of Adele: noble | |
| **Adelpha** | Sisterly (Greek) | |
| **Adi** | See **Addie** | Addy |
| **Adina** | [A-dee-na] Slender (Hebrew) | |
| **Aditi** | Infinity (Sanskrit) | |
| **Adora** | Adoration (Spanish) | |
| **Adria** | See **Adriana** | |
| **Adriana** | Female form of Adrian: man from Hadria, a town in northern Italy | Adria, Adrianna |
| **Adrienne** | French female form of Adrian: man from Hadria, a town in northern Italy | Adrianne |
| **Aegle** | Brightness, splendour (Greek) | |
| **Afon** | River (Welsh) Also a boy's name | |
| **Afra** | See **Aphra** | |
| **Agatha** | Good, honourable (Greek) It may have gained in popularity thanks to the crime writer Agatha Christie | Aggie, Aggy |
| **Aggie** | Short for Agatha or Agnes | Aggy |
| **Agnes** | Pure (Greek) Lamb (Latin) | Aggie, Aggy, Nessa, Nessie, Nest, Nesta / Annice, Annis, Ines |
| **Ahlam** | Vision of perfection (Arabic) | |
| **Aida** | [Eye-ee-da] Gift (Arabic) | Ayeeda |

| Name | Definition | Short forms/ Variations |
|------|-----------|------------------------|
| **Aifric** | Pleasant (Irish Gaelic) | |
| **Aika** | Love song (Japanese) | |
| **Aiko** | Beloved child (Japanese) | |
| **Aileen** | Scottish form of Helen: sunbeam | *Ailie, Ailleen* |
| **Ailie** | Short for Aileen | |
| **Ailis** | Noble (Irish Gaelic) | |
| **Ailsa** | Ailsa Craig is a rocky inlet off the Ayrshire coast in Scotland | |
| **Aimée** | [Ay-mee] Beloved (French) | *Amy* |
| **Aine** | Radiance (Irish Gaelic) In Celtic myth, Aine is queen of the fairies | |
| **Aisha** | [Aye-ee-sha] Alive, thriving (Arabic) | *Ayesha* |
| **Aishi** | Life (Sanskrit) | |
| **Aisling** | [Ash-ling] Dream or vision (Irish) | *Aislin, Ashling* |
| **Akemi** | Bright beauty (Japanese) | |
| **Aki** | Autumn; bright (Japanese) Also a boy's name | |
| **Akiko** | Child born in autumn (Japanese) | |
| **Akira** | Bright; dawn (Japanese) Also a boy's name | |
| **Alaina** | Female form of Alain, the French form of Alan: rock | |
| **Alana** | Female form of Alan: rock | *Alanah, Alanna, Alanis, Alannis, Alena, Alina* |
| **Alanda** | Female form of Alan: rock | *Alana, Alanah, Alanis, Alanna, Alannis, Alena, Alina* |
| **Alannah** | Child (Irish Gaelic) | *Lana / Alana, Alanah, Alanis, Alanna, Alannis, Alena, Alina* |
| **Alannis** | See **Alannah** | *Alanis* |
| **Alba** | White (Italian) | |
| **Alberga** | Noble (Teutonic) | |
| **Alberta** | Female form of Albert: noble knight | *Albertina, Albertine* |
| **Albertine** | See **Alberta** | *Albertina* |
| **Alda** | Old (German) | |
| **Aldara** | Winged gift (Greek) | |
| **Aledwen** | Female form of Aled: child | |

28

| Name | Definition | Short forms/ Variations |
|------|-----------|--------------------------|
| **Alena** | [A-lee-na] See **Alannah** | *Alina, Lena, Lina* |
| **Alessa** | Short for Alessandra | |
| **Alessandra** | Italian form of Alexandra: protector | *Alessa, Sandra, Sandy* |
| **Alethea** | Truth (Greek) | *Thea* |
| **Alette** | French pet form of Adele: noble | |
| **Alex** | Short for Alexandra or Alexandrina. Also a boy's name | *Alix* |
| **Alexa** | Short for Alexandra or Alexandrina | *Alessa, Alexia* |
| **Alexandra** | Protector (Greek) | *Alex, Alexa, Alexis, Ali, Alix, Lexie, Lexy, Sandra, Sandy, Sasha, Xandra, Zandra / Alexandria, Alexandrina, Alexandrine, Alexina* |
| **Alexandrina** | See **Alexandra** | *Alex, Alexa, Rina, Xandra, Xandrina / Alexandrine* |
| **Alexia** | See **Alexis** | |
| **Alexina** | See **Alexandra** | |
| **Alexis** | To defend (Greek) Also a boy's name | *Lexie, Lexy / Alexia* |
| **Alfreda** | See **Elfreda** | *Freda* |
| **Ali** | Short for Alexandra, Alice, Alison or Allegra | *Allie, Ally, Aly* |
| **Alice** | True (Greek) Noble (German) Became popular after the publication of Lewis Carroll's 19th-century novel *Alice's Adventures in Wonderland* | *Ali, Alicia, Alisha, Alison, Alissa, Alyce, Alys* |
| **Alicia** | [A-liss-ee-a] See **Alice** | *Alesha, Alicea, Alisa, Alisha, Alisia, Alissa, Alyssa* |
| **Alickina** | Female form of Alick, short for Alexander: to defend | *Kina* |
| **Alida** | Short for Adelaide | |
| **Alina** | [A-lee-na] Fair-haired (Scottish, Slavic) Lovely (Gaelic) | *Lena, Lina / Alena, Aline* |
| **Alisha** | See **Alice, Alicia** | *Lisha* |
| **Alison** | See **Alice** | *Ali, Allie, Ally, Ali / Allison, Allyson, Alyson* |

| Name | Definition | Short forms/ Variations |
|------|-----------|-------------------------|
| **Alissa** | See **Alice, Alicia** | |
| **Aliyya** | [Al-eye-a] Female form of the Arabic name Ali: excellent | Aaliyah, Aliyah |
| **Aliza** | Joyful (Hebrew) | |
| **Allegra** | Cheerful (Italian) Traditionally used as a musical term. Thought to have first been used as a name for the daughter of 19th-century poet Lord Byron | Ali, Allie, Ally |
| **Allie** | Short for Alison, Allegra or Allison | Ally |
| **Allison** | See **Alison** | Allie, Ally |
| **Alma** | Nourishing, kind (Latin) | |
| **Almira** | Woman from Almeira (Spanish) | |
| **Aloha** | [Al-o-a] Love (Polynesian) | |
| **Aloise** | Female form of Aloysius: fame; war | |
| **Alouette** | Lark (French) May have gained in popularity thanks to the French children's song *Alouette* (despite the fact this describes plucking a lark in preparation for eating it) | |
| **Alpa** | Small (Sanskrit) | |
| **Alpha** | The first letter of the Greek alphabet | |
| **Althea** | To heal (Greek) | Thea |
| **Alva** | White (Old Irish) | |
| **Alyson** | See **Alison** | Ali, Allie, Ally, Aly / Allison, Allyson |
| **Amabel** | Lovable (Latin) | Mabel, Mabli / Amabella, Annabel |
| **Amal** | Hope (Arabic) Also a boy's name | |
| **Amala** | Pure (Sanskrit) | |
| **Amalia** | See **Amelia** | Amélie, Emilia, Emily |
| **Amanda** | Lovable (Latin) | Mandie, Mandy |
| **Amani** | Aspirations (Arabic) | |
| **Amantha** | Combination of Amanda (lovable) and Samantha (female form of Samuel: asked of God) | |
| **Amara** | Short for Amarantha | |
| **Amarantha** | Unfading (Greek) Also the name of a flower | Amara |
| **Amaryllis** | To sparkle (Greek) | |

| Name | Definition | Short forms/Variations |
|------|------------|------------------------|
| **Amaya** | Infinite (Sanskrit) | |
| **Ambrosia** | Female form of Ambrose: immortal | |
| **Amecia** | See **Amice** | *Amicia* |
| **Amelia** | Hardworking (German) | *Amalia, Amélie, Emilia, Emily* |
| **Amélie** | French form of Amelia: hardworking | *Amalia, Emilia, Emily* |
| **Amice** | Friendship (Latin) | *Amecia, Amicia* |
| **Amie** | [Am-ee] Friend (French) Loved (Sanskrit) | |
| **Amiga** | Female friend; girlfriend (Spanish) | |
| **Amina** | Peaceful (Arabic) | *Mina* |
| **Aminta** | In Mozart's 18th-century opera *Il re pastore*, Aminta is a male shepherd – but as it is a soprano role it is always sung by a woman | |
| **Amisha** | Honest (Sanskrit) | |
| **Amity** | Friendship (Latin) | |
| **Amor** | Love (French) Also a boy's name | |
| **Amora** | Love (Spanish) | |
| **Amoret** | Beloved (Latin) | |
| **Amoretta** | Little loved one (Latin) | *Amorita* |
| **Amparo** | Protection (Spanish) | |
| **Amrit** | Immortal (Sanskrit) Nectar (Sikh) Also a boy's name | |
| **Amy** | Beloved (Old French) | *Aimée* |
| **Ana** | See **Anna** | *Anaïs, Ann, Anne* |
| **Anabel** | See **Annabel** | *Bel, Bella, Belle / Amabel, Amabella, Annabella, Annabelle* |
| **Anaïs** | [An-eye-ees] See **Anna** | *Ana, Ann, Anne* |
| **Anandi** | Bringer of joy (Sanskrit) | |
| **Anastasia** | [Ana-stay-sia or Ana-star-sia] Resurrection (Greek) | *Ana, Stasia / Anastacia, Anstace, Anstice* |
| **Andie** | Short for Andrea | *Andy* |
| **Andra** | Female form of Andrew: warrior (Greek) | |
| **Andrea** | Female form of Andreas: warrior (Greek) | *Andie, Andy, Drea* |

| Name | Definition | Short forms/ Variations |
|------|-----------|-------------------------|
| **Andromeda** | To think of a man (Greek) In Greek myth, Andromeda is the princess Perseus rescues from sacrifice to a sea monster. Andromeda is also the name of a galaxy 2.5 million light years away | |
| **Andy** | See **Andie**. Also a boy's name | |
| **Aneliese** | See **Annalise** | *Anneli, Lisa, Lise / Anelise, Annaliese, Annelies, Anneliese, Annelise* |
| **Ange** | Angel (French) | |
| **Angel** | Angel (Greek, English) Traditionally a boy's name | *Angela, Angelina, Angeline* |
| **Angela** | Angel (Greek) | *Ang, Angelita, Angie / Angelina, Angeline* |
| **Angelica** | [Anj-ell-ick-a] Angelic (Latin) | *Angélique* |
| **Angelina** | [Anj-ell-ee-na] See **Angela** | *Angie / Angel, Angeline* |
| **Angeline** | See **Angela** | |
| **Angélique** | French form of Angelica: angelic | |
| **Angelita** | Spanish pet form of Angela | |
| **Angharad** | Love (Welsh) | |
| **Angie** | Short for Angela or Angelina | *Ang* |
| **Anita** | Graceful (Sanskrit) Also the Spanish pet form of Anna: favoured by God | *Neeta, Nita* |
| **Anja** | See **Anya** | |
| **Anke** | [An-ka] German pet form of Anne | |
| **Ann** | See **Anna** | *Annie, Nan, Nancy / Ana, Anaïs, Annchen, Anne, Anouk, Nanine* |
| **Anna** | Favoured by God (Hebrew) | *Annie / Ana, Anaïs, Anita, Ann, Anne, Anneke, Annette, Anouk, Anouska, Anya* |
| **Annabel** | See **Amabel** | *Bel, Bella, Belle / Amabel, Amabella, Anabel, Annabella, Annabelle* |

| Name | Definition | Short forms/ Variations |
|------|-----------|------------------------|
| **Annalise** | [Anna-leez or Anna-leeza] Gracious (German) | *Anneli, Lisa, Lise / Aneliese, Anelise, Annaliese, Annelies, Anneliese, Annelise* |
| **Annapurna** | Goddess of harvests (Sanskrit) | |
| **Annchen** | German pet form of Ann | |
| **Anne** | see **Anna** | |
| **Anneke** | [A-na-kuh] Dutch pet form of Anna: favoured by God | *Anneka, Annika* |
| **Anneli** | [A-na-lee] Short for Annalise | *Annelie* |
| **Anneliese** | [Anna-leeze or Anna-leeza] See **Annalise** | *Anneli, Lisa, Lise / Aneliese, Anelise, Annaliese, Annalise, Annelies, Annelise* |
| **Anne-Marie** | Combination of Ann (favoured by God) and Marie (sea) | |
| **Annette** | French pet form of Ann: favoured by God | *Nettie* |
| **Annfrid** | Beautiful eagle (Old Norse) | |
| **Annie** | Pet form of Ann or Anna | |
| **Annika** | See **Anneke** | *Anneka* |
| **Annis** | See **Agnes** | *Annice, Annys* |
| **Annwen** | See **Anwen** | |
| **Annwyl** | Beloved (Welsh) | *Anwyl* |
| **Anouk** | French pet form of Ann: favoured by God | |
| **Anouska** | [An-ush-ka] Russian pet form of Anna: favoured by God | *Anushka, Anuska* |
| **Anstace** | See **Anastasia** | *Anstice* |
| **Antara** | Soul (Sanskrit) | |
| **Anthea** | Floral (Greek) | |
| **Antigone** | [An-tig-on-ee] Contrary born (Greek) In Greek myth, Antigone is a tragic figure, conceived through unintended incest, who ended her days by being buried alive | *Tiggy* |
| **Antoinette** | [An-twon-et] French female form of Antoine: of inestimable worth. May have gained in popularity thanks to Marie-Antoinette, 18th-century queen of France | *Nettie, Toinette, Toni* |

| Name | Definition | Short forms/ Variations |
|------|-----------|------------------------|
| **Antonia** | Priceless (Latin) | *Toni, Tonia, Tonya / Anthonia, Antonina* |
| **Antonina** | [An-ton-ee-na] See **Antonia** | *Nina, Toni* |
| **Anuja** | Lovable younger sister (Sanskrit) | |
| **Anupriya** | Dearly loved (Sanskrit) | |
| **Anushka** | See **Anouska** | *Anuska* |
| **Anwen** | Fair; blessed (Old Celtic) | *Annwen* |
| **Anwyl** | See **Annwyl** | |
| **Anya** | [Ann-ya or Ahn-ya or On-ya] Grace (Russian) Mercy (Hebrew) | *Anja* |
| **Aoife** | Beautiful, radiant (Irish Gaelic) | |
| **Aphra** | Woman from Africa (Latin) | *Afra* |
| **Aphrodite** | [Af-ro-dye-tee] Born of the foam (Greek) In Greek myth, Aphrodite is goddess of love and beauty | |
| **Apollonia** | Taken from Apollo, the Greek sun god | *Abelone* |
| **Arabella** | Beautiful altar (Latin) | *Bel, Bella, Belle / Arabel* |
| **Araceli** | Altar of the sky (Spanish) | |
| **Araminta** | Thought to have been invented by playwright Sir John Vanbrugh for a character in his 18th-century comedy *The Confederacy* | |
| **Archer** | Originally a surname, meaning bowman. Also a boy's name | |
| **Aretha** | [A-ree-tha] Excellence (Greek) It may have gained in popularity thanks to soul singer Aretha Franklin | |
| **Ariadne** | [A-ree-ad-nee] Holy (Greek) In Greek myth, Ariadne helped Theseus to escape from the Labyrinth after killing the Minotaur | *Arianna, Arianne* |
| **Arianna** | Italian form of Ariadne: holy | *Ariana, Arianne* |
| **Arianne** | French form of Ariadne: holy | |
| **Arianwen** | Silver and fair or blessed (Welsh) | |
| **Ariba** | Intelligent (Arabic) | |
| **Ariel** | God's lion (Hebrew) A spirit of the air in Shakespeare's *The Tempest*. Also a boy's name | *Arielle* |
| **Arlene** | Oath, promise (Irish) | |

| Name | Definition | Short forms/<br>Variations |
|---|---|---|
| **Arlette** | Eagle (Germanic) | |
| **Armani** | Originally an Italian surname, meaning free man, it may be given in homage to the fashion designer Giorgio Armani | |
| **Artemis** | Greek goddess of the moon and hunting | |
| **Aruna** | Dawn (Sanskrit) | |
| **Arwen** | An elven princess from Tolkien's novel *The Lord of the Rings*. In the book, the name means 'noble woman' | |
| **Asami** | Morning beauty (Japanese) | |
| **Asha** | Hope (Sanskrit) | |
| **Ashanti** | The name of a Ghanian ethnic group | |
| **Ashby** | Brash (Scandinavian) Also a boy's name | |
| **Ashley** | Originally an English surname, meaning ash wood. Also a boy's name | *Ash / Ashleigh* |
| **Ashling** | English form of Aisling: dream or vision | *Aislin* |
| **Ashton** | Originally a surname, meaning town or village by an ash tree. Also a boy's name | |
| **Asma** | Prestige (Arabic) | |
| **Asra** | Night journey (Arabic) According to Islamic tradition, Muhammad made a miraculous night journey from Mecca to Jerusalem where he prayed with Abraham, Moses and Jesus | *Isra* |
| **Asta** | Short for Astrid | |
| **Astarte** | A Phoenician goddess connected with fertility, sexuality and war | |
| **Aster** | Star (Latin) | |
| **Astley** | Originally a surname, meaning eastern wood. Also a boy's name | |
| **Aston** | Originally a surname, meaning eastern town or village. Also a boy's name | |
| **Astra** | Star (Greek) | |
| **Astrid** | Beautiful god (Old Norse) | *Asta, Sassa* |
| **Atalanta** | In Greek myth, Atalanta is an amazingly fast runner who refuses to marry unless the suitor can beat her in a race. Hippomenes wins by dropping three golden apples, which she stops to pick up | |

| --- | --- | --- |
| **Atarah** | Crown (Hebrew) | *Atara* |
| **Athene** | Greek goddess of wisdom | *Athena, Athina* |
| **Auda** | Rich (Old English) | |
| **Aude** | See **Audrey** | |
| **Audra** | See **Audrey** | |
| **Audrey** | Strong and noble (Old English) | *Addie, Addy, Adi / Aude, Audra, Audrie* |
| **Augusta** | Female form of Augustus: magnificent | |
| **Augustine** | Magnificent (Latin) Also a boy's name | *Gussie* |
| **Aura** | See **Aurelia** | *Auria* |
| **Aurelia** | [Aw-ree-lee-a] Golden (Latin) | *Aura, Auria, Auriel* |
| **Auriel** | [Aw-ree-el] See **Aurelia** | *Aura, Auria, Aurial, Oriel* |
| **Aurora** | Dawn (Latin) | |
| **Ava** | Bird (Latin) May have increased in popularity thanks to Hollywood film star Ava Gardner | *Eva* |
| **Avalon** | In Arthurian myth, Avalon is the island King Arthur was taken to after death | |
| **Avanti** | Modest (Sanskrit) | |
| **Aveline** | See **Evelyn** | *Avelina* |
| **Averil** | Strong and brave as a wild boar (Old English) | *Averilla, Averyl* |
| **Avice** | War refuge (Germanic) | *Avicia* |
| **Avis** | Bird (Latin) | |
| **Avital** | See **Abital** | |
| **Avril** | April (French) | |
| **Aya** | Beautiful; colourful; woven threads (Japanese) | |
| **Ayda** | Advantage (Arabic) | |
| **Ayeeda** | [Eye-eed-a] See **Aida** | |
| **Ayesha** | [Aye-ee-sha] See **Aisha** | |
| **Azalia** | Reserved by God (Hebrew) | |
| **Azania** | Heard by God (Hebrew) | |
| **Azaria** | Helped by God (Hebrew) | |
| **Azza** | Pride; power (Arabic) | |

| Name | Definition | Short forms/ Variations |
|------|-----------|-------------------------|
| **Babette** | Latin pet form of Barbara | |
| **Babita** | Born in the first part of the day (Sanskrit) | |
| **Bahiyya** | Beautiful (Arabic) | |
| **Bailey** | Originally a surname, meaning bailiff. Also a boy's name | *Bailie, Baillie* |
| **Bambi** | Short for Bambina. Usually associated with the 1942 Disney film *Bambi*, about a young roe deer | |
| **Bambina** | Young girl (Italian) | *Bambi* |
| **Barbara** | Foreigner (Latin) | *Barbie / Barbra, Biba* |
| **Barbie** | Short for Barbara | *Barb* |
| **Barindra** | Sea (Sikh) Also a boy's name | |
| **Basma** | Smile (Arabic) | |
| **Bathsheba** | Daughter of the oath (Hebrew) | *Sheba* |
| **Bea** | [Bee] Short for Beata, Beatrice, Beatrix or Beattie | |
| **Beata** | Blessed (Latin) | Bea |

| Name | Definition | Short forms/ Variations |
|------|-----------|------------------------|
| **Beatrice** | [Bee-a-triss] Bringer of joy (Latin) | *Bea, Beattie, Trissie, Trissy, Trixi, Trixie / Beatrix* |
| **Beatrix** | See **Beatrice** | *Bea, Beattie, Trixi, Trixie* |
| **Beattie** | [Bea-tee] Short for Beatrice or Beatrix | *Bea* |
| **Beau** | [Bo] Handsome (French) Traditionally a boy's name | |
| **Becca** | Short for Rebecca | |
| **Becky** | Short for Rebecca | |
| **Beile** | White (Slavic) | *Beyle* |
| **Belinda** | Combination of Belle (beautiful) and Linda (pretty) | *Bel, Bella, Belle, Linda* |
| **Belita** | Beautiful one (Spanish) | |
| **Bella** | Beautiful (Italian) | *Bel, Belle, Bellina* |
| **Bellina** | See **Bella** | |
| **Benazir** | [Ben-a-zeer] Unique (Arabic) | |
| **Benedicta** | Female form of Benedict: blessed | |
| **Benita** | [Ben-ee-ta] Female form of Benito, the Spanish form of Benedictine: blessed | *Neeta, Nita* |
| **Berenice** | [Berr-en-ees] Victory bringer (Greek) | *Bernie, Binnie / Bernice* |
| **Bernardette** | See **Bernardine** | *Berneen, Bernie / Bernadette, Detta* |
| **Bernardine** | [Bern-ud-een] Female form of Bernhard: strong bear | *Bernie / Bernadine, Bernhardine* |
| **Berneen** | Pet form of Bernardette | |
| **Bernie** | Short for Berenice, Bernardette or Bernardine | |
| **Bertha** | Bright; famous (Germanic) | |
| **Bertie** | Short for Ethelbert. Also a boy's name | |
| **Beryl** | From the gemstone | |
| **Bess** | Short for Elizabeth | *Bessie, Bessy* |
| **Bet** | Short for Elizabeth | *Bette* |
| **Beth** | Short for Elizabeth | |
| **Betha** | Life (Irish) | |

| Name | Definition | Short forms/ Variations |
|------|-----------|------------------------|
| **Bethan** | Pet form of Beth, short for Elizabeth: God is my oath | |
| **Bethany** | In the Bible, Bethany is the village just outside Jerusalem where Jesus stayed during Holy Week | *Bethanie* |
| **Bethia** | Servant of Jehovah (Hebrew) | *Bethiah* |
| **Betsy** | Short for Elizabeth | |
| **Betta** | See **Betty** | *Bette* |
| **Bette** | [Bet] Short for Elizabeth. It may have gained in popularity thanks to American movie star Bette (Ruth Elizabeth) Davis | *Bet* |
| **Bettina** | Combination of Beth or Betty and Tina | *Betty, Tina* |
| **Bettrys** | Welsh form of Beatrice: bringer of joy | |
| **Betty** | Short for Bettina or Elizabeth | *Betta, Bette, Bettie* |
| **Betula** | Birch tree (Latin) | *Betulah* |
| **Beulah** | [B'yoo-la] Married (Hebrew) | |
| **Bhupinder** | Looked after by God (Sikh) Also a boy's name | |
| **Bianca** | [Bee-anka] White (Italian) | |
| **Biba** | [Bee-bah] The nickname – and label – of 1960s fashion designer Barbara Hulanicki | |
| **Bibi** | Lively (Latin, French) Lady of the house (Persian) | |
| **Biddy** | Short for Bridget | *Biddie* |
| **Bijou** | [Bee-jhu] Jewel (French) | |
| **Billie** | Female form of Billy, short for William: protector | *Billy* |
| **Billie-Jean** | Combination of Billie (protector) and Jean (God is gracious) | *Billie-Jo* |
| **Billie-Jo** | See **Billie-Jean** | |
| **Bina** | [Bee-na] Understanding (Hebrew) | *Binah* |
| **Binnie** | Short for Berenice | |
| **Bionda** | [Bee-ondah] Blonde (Italian) | |
| **Birgit** | [Bir-jit] Scandinavian form of Brighid: the exalted one | |

| Name | Definition | Short forms/ Variations |
|------|-----------|------------------------|
| **Birgitta** | [Bir-jitta] See **Birgit**. St Birgitta (also known as St Bridgid of Sweden) is the patron saint of Europe | *Britta* |
| **Bishakha** | Famous (Sanskrit) | |
| **Bjork** | [B'yerk or B'yersh] Birch tree (Icelandic) | |
| **Blair** | Originally a surname, meaning field. Also a boy's name | |
| **Blaise** | Stuttering (Latin) Also a boy's name | *Blaze* |
| **Blanca** | White (Spanish) | |
| **Blanche** | [Blahnch] White (French) | |
| **Blathnat** | Flower (Gaelic) | |
| **Blaze** | English form of Blaise: stuttering | |
| **Blodeyn** | Flower (Welsh) | *Blodyn* |
| **Blodwen** | White or blessed flowers (Welsh) | |
| **Blondell** | Little fair-haired one (Old English) Also a boy's name | |
| **Blondie** | Pet name for someone with blonde hair. May have increased in popularity thanks to the rock group fronted by Deborah Harry | |

| Name | Definition | Short forms/ Variations |
|---|---|---|
| **Blush** | To go red (English) | |
| **Bo** | Precious (Chinese) | |
| **Bobbie** | Short for Roberta or female form of Bobby, short for Robert: bright, shining fame | *Bobbi, Bobby* |
| **Bonita** | [Bon-ee-ta] Pretty (Spanish) | *Bonnie, Bonny, Neeta, Nita* |
| **Bonnie** | Pretty (Scottish) The name of Scarlett O'Hara's daughter in Margaret Mitchell's novel *Gone with the Wind* | *Bonny* |
| **Braden** | Salmon (Irish Gaelic) Also a boy's name | *Brayden, Brydon* |
| **Brandy** | From the drink | *Brandie* |
| **Branka** | Female form of Branko: peaceful protection | |
| **Branna** | Raven (Irish Gaelic) It may be used for girls with raven-black hair | |
| **Branwen** | Fair or blessed raven (Welsh) | |
| **Brea** | Short for Breana | |
| **Breana** | See **Brianna** | *Brea, Breanna, Briana* |
| **Bree** | English form of Brighe, short for Brighid: the exalted one | *Brie* |
| **Breena** | Fairy land (Irish) | |
| **Brenda** | Sword (Old Norse) | |
| **Brenna** | Raven (Welsh) | |
| **Brennan** | Originally a surname, meaning drop of water. Also a boy's name | |
| **Bria** | [Bree-uh] Short for Brianna | |
| **Brianna** | [Bree-an-uh] Female form of Brian: noble | *Bree, Bria, Brie / Breana, Breanna, Briana* |
| **Brid** | Short for Brighid | *Bride* |
| **Bridget** | English form of Brighid: the exalted one | *Biddie, Biddy, Bridey, Bridie, Brydie / Bridgid, Bridgit, Brigid, Brigit, Brigitte, Britt* |

| Name | Definition | Short forms/ Variations |
|---|---|---|
| **Bridie** | See **Bridget** | *Bridey, Brydie* |
| **Brie** | [Bree] Short for Brianna | *Bree* |
| **Brighe** | Short for Brighid | *Bree, Brie* |
| **Brighid** | [Breed] The exalted one (Irish) | *Brid, Bride / Brigid* |
| **Brina** | Short for Sabrina | *Breena* |
| **Brionna** | Female form of Brion, a variation of Brian: noble | |
| **Britt** | See **Bridget** | |
| **Britta** | Short for Birgitta | |
| **Brodie** | Originally a Scottish surname, meaning muddy place. Also a boy's name | *Brody* |
| **Brogan** | English form of an Irish surname, meaning shoe. Also a boy's name | |
| **Bronagh** | [Bro-nah] Sorrowful (Irish Gaelic) | |
| **Brontë** | [Bron-tay] Thunder (Greek). Originally a surname, now sometimes used as a first name in homage to the 19th-century authors, sisters Charlotte, Emily and Anne Brontë | |
| **Bronwyn** | White-breasted (Welsh) | *Bronwen* |
| **Brunhild** | Maid of battle (Germanic) | *Hilda / Brunhilda* |
| **Bryanna** | Female form of Bryan: noble | |
| **Brydon** | See **Braden**. Also a boy's name | *Brayden* |
| **Brynn** | Female form of Bryn: hill | |
| **Buffy** | Short for Elizabeth. It may have gained in popularity thanks to the American TV series *Buffy the Vampire Slayer* | |

| Name | Definition | Short forms/ Variations |
|------|-----------|-------------------------|
| **Cabriole** | Goat-like leap (French) The name of a type of jump in ballet | |
| **Cachet** | [Cash-ay] Prestige (English) | |
| **Cadence** | The sound of someone's voice (English) | |
| **Caintigern** | Fair lady (Irish) | |
| **Cairenn** | Beloved little one (Irish Gaelic) | |
| **Caitlin** | Irish form of Katherine: pure | *Cait, Cate / Caitlyn, Katelyn* |
| **Calanthe** | Beautiful flower (Greek) Also the name of a type of orchid | *Calanthia* |
| **Calanthia** | See **Calanthe** | |
| **Caledonia** | A romantic name for Scotland (Latin) | |
| **Calico** | From the cotton fabric | |
| **Calista** | Cup (Latin) Fairest, most beautiful (Greek) | *Callie, Cally / Callista Kalista, Kallista* |
| **Calliope** | Beautiful face (Greek) | *Callie, Cally* |
| **Cally** | Short for Calista or Calliope | *Callie* |

| --- | --- | --- |
| **Calypso** | [Cal-ip-so] In Greek legend, a sea nymph who held Odysseus captive | |
| **Camelot** | [Cam-a-lot] In Arthurian myth, Camelot is the seat of King Arthur's court | |
| **Cameo** | [Cam-ee-oh] A pendant with a raised design, usually a woman's portrait (English) | |
| **Cameron** | Originally a surname, meaning crooked nose. Also a boy's name | *Cam / Camron* |
| **Camilla** | Noble (Latin) A warrior queen in Virgil's *Aeneid* | *Milla, Millie, Milly / Camelia, Camille* |
| **Camille** | [Cam-eel] French form of Camilla: noble | |
| **Candace** | The name of a line of queens of Ethiopia | *Candy* |
| **Candice** | [Can-dees] Whiteness (Latin) | *Candy* |
| **Candida** | White (Latin) Unfortunately, it's also the medical term for a yeast infection | *Candy* |
| **Candy** | Short for Candace or Candice | |
| **Caoimhe** | Gentleness, grace (Irish) | *Keeva* |
| **Cara** | Beloved (Italian) Friend (Gaelic) | *Careen, Carina, Carine, Kara, Karina* |
| **Careen** | See **Cara** | |
| **Carey** | See **Cary**. Also a boy's name | |
| **Caridad** | Charity (Spanish) | |
| **Carina** | [Ca-ree-nuh] See **Cara** | *Carrie, Carry, Rina / Carine, Karina* |
| **Carla** | See **Carlotta** | *Carlie, Carly* |
| **Carlotta** | Female form of Carl: free man | *Carla, Carlie, Carly Lottie / Charlotte* |
| **Carly** | Short for Carla, Carlotta or Caroline | *Carlie* |
| **Carmel** | Garden (Hebrew) Our Lady of Carmel is a title of the Virgin Mary | *Carmela, Carmella* |
| **Carmela** | Italian and Spanish form of Carmel: garden | |
| **Carmen** | Spanish form of Carmel: garden. It may have gained in popularity thanks to the tragic heroine of Bizet's 19th-century opera *Carmen* | *Carmine* |
| **Carmine** | Song (Latin) | |
| **Carol** | Female form of Carl: free man | *Carola, Carole* |
| **Carol-Ann** | Combination of Carol (free man) and Ann (favoured by God) | *Carol-Anne, Carole-Ann, Carole-Anne* |

names

c

girls'

| Name | Definition | Short forms/ Variations |
|------|-----------|------------------------|
| **Caroline** | Female form of Carl: free man | *Carlie, Carly, Caro, Carrie, Carry / Carolina, Carolyn* |
| **Carolyn** | See **Caroline** | |
| **Caron** | Love (Welsh) | |
| **Carrie** | Short for Carina or Caroline | *Carry* |
| **Carson** | Originally a surname. Also a boy's name | |
| **Cary** | Originally a surname, meaning pleasant stream. Traditionally a boy's name, which may have gained in popularity thanks to film star Cary Grant | *Carey* |
| **Carys** | [Carr-iss] Love (Welsh) | *Cerys* |
| **Cas** | Curly-haired (Irish Gaelic) | |
| **Casey** | Vigilant in war (Irish Gaelic) Traditionally a boy's name, it's sometimes given in homage to the American folk hero Casey Jones | *Casie* |
| **Cass** | Short for Cassandra, Cassia or Cassidy | *Cassie* |
| **Cassandra** | In Greek legend, a Trojan princess with the gift of prophecy | *Cass, Cassie* |
| **Cassia** | Female form of Cassius: hollow | *Cass, Cassie* |
| **Cassidy** | Originally an Irish surname, meaning curly-haired. Also a boy's name | *Cass, Cassie* |
| **Cassie** | Short for Cassandra, Cassia or Cassidy | *Cass* |
| **Cate** | Short for Catherine or Caitlin | *Cait, Kate* |
| **Caterina** | See **Katerina** | |
| **Catherine** | See **Katherine** | *Cate, Cathie, Cathy, Kate / Caitlyn, Catharine, Catrina, Catrine, Catriona, Katharine, Kathryn* |
| **Cathie** | Short for Catherine or Cathleen | *Cath / Cathy* |
| **Cathleen** | Irish form of Katherine: pure | *Cathie, Cathy* |
| **Catrin** | Welsh form of Katherine: pure | |
| **Catrine** | See **Katherine** | *Cat / Katrine* |
| **Catriona** | See **Katherine** | *Cat, Treena, Trina / Catrina, Katrina, Katriona* |
| **Cecile** | [Sess-eel] French form of Cecilia: clever | |

| Name | Definition | Short forms/ Variations |
|---|---|---|
| **Cecilia** | See **Cecily** | *Celia, Cissie, Sissie / Cecelia, Cecile, Cecilie, Cicely* |
| **Cecily** | Clever (Latin) | *Cissie, Sissie / Cecelia, Cecile, Cecilia, Cecilie Celia, Cicely, Cicily, Sighile, Síle, Sisley* |
| **Céleste** | [Sell-est] Heavenly (Latin) | *Celeste* |
| **Célestia** | [Sel-est-ee-uh] See **Céleste** | *Celestia* |
| **Célestine** | [Sel-est-een] Pet form of Céleste | *Celestine* |
| **Celia** | Heaven (Latin) | *Cecelia, Cecile, Cecilia, Cecilie, Cicely* |
| **Céline** | [Sell-een] Heaven (Latin) | *Celine* |
| **Ceri** | [Kerry] Short for Ceridwen | |
| **Cerian** | [Keh-ree-an] Love (Welsh) | |
| **Ceridwen** | [Ker-id-wen] Fair or blessed poetry (Welsh) In Celtic folklore, Ceridwen is the goddess of poetic inspiration | *Ceri* |
| **Cerys** | [Ker-iss] See **Carys** | |
| **Chablis** | [Shab-lee] A type of white wine | |
| **Chai** | Life (Hebrew) Originally a boy's name | |
| **Chakra** | Wheel, circle (Sanskrit) In Hinduism and other Asian cultures, a chakra is thought to be a type of energy in the human body | |
| **Chalice** | [Cha-liss] A large cup or goblet for wine, particularly one used during the Christian ceremony of Holy Communion (English) | |
| **Chambray** | [Shom-bray] A cotton fabric, often used in shirts, that was developed in Chambray in the Eure area of France | |
| **Chameli** | Jasmine (Sanskrit) | |
| **Chandani** | Moonlight (Sanskrit) | |
| **Chandler** | Originally a surname, meaning candle maker. Also a boy's name | |
| **Chandra** | Moon (Sanskrit) Also a boy's name | |
| **Chanel** | [Shan-el] Sometimes given in homage to fashion designer Coco Chanel | |

| Name | Definition | Short forms/ Variations |
|------|-----------|------------------------|
| **Channing** | Originally a surname, meaning church official. Also a boy's name | |
| **Chantal** | [Shan-tal] Singer (French) | *Chantel, Chantelle* |
| **Chantilly** | [Shan-tilly] A handmade lace from Chantilly, a city in the Picardie region of France | |
| **Chardonnay** | [Shar-donn-ay] A type of white wine. The name is taken from the village of Chardonnay in the Burgundy region of France | |
| **Charis** | [Kar-iss] Grace (Greek) | *Caris, Charissa, Charisse* |
| **Charlene** | [Shar-leen] Female form of Charles: free man | *Charley, Charlie* |
| **Charlie** | Short for Charlene or Charlotte. Also a boy's name | *Charley* |
| **Charlize** | Female form of Charles: free man. May have increased in popularity thanks to South African actress Charlize Theron | |
| **Charlotte** | Female form of Charles: free man | *Charley, Charlie, Chattie, Chatty, Lotte, Lottie / Carlotta* |
| **Charmaine** | [Shar-mane] See **Charmian** | |
| **Charmian** | [Shar-mee-an] Delight (Greek) | *Charmaine, Charmion* |
| **Charna** | Dark, black (Slavic) | |
| **Chase** | Originally a surname, meaning huntsman. Also a boy's name | |
| **Chattie** | Short for Charlotte | *Chatty* |
| **Chaya** | Alive (Hebrew) | |

| Name | Definition | Short forms/<br>Variations |
|---|---|---|
| **Chelle** | [Shel] Short for Michelle | *Shell* |
| **Chenda** | Intellect (Khmer) | |
| **Chenille** | [Sheh-nil] A type of plant with brightly-coloured, furry flowers. Also a soft, velvety fabric | |
| **Cher** | [Shair] Dear (French) | |
| **Cherie** | [Shuh-ree] Darling (French) | *Chérie* |
| **Cherish** | To treasure (English) | |
| **Cherokee** | From the Native American people | |
| **Cheryl** | Combination of Cherry and Beryl | *Cherith, Cheryth,*<br>*Sheryl* |
| **Cheryth** | See **Cheryl** | *Cherith* |
| **Chesney** | Originally an English surname, meaning camp. Also a boy's name | |
| **Chet** | Originally a boy's name, short for Chester | |
| **Chevy** | Short for Chevrolet, a brand of car often seen as particularly American – partly thanks to the line in Don McLean's 1971 hit *American Pie*, 'Drove my Chevy to the levee; But the levee was dry'. Also a boy's name | |
| **Cheyenne** | [Shy-en] From the Native American people | |
| **Chiara** | [Key-ah-ra] Italian form of Clara: bright, shining fame | |
| **Chiasa** | A thousand mornings (Japanese) | |
| **Chica** | [Chee-ka] Short for Francesca | |
| **Chie** | A thousand blessings (Japanese) | |
| **Chieko** | [Chi-ee-ko] Child of a thousand blessings (Japanese) | |
| **Chiquita** | [Chee-key-tuh] Little girl (Spanish) | |
| **Chlöe** | [Klo-ee] Flowering (Greek) | |
| **Chloris** | Green (Greek) In Greek myth, Khloris was a goddess of vegetation | |
| **Chrissa** | Short for Christabel, Christiana, Christianne, Christina or Christine | |
| **Chrissie** | Short for Christabel, Christiana, Christianne, Christina or Christine | *Chris / Chrissy* |
| **Christa** | Short for Christabel, Christiana, Christianne, Christina or Christine | *Chris / Krista* |

| Name | Definition | Short forms/ Variations |
|---|---|---|
| **Christabel** | Combination of Christ and Belle (beautiful) | *Bel, Bella, Belle, Chrissa, Chrissie, Chrissy, Christa, Christie / Christabelle, Christobel, Cristabel, Cristobel* |
| **Christiana** | See **Christina** | *Chris, Chrissa, Chrissie, Chrissy, Christa, Christie, Tiana / Christianna* |
| **Christianne** | Follower of Christ (Latin) | *Chris, Chrissa, Chrissie, Chrissy, Christie, Christy* |
| **Christie** | Short for Christabel, Christiana, Christianne, Christina or Christine | *Chris* |
| **Christina** | Female form of Christian: follower of Christ | *Chris, Chrissa, Chrissie, Chrissy, Christa, Christie, Tina / Christine, Kirstin* |
| **Christine** | See **Christina** | |
| **Ciara** | [Key-ah-ra] Female form of Ciaran: black | *Keira, Kiara, Kiera* |
| **Cicely** | [Siss-uh-lee] See **Cecily** | *Cissie, Sissie / Cecelia, Cecile, Cecilia, Cecilie Celia, Cicily, Sighile, Síle, Sisley* |
| **Cilla** | [Sill-a] Short for Priscilla | |
| **Cinda** | [Sin-da] Short for Lucinda | |
| **Cinderella** | In Charles Perrault's 17th-century fairy tale, Cinderella is a mocking nickname given to the heroine by her wicked stepmother and stepsisters, who force her to do domestic duties such as tending the fire. But all works out well when, thanks to the intervention of Cinderella's fairy godmother, she goes to the ball and marries the prince | |
| **Cindy** | Short for Cynthia or Lucinda | *Cindie, Sindie, Sindy* |
| **Cinta** | Short for Jacinta | |
| **Circe** | [Sur-say] In Greek myth, Circe was the sorceress who turned Odysseus's shipmates into pigs | |

| Name | Definition | Short forms/ Variations |
| --- | --- | --- |
| **Cissie** | Short for Cecilia or Cecily | |
| **Claire** | Bright, shining fame (Latin) | *Clair, Clara, Clare, Clarette, Claribel* |
| **Clara** | [Klair-uh or Klah-rah] See **Claire** | *Clare, Claribel* |
| **Clarabelle** | Combination of Clara (bright, shining fame) and Belle (beautiful) | |
| **Clarette** | See **Claire** | *Clari, Clarie, Clarrie, Clary* |
| **Claribel** | See **Claire** | |
| **Clarice** | [Klar-ees] Fame (Latin) | *Clari, Clarie, Clarrie, Clary / Claris, Clarissa* |
| **Clarinda** | Combination of Clara (bright, shining fame) and Lucinda (light) | *Clari, Clarie, Clarrie, Clary* |
| **Clarissa** | See **Clarice** | *Clari, Clarie, Clarrie, Clary, Rissa* |
| **Clarrie** | Short for Clarette, Claribel, Clarice, Clarinda or Clarissa | *Clari, Clarie, Clary* |
| **Claudette** | See **Claudia** | *Claudine* |
| **Claudia** | Lame (Latin) | *Claudette, Claudine* |
| **Claudine** | See **Claudia** | *Claudette* |
| **Clea** | Praise (Greek) | |
| **Clem** | Short for Clemence, Clementine or Clementina | |
| **Clemence** | Mercy (Latin) | *Clem, Clemmie* |
| **Clementine** | Merciful (Latin) It may have gained in popularity thanks to the 19th-century American folk ballad *Oh my darling, Clementine* | *Clem, Clemmie, Tina / Clementina* |
| **Cleo** | Glory (Greek) | *Clio* |
| **Cleopatra** | Father's glory. Given in homage to the passionate, tragic Egyptian queen | *Cleo* |
| **Cliantha** | Glorious flower (Greek) | |
| **Clio** | See **Cleo** | |
| **Cliona** | According to Irish myth, Cliona was a goddess of beauty who lived in the Land of Promise. She fell in love with a mortal and later drowned | |
| **Clodagh** | [Klo-da] The name of an Irish river | |

| Name | Definition | Short forms/Variations |
|------|-----------|------------------------|
| **Clorinda** | Renowned beauty (Persian) | |
| **Clothilde** | [Klot-ild] Famous in battle (Germanic) | *Clothilda, Clotilda, Clotilde* |
| **Coco** | Coconut (Spanish) Sometimes given in homage to French fashion designer Coco Chanel | |
| **Cody** | Originally an Irish surname, meaning prosperous. Its popularity in the US may be thanks to Buffalo Bill, the showman William Cody. Also a boy's name | |
| **Colette** | Victorious (French) | *Collette* |
| **Colina** | Female form of Colin: victorious people | |
| **Colleen** | Girl (Gaelic) | *Coleen* |
| **Columbina** | [Kol-um-byna] Little dove (Italian) A servant and Harlequin's girlfriend in the Italian *Commedia dell'Arte* | *Colombina, Columbine* |
| **Concetta** | [Kon-chetta] From the Italian for conception. The name refers to the Immaculate Conception of the Virgin Mary | |
| **Concha** | Seashell (Spanish) | *Conchita* |
| **Conchita** | Pet form of Concha | |
| **Condi** | Short for Condoleezza | |
| **Condolcezza** | With sweetness (Italian) An expression used in music | *Condoleezza* |
| **Condoleezza** | See **Condolcezza**. It may have gained in popularity thanks to American stateswoman Condoleezza Rice | *Condi* |
| **Connie** | Short for Constance or Constantia | |
| **Constantia** | Constance (Latin) | *Connie / Constanza* |
| **Constantina** | Female form of Constantine: constant | |
| **Constanza** | Spanish form of Constantia: constance | |
| **Contessa** | Countess (Italian) | |
| **Cora** | Maiden (Greek) Thought to have first been used for one of the main female characters in James Fenimore Cooper's 19th-century novel *The Last of the Mohicans* | *Corrie, Corry / Coralie* |
| **Coralie** | See **Cora** | *Corrie, Corry* |
| **Corazon** | Heart (Spanish) | *Cora, Corrie, Corry* |

| Name | Definition | Short forms/ Variations |
| --- | --- | --- |
| **Cordelia** | Heart (Latin) Thought to have first been used by Shakespeare in *King Lear*. Cordelia is the king's one good daughter | *Cordie, Cordy / Cordelita* |
| **Cordelita** | See **Cordelia** | |
| **Cordula** | Heart (Latin) | *Cordie, Cordy* |
| **Cordy** | Short for Cordelia or Cordula | *Cordie* |
| **Coretta** | See **Cora** | *Corrie, Corry* |
| **Corey** | Originally an Irish surname, meaning spear. Also a boy's name | *Cory* |
| **Corinna** | Heart (Greek) | *Corrie, Corry / Corinne* |
| **Corinne** | French form of Corinna: heart | *Corrie, Corry* |
| **Cornelia** | Female form of Cornelius: hero | |
| **Corona** | Crown (Latin) | |
| **Corrie** | Short for Cora, Coralie, Corazon, Coretta, Corinna or Corinne | *Corry* |
| **Cosima** | [Coz-ee-ma] Female form of Cosmo: order, beauty | |
| **Courtney** | From Courtenay, a place in northern France meaning Curtius's home | *Courtenay, Courteney* |
| **Cressa** | Short for Cressida | |
| **Cressida** | [Cress-idd-a] Golden (Greek) One of the lovers in Shakespeare's *The History of Troilus and Cressida* | *Cressa* |
| **Cruz** | [Crooth] Christ's cross (Spanish) Usually a girl's name, although it was used by footballer David Beckham for his third son | |
| **Cupid** | In Roman legend, Cupid is god of erotic love | |
| **Cushla** | Beat of my heart (Gaelic) | |
| **Cymbeline** | [Sim-be-line] In Shakespeare's play of the same name, Cymbeline is a king, based on a British chieftain | |
| **Cynthia** | [Sin-thea] From Mount Kynthos on the island of Delos, Greece. In Greek myth, Artemis, goddess of the moon and hunting, was born there | *Cindy* |

| Name | Definition | Short forms/ Variations |
|------|-----------|------------------------|
| **Dagmar** | Day's maid (Old Danish) | |
| **Dagna** | New day (Old Norse) | *Dagne, Dagny* |
| **Daksha** | Earth (Sanskrit) | |
| **Damaris** | Calf (Greek) | |
| **Damask** | From the fabric, which originally came from Damascus, Syria | |
| **Dana** | Wealth (Irish Gaelic) Dana is also the name of an Irish goddess | |
| **Dani** | Short for Danièle, Daniella or Danika | *Danni* |
| **Danièle** | French female form of Daniel: God is my judge | *Dani, Danni, Dannie / Daniela, Daniella, Danielle* |
| **Daniella** | Female form of Daniel: God is my judge | *Dani, Danni, Dannie / Daniela, Danièle, Danielle* |
| **Danika** | Morning star (Slavic) | *Dani, Danni, Dannie / Danica, Donica, Donika* |

| Name | Definition | Short forms/Variations |
|------|-----------|------------------------|
| **Daphne** | Laurel (Greek) In Greek myth, Daphne was turned into a laurel bush by her father | |
| **Dara** | Pearl of wisdom (Hebrew) Wise, compassionate (Sikh) Also a boy's name | |
| **Darcey** | Female form of Darcy: from the fortress. Originally a surname, it's sometimes given in homage to the hero of Jane Austen's 19th-century novel *Pride and Prejudice* | *Darcie, Darcy* |
| **Daria** | Female form of Darius: he who upholds the good | |
| **Darina** | Fruitful (Irish Gaelic) | |
| **Darla** | See **Darlene** | |
| **Darlene** | From darling (English) | *Darleen* |
| **Darya** | Great ruler (Persian) | |
| **Daryl** | Originally a surname, meaning from Airelle, Calvados, north-west France. Traditionally a boy's name | *Darrel, Darrell, Darryl* |
| **Davie** | Short for Davina. Also a boy's name | *Davey, Davy* |
| **Davina** | Female form of David: darling | *Davey, Davie, Davy / Davena, Davinia* |
| **Deandra** | See **Diana** | *Deanna, Diane, Dianne* |
| **Deanna** | See **Diana** | *Dee / Deandra, Diane, Dianne* |
| **Debbie** | Short for Deborah | *Debbi, Debby, Debi* |
| **Deborah** | Bee (Hebrew) | *Debbi, Debbie, Debby, Debi / Debra* |
| **Dee** | Originally short for any name beginning with D, particularly Deanna or Dionne | |
| **Deedee** | Sister (Hindi) | *DeeDee* |
| **Deepa** | Light (Sanskrit) | |
| **Deirbhile** | [Der-vla] Poet's daughter (Irish) | *Dervila, Dervla* |
| **Deirdre** | [Deer-dree] Raging one (Celtic) In Celtic myth, Deirdre was engaged to Conchobhar, King of Ulster, but eloped with Naoise instead. Naoise was murdered by Conchobhar and Deirdre died of a broken heart | *Deirdra* |
| **Deja** | Already (French) | |
| **Delaney** | [D'lane-ee] Dark challenger (Irish Gaelic) Also a boy's name | |

| Name | Definition | Short forms/ Variations |
|------|-----------|------------------------|
| **Delia** | From Delos, the Greek island birthplace of the goddess Artemis | |
| **Delicia** | [Del-ee-see-uh] Delight (Latin) | *Delice* |
| **Delilah** | [D'lie-luh] In the Bible, the woman who betrayed Samson to the Philistines by cutting off his hair – the source of his strength | *Lila, Lilah / Dalila, Dalilah, Delila* |
| **Delisha** | [D'lee-shah] One who brings happiness (Arabic) | *Lisha* |
| **Della** | Short for Adela or Adele | |
| **Delores** | [D'lor-ez] See **Dolores** | |
| **Delpha** | From Delphi (Greek) | |
| **Delphine** | Calmness and serenity (Greek) | *Delfina, Delfine, Delphina* |
| **Delwyn** | Neat and fair or blessed (Welsh) | |
| **Delyth** | Neat (Welsh) | |
| **Demelza** | A hamlet in north Cornwall. It may have gained in popularity thanks to Demelza Poldark, the heroine of Winston Graham's *Poldark* novels | *Demi* |
| **Demetria** | A classical goddess of fertility | *Demi* |
| **Demi** | Originally short for Demelza or Demetria | |
| **Dena** | See **Dinah** | |
| **Denise** | French female form of Dennis: follower of the Greek god Dionysos | *Denice, Dionysia* |
| **Dervila** | [Der-vla] English form of Deirbhile: poet's daughter | *Dervla* |
| **Deryn** | Blackbird (Welsh) | |
| **Desdemona** | [Dez-dem-ohn-a] Ill-omened (Greek) In Shakespeare's tragedy *Othello*, Desdemona is murdered by her husband, Othello, in a jealous rage | |
| **Desi** | Short for Desirée | |
| **Desirée** | [Dez-ray] Desired (Latin) | *Desi* |
| **Destina** | Destiny, fate (Spanish) | |
| **Destry** | Originally a surname. In the 1939 Western *Destry Rides Again*, James Stewart plays Tom Destry, an easy-going deputy sheriff trying to clean up a corrupt frontier town. Usually a boy's name | |

| Name | Definition | Short forms/ Variations |
|------|-----------|------------------------|
| **Detta** | Short for Bernardette | |
| **Devangi** | Like a goddess (Sanskrit) | |
| **Devendra** | Chief of gods (Sikh) Also a boy's name | |
| **Devi** | Goddess (Sanskrit) | |
| **Dextra** | Female form of Dexter: right-handed, skilful | |
| **Dharma** | Custom (Sanskrit) | |
| **Diana** | Roman goddess of the moon, hunting and fertility | *Di / Deandra, Deanna, Diane, Dianne* |
| **Dido** | [Die-doh] Queen of Carthage in Virgil's epic poem *The Aeneid* | |
| **Digna** | Worthy (Latin) | |
| **Dilly** | Short for Dilys or Odile | *Dillie* |
| **Dilwen** | True and fair or blessed (Welsh) | |
| **Dilys** | [Dill-iss] Genuine, true (Welsh) | *Dillie, Dilly / Dylis, Dyllis* |
| **Dima** | Torrential rain (Arabic) | |
| **Dimity** | From the cotton fabric | |
| **Dinah** | Judgment (Hebrew) The associations are not positive. In the Bible, Dinah is raped and her brothers take revenge by killing the rapist and all the men in the city | *Dena, Dina* |
| **Dionne** | [Dee-on] Female form of Dion: taken from Zeus, king of the gods in Greek legend | *Dee / Deonne, Dione* |
| **Dionysia** | See **Denise** | |
| **Dior** | [Dee-or] Sometimes given in homage to French fashion designer Christian Dior | |
| **Dita** | [Deet-a] Originally short for Perdita | *Deeta* |
| **Diva** | [Dee-vah] Goddess (Italian) | |
| **Dixie** | Girl from the southern states of the USA | |
| **Dodie** | Short for Dorothea or Dorothy | *Dodo* |
| **Dodo** | Short for Dorothea or Dorothy | *Dodie* |
| **Dolly** | Short for Dolores | |
| **Dolores** | [Dol-or-ez] Sorrows (Spanish) | *Dolly, Lola / Delores* |
| **Dominga** | Born on a Sunday (Spanish) | |
| **Dominica** | Female form of Dominic: lord | |

| Name | Definition | Short forms/ Variations |
|------|-----------|------------------------|
| **Dominique** | French female form of Dominic: lord | *Dom* |
| **Domino** | Lord, master (Latin) Also a boy's name | |
| **Donata** | Female form of Donato: given by God | |
| **Donatella** | Female form of Donato: given by God | |
| **Donella** | Female form of Donald: world rule | |
| **Donika** | See **Danika** | *Danica, Donica* |
| **Donla** | Lady of the fortress (Irish Gaelic) | |
| **Donna** | Lady (Italian) | |
| **Dora** | Short for Dorothea, Dorothy, Eudora, Isadora or Theodora | *Dory / Doreen, Dorinda* |
| **Dorcas** | [Dor-kus] Doe, a female deer (Greek) | |
| **Doreen** | See **Dora** | |
| **Dorinda** | See **Dora** | |
| **Doris** | Dorian woman; the Dorians were one of the tribes of Greece. In Greek myth, Doris was a goddess of the sea | *Dot, Dottie* |
| **Dorothea** | See **Dorothy** | *Dodie, Dodo, Dora, Dot, Dottie, Thea* |
| **Dorothy** | Gift from God (Greek) | *Dodie, Dodo, Dora, Dot, Dottie / Dorothea* |
| **Dorrit** | Amy Dorritt is the selfless heroine of Charles Dickens's 19th-century novel *Little Dorrit* | |
| **Dory** | Pet form of Dora | |
| **Dot** | Short for Doris, Dorothea or Dorothy | *Dottie* |
| **Drea** | Short for Andrea | |
| **Dreda** | Short for Etheldreda | |
| **Drew** | Traditionally a boy's name, short for Andrew: warrior | |
| **Drusilla** | From the Roman family name Drusus | *Dru* |
| **Dua** | Prayer (Arabic) | |
| **Duha** | Morning (Arabic) | |
| **Dulcie** | [Dul-see] Sweet (Latin) | *Dulcia* |
| **Dusty** | Female form of Dustin: originally a surname, meaning Thor's stone. It may have gained in popularity thanks to singer Dusty Springfield | |
| **Dymphna** | [Dimf-nuh] Fawn (Gaelic) St Dymphna is patron saint of the mentally ill | |

| Name | Definition | Short forms/ Variations |
| --- | --- | --- |
| **Eartha** | Earth (English) May have increased in popularity thanks to American singer and actress Eartha Kitt (born Eartha Mae Keith) | |
| **Ebba** | Rich fortress (Old English) | |
| **Eda** | Originally short for Edith | *Dodo* |
| **Edda** | Poetry (Old Norse) | |
| **Eddie** | Short for Edna or Edwina | *Eddi* |
| **Eden** | Place of pleasure (Hebrew) From the Biblical Garden of Eden. Also a boy's name | |
| **Edie** | [Ee-dee] Short for Edith | |
| **Edith** | Riches (Old English) | *Eda, Edie / Edyth* |
| **Edna** | Pleasure, delight (Hebrew) | *Eddi, Eddie / Edana, Edina, Ednah* |
| **Edwina** | Female form of Edwin: wealthy friend | *Eddie* |
| **Effie** | Short for Euphemia | *Ephie* |
| **Eglantine** | An alternative name for the sweetbriar flower | |
| **Eileen** | Irish form of Helen: sunbeam | *Aileen* |

| Name | Definition | Short forms/ Variations |
|------|-----------|------------------------|
| **Eilwen** | Fair brow (Welsh) | |
| **Eira** | [Eye-ra] Snow (Welsh) | |
| **Eireen** | [Irene] Irish form of Irene: peace | |
| **Eirian** | Beautiful / silver (Welsh) | |
| **Eirlys** | Snowdrop (Welsh) | |
| **Eirwen** | Fair or blessed snow (Welsh) | |
| **Eithne** | Kernel (Irish) | *Ena, Enya* |
| **Ekta** | Unity (Sanskrit) | |
| **Elaine** | See **Helen** | *Lainey, Lanie* |
| **Eleanor** | [El-en-or] See **Helen** | *Ellie, Leonore, Nell, Nellie, Nelly / Eleanora, Eleanore, Elena, Elenor, Elinor, Ellena, Ellenor* |
| **Electra** | Brilliant, radiant (Greek) In Greek myth, Electra and her brother avenge their father's murder by their mother and her lover | *Elettra* |
| **Elena** | [El-ay-nuh or El-en-uh] Italian, Portuguese and Spanish form of Eleanor: sunbeam | *Ellie, Nell, Nellie, Nelly / Eleanora, Eleanore, Elenor, Elinor, Ellena, Ellenor* |
| **Eleonora** | Italian form of Eleanor: sunbeam | *Leonora, Nora* |
| **Eleri** | The name of a Welsh river | |
| **Elettra** | Italian form of Electra: brilliant, radiant | |
| **Elfin** | Delicate, elf-like beauty (English) | |
| **Elfleda** | Noble beauty (Old English) | |
| **Elfreda** | Elf strength (Old English) | *Freda / Alfreda, Elfrida* |
| **Elgiva** | 10th-century English queen who became a saint | |
| **Eliana** | Italian form of Liane: from Aelianus, an old Roman family name | |
| **Elina** | Intelligent (Sanskrit) | |
| **Elisabeth** | See **Elizabeth** | |
| **Elisabetta** | Italian form of Elizabeth: God is my oath | |
| **Elise** | [El-eez] Short for Elizabeth | *Lise / Élise* |
| **Elita** | Elite (English) | |
| **Eliza** | [El-eye-za] Short for Elizabeth | *Liza* |

| Name | Definition | Short forms/ Variations |
|------|-----------|-------------------------|
| **Elizabeth** | God is my oath (Hebrew) | *Bess, Bessie, Bessy, Bet, Beth, Betsy, Bette, Betty, Buffy, Elise, Eliza, Elsa, Elsie, Ilsa, Ilse, Libbie, Libby, Liese, Lisbet, Lisbeth, Lisette, Liz, Liza, Lizbet, Lizbeth, Lizzie, Lizzy / Elisabeth, Elisabetta, Elspeth* |
| **Elke** | Female form of Elkan: possessed by God | *Elkie* |
| **Ella** | See **Helen** | |
| **Elle** | [El] She (French) | |
| **Ellen** | See **Helen** | *Ellie, Nell, Nellie, Nelly / Elen, Elin, Ella* |
| **Ellery** | Originally a surname. Ellery Queen is a fictional American detective in a series of novels by Frederic Dannay and Manfred Bennington Lee. Traditionally a boy's name | *Ellerie* |
| **Ellie** | Short for Ellen, Eleanor or Élodie | *Elly* |
| **Elma** | Love (Greek) Elm (Anglo Saxon) | |
| **Elmina** | Awesome fame (Germanic) | *Mina* |
| **Élodie** | Foreign riches (Visigothic) | *Elle, Ellie / Elodia* |
| **Éloise** | [El-oo-eez] Famous in battle (French) | *Eloisa, Eloise, Héloïse* |
| **Elsa** | Short for Elisabeth or Elizabeth | *Else, Elza* |
| **Elsie** | Short for Elizabeth | |
| **Elspeth** | See **Elizabeth** | |
| **Eluned** | Idol (Welsh) | *Eiluned, Luned* |
| **Elvina** | Female form of Alvin: elf friend | |
| **Elvira** | [El-veer-a] True (Germanic) | *Elle* |
| **Elysia** | [El-ee-zee-uh] Blissful (Greek) | |
| **Elza** | See **Elsa** | |
| **Emer** | [Ee-mer] In Gaelic myth, the wise and beautiful wife of the great warrior Cuchulainn | |
| **Emi** | [Em-ee] Smile (Japanese) | |
| **Emiko** | [Em-ee-ko] Smiling child (Japanese) | |

| Name | Definition | Short forms/ Variations |
|------|------------|-------------------------|
| **Emilia** | See **Amelia** | *Emmie, Emmy, Millie, Milly / Amalia, Amélie, Emily* |
| **Emily** | See **Amelia** | *Emmie, Emmy, Millie, Milly / Emilia, Emilie* |
| **Emma** | Entire (Germanic) It may have gained in popularity thanks to Jane Austen's 19th-century novel *Emma*. The spoilt but entrancing heroine can't resist matchmaking her friends but is blind when it comes to her own love life | *Emmie, Emmy / Ema, Emmeline* |
| **Emmanuelle** | French female form of Emmanuel: God is with us | |
| **Emmeline** | See **Emma** | *Emmie, Emmy / Emmelina* |
| **Emmie** | Short for Emilia, Emily, Emma or Emmeline | *Em / Emmy* |
| **Emmylou** | Combination of Emmy (entire) and Lou (fame in war) | |
| **Ena** | [Ee-nuh] English form of Eithne: kernel | |
| **Enfys** | Rainbow (Welsh) | |
| **Enid** | [Ee-nid] Purity (Celtic) In Arthurian myth, Enid's husband Geraint wrongly suspects she's been unfaithful, but she recovers his trust | |
| **Ennis** | [En-iss] See **Innis**. Also a boy's name | |
| **Enya** | English form of Eithne: kernel | *Ena* |
| **Eppie** | Short for Hephzibah | |
| **Eri** | Blessed prize (Japanese) | |
| **Erica** | Heather (Latin) | *Erika* |

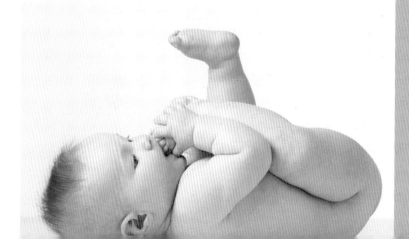

| Name | Definition | Short forms/ Variations |
|------|-----------|------------------------|
| **Erin** | Ireland (Irish) | |
| **Ermine** | [Er-min] See **Erminia**. Also the name of a small animal – part of the weasel family – whose fur turns white in winter and was used to trim royal robes | |
| **Erminia** | Female form of Ermin, from the name of a Teutonic demi-god | *Ermine* |
| **Ermintrude** | Entirely beloved (Germanic) | *Trude, Trudi, Trudie, Trudy* |
| **Ernestine** | Female form of Ernest: determined | *Tina / Ernestina* |
| **Esha** | Wish (Sanskrit) | |
| **Esmé** | [Ez-may] Valued, esteemed (French, Latin) | *Ismay* |
| **Esmerelda** | Emerald (Spanish) | *Esmé* |
| **Esperanza** | Hope (Latin) | |
| **Essie** | Short for Esther | |
| **Esta** | See **Esther** | |
| **Estella** | Star (French, Latin) A beautiful but icy young woman in Charles Dickens' 19th-century novel *Great Expectations* | *Estelle, Stella* |
| **Esther** | [Es-ta] Star (Persian) | *Essie / Esta, Hester* |
| **Esyllt** | Welsh form of Isolde, an Irish princess in Arthurian myth | *Ettie, Etty* |
| **Ethel** | Noble (Old English) | |
| **Ethelbert** | Noble splendour (Anglo Saxon) | *Bertie, Ethel* |
| **Ethelburga** | Noble protector (Anglo Saxon) | *Ethel* |
| **Etheldreda** | Noble strength (Old English) | *Dreda, Ethel / Etheldred* |
| **Ethelgiva** | Noble gift (Anglo Saxon) | *Ethel* |
| **Etta** | Short for Henrietta or Rosetta | |
| **Ettie** | Short for Esyllt | *Etty* |
| **Eudora** | [Yu-dora] Good gift (Greek) | *Dora* |
| **Eugenia** | [Yu-jhee-nee-uh] Female form of Eugene: well-born, noble | |
| **Eugénie** | [Yu-jhee-nee] French form of Eugenia: well-born, noble | *Eugenie* |
| **Eulalia** | To talk well (Greek) | *Eula, Lalie / Eulalie, Olalla* |

| Name | Definition | Short forms/ Variations |
| --- | --- | --- |
| **Eunice** | [Yu-niss] Good victory (Greek) | |
| **Euphemia** | To speak well (Greek) | *Effie, Ephie* |
| **Eurydice** | [Yu-rid-ee-chee] Wide justice (Greek) In Greek myth, Eurydice was Orpheus's wife, who died after being bitten by a serpent. Orpheus tried to rescue her from the Underworld, but failed after he disobeyed the condition that he must not look back on the way out | |
| **Eustacia** | Female form of Eustace: fruitful | |
| **Eva** | See **Eve** | |
| **Evadne** | [Ev-ad-nee] Fortunate (Greek) | *Evie* |
| **Evangeline** | Gospel (Latin) | *Eva / Evangelina* |
| **Eve** | Living (Hebrew) According to the Bible, the first woman | *Evie, Evita / Eva, Evelyn* |
| **Evelyn** | See **Eve**. Also a boy's name | *Evie / Aveline, Eveleen, Evelina, Eveline* |
| **Evie** | Short for Eve, Evelyn or Genevieve | |
| **Evita** | Spanish pet form of Eva | |

| Name | Definition | Short forms/ Variations |
|------|-----------|------------------------|
| **Fabia** | Female form of Fabian: bean | |
| **Fabienne** | French female form of Fabian: bean | |
| **Fabiola** | Female form of Fabio: bean | |
| **Faline** | See **Felina** | |
| **Fallon** | Originally an Irish surname, meaning grandchild of the ruler | |
| **Farah** | Joy (Arabic) | *Farrah* |
| **Fatima** | Chaste (Arabic) The name of Muhammad's daughter, known as the mother of all Muslims | |
| **Faustina** | Fortunate (Latin) | |
| **Fay** | Fairy (Old English) | *Faye, Fayette* |
| **Fayette** | See **Fay** | |
| **Felice** | [Fel-eece] French female form of Felix: happy, lucky | |
| **Felicia** | [Fel-iss-ee-uh] Female form of Felix: happy, lucky | *Flic, Flick* |
| **Felicity** | Good fortune (French, Latin) | *Flic, Flick* |
| **Felina** | Feline, cat-like (Latin) | *Faline* |

| Name | Definition | Short forms/Variations |
|---|---|---|
| **Fenella** | English form of Fionnuala: white shoulders | *Finella* |
| **Fernanda** | Spanish female form of Ferdinand: ready for the journey | |
| **Ffion** | [Fee-on] Welsh form of Fiona: white, fair | |
| **Fiamma** | [Fee-am-uh] Flame (Italian) | *Fiammetta* |
| **Fiammetta** | Pet form of Fiamma | |
| **Fianna** | [Fee-an-uh] Warrior (Irish Gaelic) | |
| **Fidela** | [Fid-ay-luh] Female form of Fidelis: faithful | |
| **Fidelma** | Constancy (Irish Gaelic) | |
| **Fiesta** | Celebration (Spanish) | |
| **Fifi** | [Fee-fee] Short for Fiona or Josephine | |
| **Fina** | [Fee-nuh] Short for Rufina | |
| **Finola** | English form of Fionnuala: white shoulders | *Nola / Fenella, Finella* |
| **Fiona** | White, fair (Gaelic) | *Fi, Fifi / Ffion* |
| **Fionnuala** | White shoulders (Irish Gaelic) | *Nuala / Finola* |
| **Fiorella** | Flower (Italian) | |
| **Flavia** | [Flah-vee-a] Yellow-haired (Latin) | |
| **Fleur** | Flower (French) | |
| **Flick** | Short for Felicia or Felicity | *Flic* |
| **Flo** | Short for Flora, Florence or Florentia | |
| **Floella** | Combination of Flo (short for Florence: blossoming) and Ella (sunbeam) | |
| **Flora** | Roman goddess of flowers | *Flo, Florrie, Flossie* |
| **Florence** | Blossoming (Latin) | *Flo, Flora, Florrie, Flossie / Florentia* |
| **Florentia** | Blossoming (Latin) | *Flo, Flora, Florrie, Flossie / Florence* |
| **Florrie** | Short for Flora, Florence or Florentia | *Flo* |
| **Flossie** | Short for Flora, Florence or Florentia | *Flo* |
| **Flynn** | Red, ruddy (Gaelic) Traditionally a boy's name | |
| **Foula** | One of the Shetland Isles | |
| **Fran** | Short for Frances, Francesca, Francine or Francoise. Also a boy's name | |

| Name | Definition | Short forms/ Variations |
|------|-----------|------------------------|
| **Franca** | [Fran-kuh] Female form of Franco, short for Francesco: Frenchman | |
| **Frances** | Frenchman (Latin) | *Fran, Frankie / Francesca* |
| **Francesca** | [Fran-chess-ka] See **Frances** | *Cesca, Chica, Fran, Frankie* |
| **Francine** | [Fran-seen] Pet form of Francoise: Frenchman | *Fran, Frankie* |
| **Francoise** | [Fran-swahz] French form of Frances: Frenchman | *Fran, Frankie* |
| **Frankie** | Short for Frances, Francesca, Francine or Francoise. Also a boy's name | |
| **Freda** | Short for Alfreda or Elfreda | |
| **Freddie** | Short for Frederica, Frieda, Winfred or Winifred. Also a boy's name | *Fred* |
| **Frederica** | [Fred-er-eek-a] Female form of Frederick: peaceful ruler | *Fred, Freda, Freddie* |
| **Freya** | [Fray-uh] Lady (Germanic) In Scandinavian myth, the goddess of love | |
| **Frieda** | [Free-duh] Peace (German) | *Freddie / Freda, Frida, Friede* |

| Name | Definition | Short forms/ Variations |
|------|-----------|------------------------|
| **Gabir** | A helper in time of need (Arabic) | *Jabir* |
| **Gabrielle** | Female form of Gabriel: man of God | *Gabi, Gaby / Gabriel, Gabriela, Gabriella* |
| **Gaby** | [Gabb-ee] Short for Gabriella or Gabrielle | *Gabi* |
| **Gaia** | [Guy-a] Earth (Greek) | |
| **Gail** | Originally short for Abigail | *Gael, Gale, Gayle* |
| **Gala** | Short for Galina | |
| **Galaxy** | A large group of stars and planets (English) | |
| **Galina** | Calm (Greek) | *Gala* |
| **Gattie** | Short for Gertrude | *Gatty* |
| **Gavotte** | A dance popular in France in the 18th century | |
| **Gaynor** | Medieval form of Guinevere: King Arthur's wife and Lancelot's lover | |
| **Geena** | See **Gina** | |
| **Gemma** | Gem, jewel (Italian) | *Gem / Jemma* |
| **Genesis** | Birth; beginning; source, origin (Greek, Hebrew) | |

| Name | Definition | Short forms/ Variations |
| --- | --- | --- |
| **Genevieve** | Woman (Celtic, French) | *Eve, Evie, Genny, Veva* |
| **Genevra** | English form of Guinevere: white wave | *Gen, Genny* |
| **Genny** | Short for Genevieve, Genevra or Guinevere | *Gen* |
| **Gentille** | [Jon-teel] Kind (French) | *Yentl* |
| **Georgette** | French female form of George: farmer | *George, Georgie* |
| **Georgia** | Female form of George: farmer | *Georgie / Georgiana, Georgina* |
| **Georgianne** | Combination of Georgia (female form of George: farmer) and Ann (favoured by God) | *Georgie / Georgianna* |
| **Georgie** | Short for Georgette, Georgia, Georgiana, Georgianna, Georgianne or Georgina | *George* |
| **Georgina** | See **Georgia** | *George, Georgie / Georgiana, Georgine, Gina* |
| **Geraldine** | Female form of Gerald: spear; rule | *Geri, Gerri, Gerrie, Gerry* |
| **Gerd** | Stronghold (Old Norse) In Norse myth, Gerd was a fertility goddess | |
| **Geri** | Short for Geraldine | *Gerri, Gerrie, Gerry* |
| **Germaine** | Female form of Germain: brother | |
| **Gertie** | Short for Gertrude | |
| **Gertrude** | Spear strength (Germanic) | *Gattie, Gatty, Gertie, Trude, Trudi, Trudie Trudy* |
| **Gethsemane** | In the Bible, the name of the garden where Jesus prayed and was betrayed by Judas Iscariot | |
| **Ghislain** | See **Giselle** | *Ghislaine* |
| **Ghufran** | Forgiveness (Arabic) | |
| **Giachetta** | Female form of Giacomo, the Italian form of James: supplanter | *Jacquetta* |
| **Gianna** | [Jee-anna] Short for Giovanna | |
| **Giannina** | [Jee-uh-nee-nuh] Female form of Giannino, a pet form of Giovanni: God is gracious | |
| **Gigi** | Short for Giselle | |
| **Gilda** | Sacrifice (Germanic) A femme fatale played by Rita Hayworth in the 1946 film *Gilda* | |

names

girls'

g

| Name | Definition | Short forms/ Variations |
|---|---|---|
| **Gillian** | See **Julian** | *Gill, Gilly, Jill, Jilly / Jillian* |
| **Gilly** | Short for Gillian | *Gill* |
| **Gina** | Short for Georgina | *Geena* |
| **Ginevra** | Italian form of Genevieve: King Arthur's wife and Lancelot's lover | *Ginnie, Ginny* |
| **Ginger** | Short for Virginia. It may have increased in popularity thanks to American movie star and dancer Ginger (Virginia) Rogers | |
| **Ginny** | Short for Ginevra or Virginia | *Ginnie* |
| **Gioconda** | Happy (Italian) | |
| **Giovanna** | Female form of Giovanni, the Italian form of John: God is gracious | *Gianna* |
| **Girzie** | Short for Griselda, Griseldis or Grizel | |
| **Giselle** | Pledge (Germanic) Became popular after the 19th-century ballet of the same name | *Gigi / Ghislain, Ghislaine, Gisele* |
| **Gita** | [Ghee-ta] Song (Sanskrit) | |
| **Gladys** | Princess (Welsh) | |
| **Glaw** | Rain (Welsh) Also a boy's name | |
| **Glenda** | Pure and good (Welsh) | |
| **Glenna** | Female form of Glen: valley | |
| **Glenys** | Pure, holy (Welsh) | *Glenis, Glennis, Glennys, Glynis, Glynnis* |
| **Gloria** | Glory (Latin) | |
| **Glynis** | See **Glenys** | |
| **Godiva** | Gift from God (Old English) According to legend, in the 11th century Lady Godiva rode naked through the streets of Coventry in protest at her husband's wish to impose a heavy tax on the people | |
| **Golda** | Gold (Yiddish) | |
| **Goneril** | [Gon-uh-ril] The associations are not positive. Goneril is the king's treacherous eldest daughter in Shakespeare's *King Lear* | |
| **Grace** | From 'gratia' (Latin): grace and thanks | *Gracie* |
| **Gracia** | Spanish form of Grace | *Graciela / Grazia* |
| **Gracie** | Pet form of Grace | |
| **Graciela** | Pet form of Gracia | |

| Name | Definition | Short forms/ Variations |
|------|------------|-------------------------|
| **Grazia** | Italian form of Grace | *Graziella* |
| **Graziella** | Pet form of Grazia | *Graziela* |
| **Greer** | Originally a Scottish surname, meaning vigilant | |
| **Greta** | Originally short for Margareta, a variation of Margaret. Sometimes used in homage to the actress Greta Garbo | *Gretel / Grete* |
| **Gretchen** | German pet form of Margaret: pearl | |
| **Gretel** | Pet form of Greta. In the fairy story *Hansel and Gretel*, the brother and sister are left to starve in the forest by their father and stepmother. They're then caught by a witch who plans to eat them, but they manage to kill her and return home | |
| **Griet** | Short for Margriet, the Dutch form of Margaret: pearl | |
| **Griselda** | [Griz-el-duh] Grey (Germanic) | *Girzie, Zelda / Griseldis* |
| **Griseldis** | [Griz-el-diss] Grey battle maid (Teutonic) | *Girzie / Griselda* |
| **Grizel** | Scottish form of Griseldis: grey battle maid | *Girzie / Grizell, Grizzell* |
| **Gudrun** | [Good-run] God's rune (Old Norse) | |
| **Guinevere** | [Gwin-ih-veer] White wave (Celtic) In Arthurian myth, Guinevere was King Arthur's wife but had an affair with Lancelot | *Genny, Gwen, Gwynnie / Guenevere, Grete* |
| **Gulika** | Pearl (Sanskrit) | |
| **Gwen** | Short for Guinevere, Gwendolen or Gwenfrewi | |
| **Gwenda** | Good and fair or blessed (Welsh) | |
| **Gwendolen** | Holy ring (Welsh) | *Gwen, Wendy / Gwendolin, Gwendolyn* |
| **Gwenfrewi** | Blessed reconciliation (Welsh) | *Gwen / Winifred* |
| **Gwyn** | See **Gwynne** | |
| **Gwyneira** | Fair or blessed snow (Welsh) | |
| **Gwyneth** | From Gwynedd, a county in north Wales | *Gwynnie / Gwynneth* |
| **Gwynne** | Fair or blessed (Celtic) | *Gwyn* |
| **Gwynnie** | Short for Guinevere or Gwyneth | |
| **Gypsy** | Traveller (English) | |
| **Gytha** | [Gith-uh] War (Old English) | |

| Name | Definition | Short forms/ Variations |
|------|-----------|------------------------|
| **Hadil** | Cooing of doves (Arabic) | |
| **Hadley** | Originally an English surname, meaning heather wood. Also a boy's name | *Hadlee, Hadleigh* |
| **Hagar** | Flight (Hebrew) In the Bible, Hagar was a slave. Her mistress, Sarah, couldn't conceive, so gave Hagar to her husband to conceive in her place. She then treated Hagar so badly that she ran away | *Hagir* |
| **Haidee** | Modest (Greek) | *Haydee* |
| **Hailey** | See **Haley** | |
| **Haimi** | Golden (Sanskrit) | |
| **Hala** | The halo around the moon (Arabic) | |
| **Halcyon** | Kingfisher (Greek) The phrase 'halcyon days' refers to a time that was happy and peaceful, or successful | *Hallie, Hally / Halcyone* |
| **Haley** | Originally a surname, meaning hay meadow. Also a boy's name | *Hailey, Hayley* |
| **Halina** | Polish form of Helen: sunbeam | *Hallie, Hally* |
| **Halle** | Female form of Hal, short for Hallam, Halley, Harry or Henry | *Hal* |

| Name | Definition | Short forms/ Variations |
| --- | --- | --- |
| **Hallie** | Short for Halcyon or Halina | *Hally* |
| **Hana** | Bliss (Arabic) | |
| **Hannah** | Favoured by God (Hebrew) | *Nan / Hanna, Hana* |
| **Hansa** | Beautiful swan (Sanskrit) | |
| **Hansine** | Female form of Hans, a German form of John: God is gracious | |
| **Harinder** | Lord (Sikh) Also a boy's name | |
| **Harlequin** | A male servant in the Italian *Commedia dell'Arte* | |
| **Harley** | Originally a surname, meaning hare wood. Sometimes used in reference to Harley Davidson motorbikes. Also a boy's name | |
| **Harper** | Originally a surname, meaning someone who played the harp. May have gained in popularity as a girl's name thanks to American novelist Harper Lee, author of *To Kill a Mockingbird*. Also a boy's name | |
| **Harriet** | Female form of Harry, short for Henry: home ruler | *Harry, Hattie, Hatty* |
| **Haruko** | Springtime child (Japanese) | |
| **Harumi** | Springtime beauty (Japanese) | |
| **Harvir** | Brave Lord (Sikh) Also a boy's name | |
| **Hattie** | Short for Harriet or Henrietta | *Hatty* |

| Name | Definition | Short forms/Variations |
|------|-----------|------------------------|
| **Haydee** | See **Haidee** | |
| **Hayley** | See **Haley** | *Hailey, Haley* |
| **Hebe** | [Hee-bee] Young (Greek) | |
| **Hedda** | Short for Hedwig | |
| **Hedwig** | War (Germanic) | *Hedda / Hedvig* |
| **Heidi** | Short for Adelheid. It gained in popularity thanks to Johanna Spyri's 19th-century children's novel *Heidi* | |
| **Helen** | Sunbeam (Greek) Helen of Troy was a famous beauty in Greek myth | *Nell, Nellie, Nelly / Eileen, Elaine, Eleanor, Ella, Ellen, Halina, Helena, Hélène, Ileana, Ilona, Yelena* |
| **Helena** | See **Helen** | *Lena, Nell, Nellie, Nelly / Elaine, Eleanor, Ellen* |
| **Helga** | Rich and successful / blessed (Old Norse) | *Helge* |
| **Héloïse** | [Hel-oo-eez] See **Éloise** | *Heloisa* |
| **Henrietta** | Female form of Henry: home ruler | *Etta, Hattie, Hatty, Hetta, Hettie, Hetty / Henriette* |
| **Hephzibah** | My delight is in her (Hebrew) | *Eppie / Hepzibah* |
| **Hermes** | [Her-meez] The Greek messenger god | |
| **Hermia** | Taken from Hermes, the Greek messenger god. One of the lovers in Shakespeare's *A Midsummer Night's Dream* | |
| **Hermione** | [Her-my-on-ee] Taken from Hermes, the Greek messenger god. It may have gained in popularity thanks to the character of Hermione Grainger, Harry's brainy friend in JK Rowling's Harry Potter novels | |
| **Hermosa** | Beautiful (Spanish) | |
| **Hero** | In Greek myth, Hero is a priestess of Aphrodite, the goddess of love. She commits suicide after her lover, Leander, is drowned in a storm | |
| **Hester** | See **Esther** | |
| **Hetta** | Short for Henrietta | |

girls'

h

names

| Name | Definition | Short forms/ Variations |
|---|---|---|
| **Hettie** | Short for Henrietta | *Hetty* |
| **Heulwen** | Sunshine (Welsh) | |
| **Hilaria** | See **Hilary** | |
| **Hilary** | Cheerful (Latin) Also a boy's name | *Hilaria, Hillary, Ilaria* |
| **Hilda** | Battle (Germanic) | *Hilde* |
| **Hildegard** | Battle enclosure (Germanic) | *Hilda* |
| **Himani** | Snow (Sanskrit) | |
| **Hira** | Diamond (Sanskrit) | |
| **Hiro** | [Hee-ro] Abundant (Japanese) Also a boy's name | |
| **Honoria** | Honour (Latin) | *Nora / Honora* |
| **Horatia** | [Hor-ay-she-uh] Female form of Horace. The Horatians were a noble clan in Ancient Rome. The name is sometimes used in homage to Britain's greatest naval hero, Admiral Horatio Nelson | |
| **Hortense** | Taken from the Roman family name Hortensius | *Hortensia* |
| **Huan** | Happiness (Chinese) Also a boy's name | |
| **Hulda** | Lovable (Scandinavian) | |
| **Hunter** | Originally a surname. Traditionally a boy's name | |

| Name | Definition | Short forms/ Variations |
|---|---|---|
| **Ianthe** | [Eye-an-thee] Violet flower (Greek) | *Iolanthe* |
| **Ida** | Work (Germanic) | |
| **Idony** | Again (Old Norse) | |
| **Idyll** | [Id-ill] A place where everyone is happy (English) | |
| **Igraine** | In Arthurian myth, Igraine was the wife of Uther Pendragon and the mother of King Arthur | *Ygrayne* |
| **Iksha** | Foresight (Sanskrit) | |
| **Ilana** | Female form of Ilan: tree | |
| **Ilaria** | Italian form of Hilary: cheerful | |
| **Ileana** | Romanian form of Helen: sunbeam | |
| **Ilene** | Combination of Aileen (sunbeam) and Irene (peace) | |
| **Ilona** | Hungarian form of Helen: sunbeam | |
| **Ilsa** | Short for Elizabeth | *Ilse* |
| **Iman** | [Im-an] Faith (Arabic) Also a boy's name | |
| **Imani** | Trustworthy (Sanskrit) | |

| Name | Definition | Short forms/ Variations |
|---|---|---|
| **Imelda** | Whole battle (Germanic) | |
| **Immy** | Short for Imogen | *Imo* |
| **Imogen** | [Immo-jen] Maiden (Gaelic) First used in Shakespeare's *Cymbeline* | *Immy, Imo* |
| **Ina** | [Ee-na] Short form of any name ending in 'ina' | |
| **Inanna** | The Mesopotamian goddess of love and war | |
| **Inca** | Taken from the South American civilisation and empire | |
| **Indira** | Prosperity; splendour (Sanskrit) | |
| **Indra** | Possessing drops of rain (Sanskrit) Indra is the Hindu warrior god of the sky and rain. Also a boy's name | |
| **Ines** | [In-eth] Spanish form of Agnes: pure or lamb | *Inés, Inez* |
| **Inge** | [In-ga] Taken from Ing, the Old Norse fertility god. Also a boy's name | *Inka* |
| **Ingemar** | [Ing-mar] Taken from Ing, the Old Norse fertility god | *Inga, Inge* |
| **Ingrid** | Beautiful Ing – the Old Norse fertility god. Sometimes given in homage to *Casablanca* actress Ingrid Bergman | *Inga, Inge* |
| **Inka** | Finnish form of Inge | |
| **Innis** | Originally a Scottish surname, meaning island. Also a boy's name | *Ennis, Innes* |
| **Iola** | [Eye-o-la] See **Iole** | |
| **Iolanthe** | [Eye-o-lanth-ee] See **Ianthe** | |
| **Iole** | [Eye-oh-lee] Violet (Greek) | *Iola* |
| **Ione** | [Eye-oh-nee] Ionian Greece | *Nonie* |
| **Iphigenia** | [If-ij-en-eye-uh] In Greek myth, Iphigenia's father, Agamemnon, was told he had to sacrifice his daughter to the goddess Artemis to ensure favourable winds for his ships, which were heading for Troy. Sources differ as to whether he did so | *Iphigenie* |
| **Irene** | [Eye-reen or Eye-reen-ee] Peace (Greek) | *Reenie, Rene / Eireen, Eirene, Irena, Irina* |
| **Irina** | [Ih-ree-na] See **Irene** | *Reenie, Rene, Rina / Eireen, Eirene, Irena* |

| Name | Definition | Short forms/ Variations |
|------|-----------|------------------------|
| **Irma** | [Uhr-ma] Entire (Germanic) | |
| **Isabel** | Spanish form of Elizabeth: God is my oath | *Bella, Belle, Issie, Issy, Izzie, Izzy, Tibbie, Tibby / Isabella, Isabelle, Ishbel, Isobel, Isobelle, Isobella* |
| **Isabella** | See **Isabel** | *Sabella* |
| **Isadora** | See **Isidora** | |
| **Isaura** | Woman from Isauria in Asia Minor | |
| **Iseabail** | [Ish-bel] Scottish Gaelic form of Isabel: God is my oath | *Ishbel* |
| **Iseult** | See **Isolde** | *Issie, Issy, Izzie, Izzy / Yseult, Ysolt* |
| **Isha** | God: life (Sanskrit) | |
| **Ishbel** | See **Isabel** | |
| **Ishya** | Spring (Sanskrit) | |
| **Isidora** | Gift of the goddess Isis (Greek) | *Dora, Issie, Issy, Izzie, Izzy / Isadora* |
| **Isis** | [Eye-sis] A Greek goddess | |
| **Isla** | [Eye-la] From Islay, an island in the Hebrides | |
| **Ismay** | [Iz-may] See **Esmé** | |
| **Ismene** | [Iz-meen] In Greek myth, Ismene is Antigone's sister and one of Oedipus's daughters | |
| **Isolde** | [Iz-oll-da] An Irish princess in Arthurian myth | *Issie, Issy, Izzie, Izzy / Iseult, Isold, Isolda, Izolde, Yseult* |
| **Isra** | Night journey (Arabic) According to Islamic tradition, Muhammad made a miraculous night journey from Mecca to Jerusalem where he prayed with Abraham, Moses and Jesus | *Asra* |
| **Issy** | Short for Isabel, Iseult, Isidora, Isolde or Yseult | *Issie* |
| **Ivanna** | Female form of Ivan: God is gracious | |
| **Ivonne** | German form of Yvonne: yew | *Iwona* |
| **Izolde** | [Iz-ol-da] See **Isolde** | |
| **Izzy** | Short for Isabel, Iseult, Isidora, Isolde or Yseult | *Izzie* |

girls'

i

names

| Name | Definition | Short forms/ Variations |
|------|-----------|------------------------|
| **Jacinta** | [Ja-sin-ta] Hyacinth (Spanish) | *Cinta* |
| **Jackie** | Short for Jacqueline or Jacquetta | *Jacqui, Jacquie* |
| **Jacobina** | Female form of Jacob: supplanter | |
| **Jacqueline** | Female form of Jacques: supplanter | *Jackie, Jacqui, Jacquie / Jacquelyn* |
| **Jacquetta** | [Jack-ett-a] See **Giachetta** | *Jackie, Jacqui, Jacquie* |
| **Jacqui** | Short for Jacqueline | |
| **Jada** | [Jay-da] He knows (Hebrew) | |
| **Jadon** | [Jay-don] He will judge (Hebrew) Usually used as a boy's name | *Jaden, Jayden, Jaydon* |
| **Jae** | Female form of Jay: victory | |
| **Jael** | See **Yael** | |
| **Jaime** | Spanish form of James: supplanter. Also a boy's name | *Jaimie* |
| **Jamesina** | Female form of James: supplanter | |
| **Jamie** | Traditionally a boy's name, short for James: supplanter | *Jaimie* |
| **Jamila** | Beautiful, graceful (Arabic) | *Jamilla* |

| Name | Definition | Short forms/ Variations |
|------|-----------|------------------------|
| **Jan** | Short for Jancis, Janelle, Janet, Janice or Janna | |
| **Jana** | Female form of Jan: God is gracious | |
| **Jancis** | Combination of Jan (short for Janet or Janice: God is gracious) and Frances (from France) | *Jan, Jancy* |
| **Jancy** | Short for Jancis | |
| **Jane** | Female form of John: God is gracious | *Janey, Janie / Janelle, Janet, Janice, Jayne, Jean, Jeanette* |
| **Janelle** | See **Jane** | *Jan* |
| **Janet** | See **Jane** | *Jan / Janetta, Janette* |
| **Janice** | See **Jane** | *Jan / Janis* |
| **Janie** | Pet form of Jane | *Janey* |
| **Janine** | See **Jeannine** | |
| **Janis** | See **Janice** | |
| **Janisha** | Knowledgeable (Sanskrit) | |
| **Janna** | See **Joan** | *Jan* |
| **Jarul** | Beautiful flower queen (Sanskrit) | |
| **Jasminder** | Lord's glory (Sikh) Also a boy's name | *Jazz* |
| **Jaswant** | Admirable; victorious (Sikh) Also a boy's name | *Jazz* |
| **Jaswinder** | Indra (god of the sky) of the thunderbolt (Sanskrit) | *Jazz* |
| **Jaya** | Female form of Jay: victory | |
| **Jayden** | See **Jadon** | |
| **Jaye** | Female form of Jay: victory | |
| **Jayla** | Female form of Jay: victory | |
| **Jayne** | See **Jane** | |
| **Jazz** | Short for Jasminder, Jasmine, Jaswant or Jaswinder | |
| **Jean** | See **Jane** | *Jeanie, Jeannie / Jeanette, Jeanne, Jeannette* |
| **Jeanette** | See **Jane** | *Nettie / Janette, Jannette, Jeannette* |
| **Jeanie** | Pet form of Jean | |
| **Jeanne** | French female form of John: God is gracious | |
| **Jeannine** | French pet form of Jeanne | *Janine, Jeanine* |

| Name | Definition | Short forms/ Variations |
|------|-----------|------------------------|
| **Jecca** | Short for Jessica | |
| **Jemima** | Dove / bright as day (Hebrew) | *Jem, Jemma / Jemimah* |
| **Jemma** | See **Gemma** | *Jem* |
| **Jenna** | See **Jennifer** | *Jen* |
| **Jennifer** | Cornish form of Guinevere | *Jen, Jeni, Jenni, Jennie, Jenny, Jinny / Jenna* |
| **Jenny** | Short for Jennifer | *Jen / Jeni, Jenni, Jennie* |
| **Jess** | Short for Jessamine, Jessamy, Jesse, Jessica or Jessie | |
| **Jessa** | Short for Jessamine or Jessamy | |
| **Jessamine** | A variation of Jasmine | *Jess, Jessa / Jessamy* |
| **Jessamy** | A variation of Jasmine | *Jess, Jessa / Jessamine* |
| **Jesse** | [Jess] Gift (Hebrew) Also a boy's name | *Jess / Jessie* |
| **Jessica** | God is looking (Hebrew) Thought to have first been used in Shakespeare's *The Merchant of Venice* for Shylock's daughter | *Jecca, Jess, Jesse, Jessie* |
| **Jessie** | Short for Jessica | *Jess* |
| **Jeudi** | Thursday (French) | |
| **Jeune-fille** | [Jeun-fee] Young girl (French) | |
| **Jezebel** | Not exalted (Hebrew) The associations are not positive. In the Bible, Jezebel is an evil queen who ends up being thrown out of a window and eaten by dogs | |
| **Jia** | Beautiful (Chinese) | |
| **Jill** | Short for Jillian | *Gill* |
| **Jillian** | See **Julian** | *Gill, Gilly, Jill, Jilly / Gillian* |
| **Jilly** | Short for Jillian | *Jill* |
| **Jinan** | Paradise (Arabic) Also a boy's name | |
| **Jinny** | Short for Jennifer | |
| **Jinx** | A curse / someone or something that brings bad luck (English) | |
| **Joan** | Female form of John: God is gracious | *Joanie, Joni / Janna* |
| **Joanie** | Pet form of Joan | *Joni* |

| Name | Definition | Short forms/Variations |
|---|---|---|
| **Jo-Ann** | Combination of Jo and Ann (favoured by God) | *Jo-Anne* |
| **Joanne** | Female form of John: God is gracious | *Jo / Joanna, Johanne, Johanna* |
| **Jocasta** | In Greek myth, Jocasta marries Oedipus and has children with him, before discovering he's her own son | |
| **Jocelyn** | [Joss-lin] Taken from the Gauts, a Germanic tribe. Also a boy's name | *Joss / Joceline, Joseline, Joselyn, Josline, Joslyn* |
| **Jody** | Pet form of Judith. Also a boy's name | *Jodi, Jodie* |
| **Joelle** | Female form of Joel: Yaweh is God | *Jo / Joely, Jolene* |
| **Joely** | See **Joelle** | |
| **Johanna** | See **Joanne** | *Jo / Joanna, Johanne* |
| **Jolanda** | Italian form of Yolanda: violet flower | *Jolande* |
| **Jolene** | See **Joelle** | *Jo / Joleen* |
| **Jolie** | Pretty (French) | |
| **Jonelle** | Female form of John: God is gracious | |
| **Joni** | [Jo-nee] See Joan. Sometimes given in homage to Canadian singer Joni Mitchell | *Joanie* |
| **Jordana** | Obviously female form of Jordan | |
| **Jory** | Short for Marjorie | *Jorie* |
| **Josefina** | See **Josephine** | *Fifi, Jo, Josette, Josie / Josefine, Josephina* |
| **Joselyn** | See **Jocelyn** | *Joss / Joceline, Joseline, Josline, Joslyn* |
| **Josepha** | Female form of Joseph: God shall add | *Jo / Josephine* |
| **Josephine** | Female form of Joseph: God shall add | *Fifi, Jo, Josette, Josie / Josephina* |

| Name | Definition | Short forms/ Variations |
|---|---|---|
| **Josette** | French short form of Josephine | *Jo, Josie* |
| **Joshika** | Young woman (Sanskrit) | |
| **Josie** | [Jo-see or Jo-zee] Short for Josephine or Josette | *Jo* |
| **Joslyn** | See **Jocelyn** | *Joss / Joceline, Joseline, Joselyn, Josline* |
| **Joss** | Short for Jocelyn. Also a boy's name | |
| **Joyce** | Joyful (Latin) | |
| **Ju** | Chrysanthemum (Chinese) | *Hajar* |
| **Juan** | Graciousness (Chinese) | |
| **Juanita** | [Wan-ee-ta] Female form of Juan: God is gracious | *Neeta, Nita* |
| **Jubilee** | A celebration for a special occasion, such as an anniversary (English) | |
| **Jude** | Short for Judith | |
| **Judit** | Hungarian and Spanish form of Judith: Jewish woman | |
| **Judith** | Jewish woman (Hebrew) | *Jody, Jude, Judi, Judie, Judy, Jutte / Judit, Julitta* |
| **Judy** | Short for Judith | *Jude / Judi, Judie* |
| **Jules** | Short for Julia, Julian, Julie, Juliet or Juliette. Also a boy's name | *Jools* |
| **Julia** | Female form of Julius, a Roman family name | *Jools, Jules / Julie* |
| **Julian** | From the Roman family name Julius. Usually a boy's name | *Jools, Jules, Julie / Gillian, Jillian, Juliana* |
| **Juliana** | Obviously female form of Julian | *Uliana* |
| **Julianne** | Combination of Julie (from Julius, a Roman family name) and Anne (favoured by God) | *Julianna* |
| **Julie** | See **Julia** | *Jools, Jules* |
| **Juliet** | See Julia. The tragic heroine of Shakespeare's *Romeo and Juliet* | *Ju, Jools, Jules / Juliette* |
| **Juliette** | French form of Juliet: from Julius, a Roman family name | *Ju, Jools, Jules* |
| **Julitta** | Italian form of Judith: Jewish woman | *Julita* |
| **Juno** | A Roman goddess | |
| **Justine** | Female form of Justin: just and fair | |
| **Jutte** | [Yutt-a] German short form of Judith | *Jutta* |

| Name | Definition | Short forms/ Variations |
|------|------------|-------------------------|
| **Kai** | Sea (Hawaiian) | |
| **Kaja** | Scandinavian form of Katherine | |
| **Kalpana** | Imagination (Sanskrit) | |
| **Kalyani** | Lucky (Sanskrit) | |
| **Kamala** | Female form of Kamal: perfection (Arabic) or red (Sanskrit) | |
| **Kamaria** | Like the moon (Swahili) | |
| **Kara** | See **Cara** | |
| **Karam** | Generosity (Arabic) Also a boy's name | |
| **Kareema** | Kind; dignified (Arabic) | |
| **Kareena** | Pure; dear (Sanskrit) | |
| **Karen** | Danish form of Katherine: pure | *Karin* |
| **Karenza** | Loving (Cornish) | *Carenza* |
| **Kari** | Norwegian form of Katherine: pure | |
| **Karima** | Female form of Karim: generosity | |
| **Karin** | See **Karen** | *Karina* |
| **Karina** | Polish form of Karin: pure | |

| Name | Definition | Short forms/ Variations |
| --- | --- | --- |
| **Karishma** | Miracle (Sanskrit) | |
| **Karita** | Charity (Latin) | |
| **Karla** | Female form of Karl: free man | |
| **Karma** | Action; performance (Sanskrit) The concept that the way you behave in this life will affect future lives | |
| **Kat** | Short for Katerina | |
| **Katarina** | See **Katerina** | |
| **Kate** | Short for Katherine | *Katie, Katy / Cate* |
| **Katelyn** | See **Caitlin** | *Caitlyn* |
| **Katerina** | Russian form of Katherine: pure | *Kat, Katya, Rina / Caterina, Katarina, Katherina, Katrina* |
| **Katherine** | Pure (Greek) | *Kate, Kathie, Kathy, Katie, Katy, Kit, Kittie, Kitty / Caitlyn, Catharine, Catherine, Cathleen, Kaja, Kari, Katerina, Katharine, Kathleen, Kathlyn, Kathryn, Katrina, Katrine* |
| **Kathie** | Short for Katherine or Kathleen | *Kath / Kathy* |
| **Kathleen** | Irish form of Katherine: pure | *Kath, Kathie, Kathy / Cathleen, Kathlyn* |
| **Kathryn** | See **Katherine** | |
| **Kathy** | Short for Katherine or Kathleen | *Kathie* |
| **Katia** | See **Katya** | |
| **Katie** | Short for Katherine | *Katy* |
| **Katinka** | Pet form of Katya | |
| **Katrina** | See **Katerina** | *Kat, Treena, Trina / Catrina, Catrine, Catriona, Katrine, Katriona* |
| **Katy** | See **Katie** | |
| **Katya** | Originally short for Katerina | *Katinka / Katia, Katja* |
| **Kay** | Originally short for Michaela, or any name beginning with K. Also a boy's name | *Kaye* |
| **Kayla** | Originally short for Michaela | |

| Name | Definition | Short forms/ Variations |
|------|-----------|------------------------|
| **Kayley** | Originally an Irish surname | *Kaylee, Kayleigh* |
| **Kazumi** | Harmonious beauty (Japanese) | |
| **Keeley** | Good looking / graceful (Irish Gaelic) Also a boy's name | *Keelie, Keely* |
| **Keeva** | English form of Caoimhe: gentleness, grace | |
| **Keira** | [Keer-a] See **Ciara** | *Kiara, Kiera* |
| **Keisha** | [Kay-sha] Favourite daughter (African) | |
| **Kelly** | Originally a boy's name. English form of the boy's name Ceallach: bright head | |
| **Kelsey** | Originally an English surname, meaning ship's victory. Also a boy's name | *Kelsie* |
| **Kendra** | Female form of Kendrick: originally a surname, meaning chief man | |
| **Kennedy** | Originally a surname, it's sometimes given in homage to the assassinated American president John F Kennedy. Traditionally a boy's name | |
| **Keren** | In the Bible, Keren is one of Job's daughters | |
| **Kerry** | From the Irish county. Also a boy's name | *Kerrie* |
| **Keturah** | Incense (Hebrew) | |
| **Kezia** | [Kee-zee-a] From the cassia tree (Hebrew) | *Kizzie, Kizzy; Keziah* |
| **Kia** | From the Maori greeting 'Kia ora', meaning 'Be well' | |

| Name | Definition | Short forms/ Variations |
|---|---|---|
| **Kiara** | [Key-ah-ra] See **Ciara** | |
| **Kiki** | Originally short for any name beginning with K | |
| **Kiku** | Chrysanthemum (Japanese) | |
| **Kim** | Short for Kimberley. | |
| **Kimberley** | From a town in South Africa, besieged by the Boers during the Boer War. Also a boy's name | Kim, Kym / Kymberley |
| **Kimi** | Short for Kimiko | |
| **Kimiko** | Sovereign (Japanese) | Kimi |
| **Kina** | Short for Alickina | |
| **Kira** | See **Kyra** | |
| **Kiran** | Ray of light (Sanskrit) Traditionally a boy's name | |
| **Kirpal** | Kind; merciful (Sikh) Also a boy's name | |
| **Kirstie** | Pet form of Kirstin | Kirsty |
| **Kirstin** | Scottish form of Christine | Kirstie / Kirsten, Kristen, Kristin |
| **Kit** | Short for Katherine | Kittie, Kitty |
| **Kitty** | Short for Katherine | Kit / Kittie |
| **Kiyoko** | Pure child (Japanese) | |
| **Kiyomi** | Pure beauty (Japanese) | |
| **Kizzie** | Short for Kezia | Kizzy |
| **Krissi** | Short for Kristina | Krissie |
| **Krista** | Short for Kristina | |
| **Kristen** | See **Kirstin** | |
| **Kristie** | Short for Kristina | |
| **Kristin** | See **Kirstin** | |
| **Kristina** | Swedish and Czech form of Christina: follower of Christ | Krissi, Krissie, Krista, Kristie |
| **Kulvinder** | Hero of the family (Sikh) Also a boy's name | |
| **Kumiko** | Long-lived, beautiful child (Japanese) | |
| **Kveta** | Blossom (Czech) | |
| **Kyla** | Female form of Kyle: narrow channel | |
| **Kylie** | Boomerang (Aboriginal) | |
| **Kyoko** | Child of the capital city (Japanese) | |
| **Kyra** | Lady (Greek) | Kira |

names

k

girls'

| Name | Definition | Short forms/ Variations |
|------|------------|-------------------------|
| **La Toya** | Toyah is a small town in Texas. May have gained in popularity thanks to singer La Toya Jackson | *LaToya, Latoya* |
| **Lacey** | Originally short for Larissa | *Lacie, Lacy* |
| **Laetitia** | **[Leh-tish-uh]** Gladness (Latin) | *Lettie, Letty, Tia, Tisha / Latisha, Letitia, Lettice* |
| **Lainey** | Pet form of Elaine | *Lanie* |
| **Lakshmi** | Lucky omen (Sanskrit) In Hindu tradition, Lakshmi is the goddess of wealth and the wife of Lord Vishnu | |
| **Lalage** | **[Lal-a-gee or Lal-a-jee]** To chatter (Greek) | *Lallie, Lally* |
| **Lalana** | Beautiful woman (Sanskrit) | |
| **Lali** | Blushing; loved (Sanskrit) | |
| **Lalie** | **[Lay-lee]** Short for Eulalia | |
| **Lalima** | Blush; glow (Sanskrit) | |
| **Lalita** | Playful (Sanskrit) | |
| **Lally** | Short for Lalage or Leila | *Lallie* |
| **L'Amour** | Love (French) | |

| Name | Definition | Short forms/ Variations |
|------|-----------|------------------------|
| **Lan** | Orchid (Chinese) | |
| **Lana** | Short for Alannah or Svetlana | |
| **Lanfen** | Orchid fragrance (Chinese) | |
| **Lani** | [Lah-nee] Heaven (Polynesian) | |
| **Lanie** | [Lay-nee] Pet form of Elaine | *Lainey* |
| **Lara** | Originally short for Larissa | |
| **Larissa** | Cheerful maiden (Greek) | *Lacey, Lacie, Lacy, Lara, Larry, Rissa / Larisa* |
| **Lateefa** | Gentle; sociable (Arabic) | *Latifa, Latifah* |
| **Latisha** | See **Laetitia** | *Tisha* |
| **Laura** | Laurel (Latin) | *Laurie, Lolly, Loretta / Lauretta, Laurinda, Lowri* |
| **Lauren** | [Lorr-en] Female form of Laurence: man from Laurentum. Sometimes given in homage to the actress Lauren Bacall | *Laurie, Lolly / Lorena* |
| **Laurentia** | Female form of Laurence: man from Laurentum | |
| **Lauretta** | Italian pet form of Laura | |
| **Laurie** | Short for Laura or Lauren | *Lori* |
| **Laurinda** | See **Laura** | |
| **Laverne** | Female form of Vernon: originally an aristocratic French surname, meaning place of alders | |
| **Lavinia** | In Roman myth, Lavinia was the wife of Aeneas and the mother of the Roman people | |
| **Layla** | [Lay-luh] Wine (Arabic) | |
| **Lea** | [Lee-uh] German form of Leah: languid | *Léa, Leia, Lia* |
| **Leah** | [Lee-uh] Languid (Hebrew) | *Lea, Léa, Leia, Lia* |
| **Leander** | [Lee-an-duh] Lion man (Greek) Traditionally a boy's name | |
| **Leandra** | [Lee-an-druh] Obviously female form of Leander: lion man | |
| **Leanne** | [Lee-ann] See **Liane** | *Leanna* |
| **Leda** | [Lee-duh] In Greek myth, Leda was seduced by the god Zeus while he was in the form of a swan | |

| Name | Definition | Short forms/ Variations |
|---|---|---|
| **Leigh** | [Lee] Female version of Lee: wood or clearing | |
| **Leila** | [Lie-luh] Night (Arabic) | *Lally / Laila, Layla, Leilah, Leyla* |
| **Leilani** | [Lay-lah-nee] Flower of heaven (Polynesian) | |
| **Lena** | [Lee-na] Originally short for Alena or Helena | |
| **Leocadia** | Bright, clear (Greek) | |
| **Leona** | Female form of Leo: lion | |
| **Léonie** | [Lay-on-ee or Lee-on-ee] Lion (Latin) | *Léo, Leo / Leoni, Leonie* |
| **Leonora** | Short for Eleonora | *Lora, Nora / Leonore* |
| **Leontina** | Female form of Leonzio: lion | |
| **Lesley** | Female form of Leslie. Originally a Scottish surname, meaning garden of holly trees | |
| **Lettice** | Medieval form of Laetitia: gladness | *Lettie, Letty* |
| **Letty** | Short for Laetitia or Lettice | *Lettie* |
| **Levi** | [Lee-vigh] Joined (Hebrew) Traditionally a male name, it's occasionally used for girls | |
| **Lexie** | Short for Alexandra or Alexis | *Lexine, Lexy* |
| **Lexine** | See **Lexie** | |
| **Li** | [Lee] Strength (Chinese) Also a boy's name | |
| **Lia** | [Lee-uh] Italian form of Leah: languid | *Lea, Léa, Leia* |
| **Liane** | From Aelianus, an old Roman family name | *Leanne, Lianne / Eliana* |
| **Libby** | Short for Elizabeth | *Libbie* |
| **Lida** | People's love (Slavonic) | |
| **Liddy** | Short for Lydia or Lidwina | *Liddie, Lyddie* |
| **Lidwina** | People's friend (Germanic) | *Liddie, Liddy* |
| **Lien** | Lotus (Vietnamese) | |
| **Liese** | [Lee-za] German short form of Elizabeth or Lieselotte | *Lise* |
| **Lieselotte** | [Lee-za-lot-uh] Combination of Liese (short for Elizabeth: God is gracious) and Lotte (short for Charlotte, a female form of Charles: free man) | *Liese, Lise / Liselotte* |
| **Lila** | English form of Leila: night | *Lyla* |
| **Lilah** | [Ly-luh] Originally short for Delilah | *Lila* |

| Name | Definition | Short forms/ Variations |
|---|---|---|
| **Lilia** | [Lil-ee-uh] From Lily | |
| **Lilian** | Lily (Latin) | *Lil, Lilie, Lillie, Lilly, Lily / Liliana, Lillian, Lilliana* |
| **Lilias** | Scottish form of Lilian: lily | |
| **Liling** | The beautiful sound of tinkling jade (Chinese) | |
| **Lilith** | Screech owl (Hebrew) | *Lil, Lily* |
| **Lillibeth** | Combination of Lilli (Lily) and Beth (short for Elizabeth: God is my oath) | *Lilibeth* |
| **Lin** | Beautiful jade (Chinese) | |
| **Lina** | [Lee-nuh] Palm tree (Arabic) | |
| **Linda** | Pretty (Spanish) | *Lin, Lindie, Lindy, Lyn, Lynn, Lynne / Lynda* |
| **Linden** | Lime tree (Old English) | |
| **Lindis** | From the holy island of Lindisfarne off the north-east coast of England | |
| **Lindsay** | Originally a surname. Also a boy's name | *Lin, Lyn / Lindsey, Linsay, Linsey, Lyndsay, Lyndsey, Lynsay, Lynsey* |
| **Lindy** | Pet form of Linda | *Lin / Lindie* |
| **Ling** | The sound of tinkling jade (Chinese) | |
| **Linsey** | See **Lindsay** | |
| **Liora** | [Lee-or-uh] Female form of Lior: my light | |
| **Lisa** | [Lee-suh] Originally short for Annalise | *Leesa, Lise* |
| **Lisa-Marie** | [Lee-suh-m'ree] Combination of Lisa (originally short for Annalise: gracious) and Marie (sea) | |
| **Lisbeth** | [Liz-beth] Short for Elizabeth | *Lisbet, Lizbet, Lizbeth* |
| **Lise** | Short for Annelise, Elise or Liselotte | |
| **Lisette** | French pet form of Elisabeth | |
| **Lisha** | Short for Alisha or Delisha | |
| **Lissa** | Short for Melissa | |
| **Lita** | [Lee-tuh] Short for Melita | *Leeta* |
| **Liv** | Life (Norwegian) | |
| **Livia** | [Liv-ee-uh] From Livius, an old Roman family name | |

| Name | Definition | Short forms/ Variations |
|------|-----------|-------------------------|
| **Liz** | Short for Elizabeth | |
| **Liza** | [Ly-za] Short for Eliza | *Leesa, Lisa, Lise, Liese* |
| **Lizbeth** | Short for Elizabeth | *Lisbet, Lisbeth, Lizbet* |
| **Lizzie** | Short for Elizabeth | *Liz; Lizzy* |
| **Llewella** | [Lew-ell-uh or Clew-ell-uh] Female form of Llewelyn: lion | |
| **Logan** | Originally a Scottish surname. Also a boy's name | |
| **Lois** | [Lo-iss] Good (Greek) May have gained in popularity thanks to Superman's girlfriend Lois Lane | |
| **Lola** | Originally short for Dolores | |
| **Lolita** | [Low-lee-tuh] Pet form of Lola. In Vladimir Nabokov's novel *Lolita*, the 12-year-old of the title (real name Dolores) is abused by the narrator, Humbert Humbert | *Lo* |
| **Lolly** | Short for Laura or Lauren | |
| **Lora** | Short for Leonora | |
| **Lorelei** | [Lora-lie] In German legend, Lorelei is a siren who lives on a rocky headland on the Rhine river and lures sailors to their death with her song | |

| Name | Definition | Short forms/ Variations |
|------|-----------|-------------------------|
| **Lorena** | Spanish form of Lauren, a female form of Laurence: man from Laurentum | *Lori, Lory* |
| **Loretta** | Pet form of Laura | *Lori, Lory* |
| **Lori** | Short for Lorena, Loretta or Lorraine. Also a boy's name | *Lory* |
| **Lorimer** | Originally a surname, meaning someone who makes spurs. Also a boy's name | |
| **Lorna** | Lost (Anglo Saxon) Thought to have first been used by RD Blackmore for his 19th-century novel *Lorna Doone*. Lorna is a child captive who turns out to be an heiress | *Lorne* |
| **Lorraine** | Originally a surname; taken from the region in eastern France | *Lori, Lory* |
| **Lottie** | Short for Carlotta or Charlotte | |
| **Lou** | Short for Louella, Louisa or Louise. Also a boy's name | |
| **Louella** | Combination of Louise (fame in war) and Ella (sunbeam) | *Lou / Luella* |
| **Louisa** | Female form of Louis: fame in war | *Lou, Lulu / Louise, Luisa* |
| **Lourdes** | [Lourd] Usually given as an expression of Christian faith, it refers to the French town of that name, where Catholics believe the Virgin Mary appeared to a local girl in the 19th century | |
| **Lucasta** | See **Lucia** | |
| **Lucetta** | [Lou-chett-a] See **Lucia** | |
| **Lucia** | [Lou-chee-a] Female form of Lucius: light | *Lucasta, Lucetta, Lucie, Lucilla, Lucille, Lucienne, Lucinda, Lucy* |
| **Luciana** | [Lou-cha-na] Female form of Lucian: light | *Lucie* |
| **Lucienne** | French female form of Lucian: light | |
| **Lucilla** | See **Lucia** | *Lucille* |
| **Lucinda** | See **Lucia** | *Cinda, Cindie, Cindy, Sindie, Sindy / Lucie, Lucy* |
| **Lucja** | Polish female form of Lucius: light | |

| Name | Definition | Short forms/ Variations |
|------|------------|-------------------------|
| **Lucretia** | [Lou-cree-shuh] From Lucretius, an old Roman family name. The associations are not positive: in Roman myth, Lucretia was raped by the King of Rome and committed suicide. And the 16th-century Italian noblewoman Lucrezia Borgia is believed to have been an incestuous poisoner | *Tia / Lucrezia* |
| **Lucy** | See **Lucia** | *Lucie* |
| **Luella** | See **Louella** | |
| **Luisa** | Spanish and Italian form of Louisa: fame in war | |
| **Lula** | Originally short for Tallula | |
| **Lulani** | Combination of Luna (moon) and Leilani (flower of heaven) | |
| **Luli** | Dewy jasmine (Chinese) | |
| **Lulu** | Originally short for Louisa or Louise | |
| **Luna** | Moon (Latin) | |
| **Luned** | See **Eluned** | |
| **Lux** | Light (Latin) Also a boy's name | |
| **Luz** | [Luth] Light (Spanish) | |
| **Lydia** | [Lid-ee-uh] Woman from Lydia, an area of Asia Minor (Greek) | *Liddie, Liddy, Lyddie* |
| **Lyla** | See **Lila** | |
| **Lynda** | See **Linda** | *Lin, Lindie, Lindy, Lyn, Lynn, Lynne* |
| **Lyndsay** | See **Lindsay** | |
| **Lynette** | Pet form of Lynn | *Nettie / Linnet* |
| **Lynn** | Short for Linda or Lindsay | *Lyn, Lynne, Lynette* |
| **Lynsey** | See **Lindsay** | |
| **Lyra** | Lyre, a musical instrument (Latin) May have gained in popularity thanks to the quick-witted heroine of novelist Philip Pullman's trilogy, *His Dark Materials* | |
| **Lyric** | Words to a song (English) | |
| **Lys** | [Liss] Lily (French) | |
| **Lysandra** | Female form of Lysander: free | |

girls'

l

names

# M

| Name | Definition | Short forms/Variations |
|------|-----------|------------------------|
| **Mab** | In English folklore, Queen Mab is a fairy who drives her chariot over people's faces as they sleep, making them dream of what they wish for | |
| **Mabel** | Originally short for Amabel | *Mab, Maybelline / Maybelle* |
| **Mabli** | Short for Amabel | |
| **Macario** | Blessed (Greek) | |
| **Macey** | Originally a surname | *Macie, Macy* |
| **Mackenzie** | Originally a Scottish clan name and surname. Also a boy's name | *Mac, Mack* |
| **Madchen** | Girl (German) | |
| **Maddie** | Short for Madeleine | *Maddy* |
| **Maddox** | Benefactor's son (Welsh) More commonly used for boys | |
| **Madeleine** | Magdalene (French) In the Bible, Mary Magdalene was a follower of Jesus | *Maddie, Maddy / Madalene, Maddalene, Madelaine, Madelene, Madeline* |

| Name | Definition | Short forms/Variations |
|------|-----------|------------------------|
| **Madge** | Short for Margaret | |
| **Madhu** | Sweet (Sanskrit) | *Madhur* |
| **Madison** | Originally a surname. Often connected with the famous New York locations, Madison Avenue and Madison Square. In the US, it may be given in homage to former president James Madison. Also a boy's name | *Maddison* |
| **Madonna** | My lady (Italian) Originally given in homage to the Virgin Mary | |
| **Madrona** | Mother (Jewish) | |
| **Maeve** | [Mayv] Intoxicating (Irish) | |
| **Mafalda** | Italian form of Matilda: might in battle | |
| **Magda** | Short for Magdalen | |
| **Magdalen** | [Mag-da-len or Mawd-lin] Old English form of Madeleine.In the Bible, Mary Magdalene was a follower of Jesus | *Magda / Magdalena, Magdalene* |
| **Magdalena** | German, Scandinavian and Spanish form of Magdalene | |
| **Maggie** | Short for Margaret | |
| **Maha** | Oryx, a type of antelope (Arabic) | |
| **Mahala** | Tenderness (Hebrew) | *Mahalia* |
| **Mahika** | The earth (Sanskrit) | |
| **Maia** | A Roman goddess | *Maya* |
| **Maida** | Originally given after the 19th-century Battle of Maida, in Italy | *Maidie* |
| **Maidie** | Pet form of Maida | |
| **Maiko** | Dancing child (Japanese) | |
| **Maire** | Irish form of Mary: sea | *Mair, Moira, Moya* |
| **Mairéad** | Scottish Gaelic form of Margaret: pearl | *Maretta* |
| **Mairi** | Scottish Gaelic form of Mary: sea | |
| **Mairwen** | Blessed Mary (Welsh) | |
| **Maisie** | Originally short for Margaret | *Maisy* |
| **Maitland** | Originally a French surname, meaning bad temper. Also a boy's name | |
| **Maja** | [Mee-uh] German pet form of Maria | |
| **Makoto** | True (Japanese) | |

| Name | Definition | Short forms/ Variations |
|------|-----------|------------------------|
| **Mala** | Necklace (Sanskrit) | |
| **Malaika** | Angel (Sanskrit) | |
| **Malak** | Angel (Arabic) | |
| **Malati** | Blossom (Sanskrit) | |
| **Malika** | Flower (Sanskrit) | |
| **Malkah** | Queen (Hebrew) | *Malka* |
| **Mall** | Short for Matilda | |
| **Mallory** | Originally a French surname, meaning bad temper. Also a boy's name | *Malory* |
| **Malvina** | [Mal-vee-na] Smooth brow (Gaelic) | |
| **Mame** | Originally short for Margaret. May have increased in popularity thanks to Rita Hayworth's sultry rendition of 'Put the Blame on Mame' in the 1946 film *Gilda* | *Mamie* |
| **Mandeep** | Light of the mind (Sikh) Also a boy's name | |
| **Mandira** | Pure; melody (Sanskrit) | |
| **Mandy** | Short for Amanda | *Mandie* |
| **Manika** | Jewel (Sanskrit) | |
| **Manisha** | Intellect (Sanskrit) | |
| **Manon** | French pet form of Marie: sea | |
| **Mara** | Bitter (Hebrew) | |
| **Marcella** | Female form of Marcus: from Mars, the Roman god of war | *Marcie, Mars* |
| **Marcellette** | Female pet form of Marcellus | |
| **Marcelline** | Female form of Marcellus: taken from Mars, the Roman god of war | |
| **Marcena** | Female form of Marcin: taken from Mars, the Roman god of war | *Marcina* |
| **Marcia** | [Marsh-a] Female form of Marcius: from Mars, the Roman god of war | *Marcie / Marsha* |
| **Marcie** | [Mar-see] Short for Marcella or Marcia | |
| **Maretta** | See **Margaret** | |

names

m

girls'

| Name | Definition | Short forms/ Variations |
|------|------------|------------------------|
| **Margaret** | Pearl (Hebrew) | *Greta, Gretchen, Madge, Maggie, Maisie, Mamie, Margot, May, Meg, Peggoty, Peggy / Maretta, Margareta, Margaretta, Margarita, Marged, Margeurite, Marjorie* |
| **Margarita** | Spanish form of Margaret: pearl | *Margie, Rita / Margherita* |
| **Marged** | Welsh form of Margaret: pearl | |
| **Margeurite** | [Marg-yur-eet] French form of Margaret: pearl | *Margot, Rita / Margeurita* |
| **Margie** | Short for Margarita or Margery | *Marge* |
| **Margot** | [Mar-go] Originally short for Margeurite | *Margo* |
| **Margriet** | Dutch form of Margaret: pearl | *Griet* |
| **Mari** | Welsh form of Mary: sea | |
| **Maria** | [Muh-ree-a or Muh-rye-a] See **Mary** | *Maja, Mariska, Mia, Mimi, Mitzi, Ria / Mariah, Marilla* |
| **Maria-Lourdes** | Combination of Maria and Lourdes | |
| **Marian** | See **Marion** | |
| **Maria-Teresa** | Combination of Maria, as in the Virgin Mary, and Teresa, as in St Teresa. Usually given as an expression of Christian faith | |
| **Maribel** | Spanish contracted form of Maria Isabel | *Maribelle* |
| **Marie** | See **Mary** | *Maria, Maureen* |
| **Mariel** | See **Muriel** | |
| **Mariella** | Italian pet form of Maria: sea | |
| **Marielle** | French pet form of Marie: sea | |
| **Marietta** | Italian pet form of Maria: sea | *Marieta, Mariette* |
| **Marika** | [Muh-ree-ka] Slavic pet form of Maria: sea | |
| **Marilla** | See **Maria** | |
| **Marilyn** | Combination of Mary (sea) and Lynn (short for Linda: pretty) | *Marylyn* |
| **Marina** | Of the sea (Latin) | *Marinella, Marna, Marnie, Rina* |
| **Marinella** | Pet form of Marina | |

girls'

m

names

| Name | Definition | Short forms/Variations |
|------|-----------|------------------------|
| **Marion** | Probably the most famous example is Maid Marion of the Robin Hood legend. It's also a boy's name and – unlikely as it may seem – was the real name of the actor John Wayne | *Marnie / Marian, Mariana, Marianna, Marianne* |
| **Maris** | Of the sea (Latin) | |
| **Marisa** | See **Mary** | *Marissa* |
| **Mariska** | Hungarian pet form of Maria | |
| **Marjie** | Short for Marjorie | *Marj, Marje* |
| **Marjorie** | See **Margaret** | *Jorie, Jory, Marge, Margie, Marj, Marje, Marjie / Margerie, Margery, Marjory* |
| **Marla** | See **Marlene** | |
| **Marlene** | [Mar-lay-na or Mar-leen] Thought to have first been used by the German-born film star Marlene Dietrich, who used it as a contraction of her full name, Maria Magdalene | *Marla* |
| **Marna** | Short for Marina | |
| **Marnie** | Short for Marianna, Marianne or Marina | |
| **Marsaili** | Scottish Gaelic form of Marcella, a female form of Marcus: from Mars, the god of war | |
| **Marta** | Italian form of Martha: lady | *Martita* |
| **Martha** | Lady (Aramaic) | *Marta* |
| **Marti** | Short for Martina | *Marty* |
| **Martina** | Female form of Martin, from Mars, god of war | *Marti, Marty, Tina / Martine* |
| **Martita** | Pet form of Marta | |
| **Mary** | Sea (Latin) Often given in homage to the Virgin Mary, the mother of Christ | *May, Molly, Polly / Mair, Maire, Mari, Maria, Marian, Marie, Marisa, Maura, Merissa* |
| **Masumi** | Increasing beauty (Japanese) | |
| **Matilda** | Might in battle (Germanic) | *Mall, Tilda, Tillie, Tilly / Mathilda, Mathilde, Matilde* |
| **Maud** | Medieval form of Matilda: might in battle | *Maude* |
| **Maura** | Irish form of Mary: sea | |
| **Maureen** | See **Marie** | *Mo / Maurine* |

| Name | Definition | Short forms/ Variations |
|------|------------|------------------------|
| **Mavis** | Song thrush (Old French) | |
| **Maxine** | Female form of Max: greatest | |
| **Maya** | See **Maia** | |
| **Maybelle** | Combination of May and Belle (beautiful); or an elaborated form of Mabel | |
| **Maybelline** | Pet form of Mabel | |
| **Maysa** | Proud and graceful walk (Arabic) | |
| **Mead** | A sweet alcoholic drink made from honey (English) | |
| **Meara** | Merry (Celtic) | |
| **Medea** | To reflect (Greek) The associations are not positive. In Greek myth, Medea was abandoned by Jason and killed their two children in revenge | |
| **Meena** | Jewel; or Pisces, the sign of the fish (Sanskrit) | *Mina* |
| **Meera** | Sea (Sanskrit) | *Mira* |
| **Meeta** | Friend (Sanskrit) | *Mita* |
| **Meg** | Short for Margaret | *Peggy / Megan* |

| Name | Definition | Short forms/ Variations |
| --- | --- | --- |
| **Megan** | [Meg-an or Meeg-an] See **Meg** | |
| **Megumi** | Blessing (Japanese) | |
| **Mehetabel** | God makes happy (Hebrew) | *Mehitabel* |
| **Meinir** | Long and slender (Welsh) | |
| **Meinwen** | Slender and fair or blessed (Welsh) | |
| **Meiriona** | Female form of Meirion: taken from Mars, the Roman god of war | |
| **Melanie** | Dark, black (Greek) | *Mel, Mellie, Melly / Melloney, Mellony, Meloney* |
| **Melba** | Sometimes given in homage to Australian opera singer Dame Nellie Melba. Born Helen Porter Mitchell, she took her stage name from her home city of Melbourne. The name is now also associated with melba toast and the dessert peach melba, both of which were named after her | |
| **Melia** | Ash tree (Greek) | |
| **Melina** | Honey (Greek) | |
| **Melinda** | Combination of Melanie (dark, black) and Linda (pretty) | *Mindy* |
| **Mélisande** | French form of Millicent: strong labour | |
| **Melissa** | Honey bee (Greek) | *Lissa, Mel / Melita, Melitta* |
| **Melita** | See **Melissa** | *Lita, Mel / Melitta* |
| **Mellie** | Short for Melanie | *Mel / Melly* |
| **Melody** | The main tune in a piece of music (English) | |
| **Mercedes** | [Mer-say-deez] Ransom (Latin) Often used by Roman Catholics, who see Christ's death as a ransom for human sin | |
| **Mercia** | Mercy (Latin) Woman from the border country (Anglo Saxon) | |
| **Meredith** | Lord (Old Welsh) Originally a boy's name | |
| **Merete** | Danish form of Margareta | |
| **Meriel** | Medieval form of Muriel: bright sea | *Merry* |
| **Merioth** | Rebellious (Hebrew) Traditionally a boy's name | |
| **Merissa** | See **Mary** | *Rissa* |

names

m

girls'

| Name | Definition | Short forms/ Variations |
|---|---|---|
| **Merle** | [Murl] Blackbird (Old French). Also a boy's name | |
| **Merlyn** | Female form of Merlin: sea; fort. In legend, Merlin is a magician who guides King Arthur. A merlin is also a small falcon | |
| **Merrill** | Originally a surname. Also a boy's name | |
| **Meryl** | Possibly first used by actress Meryl Streep as a contraction of her first names, Mary (sea) and Louise (fame in war) | |
| **Meta** | Danish form of Margareta | |
| **Mia** | [Mee-uh] Originally short for Maria | |
| **Michaela** | [Mick-ay-la] Female form of Michael: who is like God | *Kay, Kayla, Mickie, Micky / Mikayla* |
| **Michelle** | [Mih-shell] French female form of Michael: who is like God | *Chelle, Mishy / Michèle* |
| **Michi** | Pathway (Japanese) Also a boy's name | |
| **Michiko** | Child of a thousand beauties (Japanese) | |
| **Mickie** | Short for Michaela | *Micky* |
| **Mieko** | Child of beautiful blessings (Japanese) | |
| **Mignon** | [Meen-yon] Sweet (French) | *Mignonette, Minette* |
| **Mignonette** | [Meen-yon-ette] French pet form of Mignon: sweet | *Minette, Nettie* |
| **Mika** | Beautiful fragrance (Japanese) | |
| **Mildred** | Gentle strength (Old English) | *Millie, Milly / Mildrid* |
| **Milena** | Gracious (Slavic) | |
| **Mili** | Meeting (Sanskrit) | |
| **Milla** | Originally short for Camilla | *Millie, Milly* |
| **Millicent** | Strong labour (Germanic) | *Millie, Milly / Mélisande, Milicent* |
| **Milly** | Short for Camilla, Emilia, Emily, Mildred or Millicent | *Milla, Millie* |
| **Mimi** | Originally short for Maria | |
| **Mina** | [Mee-na] Short for Amina, Elmina, Normina, Wilhelmina, Yasmina or Yasmine | *Mena, Minna, Minnie* |
| **Mindy** | Short for Melinda. May have gained in popularity thanks to American sitcom *Mork & Mindy* | |

girls'

m

names

| Name | Definition | Short forms/Variations |
|------|------------|------------------------|
| **Minerva** | Intellect (Latin) In Roman myth, Minerva was goddess of wisdom | |
| **Minette** | Short for Mignonette, the French pet form of Mignon: sweet | *Nettie* |
| **Minna** | Scottish form of Minnie, originally short for Wilhelmina | |
| **Minnie** | Originally short for Wilhelmina | *Mina, Minna* |
| **Mione** | Small (Greek) | |
| **Mira** | See **Myra** | |
| **Mirabelle** | Admirable (Latin) | *Bella / Mirabel, Mirabella* |
| **Miranda** | Admirable (Latin) Thought to have been invented by Shakespeare for the heroine of *The Tempest* | |
| **Mireille** | To admire (French) | *Mirella* |
| **Mirella** | Italian form of Mireille: to admire | |
| **Miriam** | Bitter (Hebrew) In the Bible, Miriam was the elder sister of Moses. Pharoah had ordered that all Hebrew baby boys should be killed, so Miriam hid her baby brother in the bullrushes by the river | *Mariam, Miryam* |
| **Mishy** | Short for Michelle | |
| **Mitsuko** | Bright, shining child (Japanese) | |
| **Mittens** | In Beatrix Potter's 1907 children's story *The Tale of Tom Kitten*, Mittens is a naughty kitten – although not nearly so naughty as her brother Tom | |
| **Mitzi** | German pet form of Maria | |
| **Miu** | Beautiful feather (Japanese) | |
| **Mocha** | [Moe-ka] A mixture of coffee and chocolate (English) | |
| **Moët** | [Mo-ay] Originally a French surname, now associated with Moët & Chandon champagne | |
| **Moggy** | Pet form of Molly | *Mog / Moggie* |
| **Moira** | English form of Maire: sea | |
| **Moll** | Short for Molly. Moll Flanders is an immoral but entertaining character in Daniel Defoe's 18th-century novel *The Fortunes and Misfortunes of the Famous Moll Flanders* | |

| Name | Definition | Short forms/ Variations |
|---|---|---|
| **Molly** | Originally short for Mary | *Moggy, Moll / Mollie, Polly* |
| **Momo** | Peach (Japanese) | |
| **Momoe** | A hundred blessings (Japanese) | |
| **Mona** | Alone (Sanskrit) Or the English form of Muadhnait: noble | |
| **Monica** | To counsel (Latin) | *Monique, Monika* |
| **Monique** | [Mon-eek] French form of Monica: to counsel | |
| **Morag** | Great (Scottish Gaelic) | |
| **Morgan** | Completion (Old Celtic) In Arthurian legend, Morgan le Fay, a sorceress, was King Arthur's jealous half-sister. Also a boy's name | *Morgana* |
| **Morna** | English form of Muirne: beloved | |
| **Morven** | Mountain peak (Gaelic) Morven is the name of a mountain in Caithness in the Scottish Highlands | |
| **Morwenna** | Maiden (Welsh) | |
| **Moya** | See **Maire** | |
| **Muadhnait** | Noble (Irish) | *Mona* |
| **Muireann** | As beautiful as the sea (Irish Gaelic) | |
| **Muirne** | Beloved; high-spirited (Irish) | *Morna, Myrna* |
| **Muna** | Wish (Arabic) | |
| **Munira** | Illuminating (Arabic) | |
| **Muriel** | Bright sea (Old Celtic) | *Mariel, Meriel* |
| **Myfanwy** | [M'van-wee] Woman (Welsh) | *Myvanwy* |
| **Myla** | Female form of Myles: soldier | *Myleen, Mylene* |
| **Myleen** | See **Myla** | *Mylene* |
| **Myra** | To admire (Latin) | *Mira* |
| **Myrna** | English form of Muirne: beloved | |
| **Myrtille** | French form of Myrtle | *Myrtilla* |

girls'

m

names

| Name | Definition | Short forms/ Variations |
|------|-----------|------------------------|
| **Nadezna** | Hope (Russian) | *Nadia, Nadine, Nadya* |
| **Nadia** | See **Nadya** | |
| **Nadine** | See **Nadya** | |
| **Nadiyya** | Moist with dew (Arabic) | |
| **Nadya** | Hope (Russian) | *Nadezna, Nadia, Nadine* |
| **Nahla** | Thirst-quenching drink (Arabic) | |
| **Naima** | Happy (Arabic) | |
| **Naiya** | Water nymph (Sanskrit) | |
| **Nalini** | Lotus; lovely (Sanskrit) | |
| **Nan** | Short for Ann or Hannah | |
| **Nancy** | Originally a pet form of Ann | |
| **Nandana** | Cheeful (Sanskrit) | *Nandita* |
| **Nandita** | See **Nandana** | |
| **Nanette** | Pet form of Annette or Nan | *Nan, Nettie* |
| **Nanine** | French pet form of Ann | |
| **Naomh** | A saint (Irish Gaelic) | |

| Name | Definition | Short forms/ Variations |
|------|-----------|------------------------|
| **Naomi** | Pleasant (Hebrew) | |
| **Napia** | Girl of the valley (Latin) | *Napea* |
| **Narcissa** | Female form of Narcissus: sleep, numbness. The associations are not positive. In Greek myth, Narcissus was a handsome but vain youth who fell in love with his own reflection in a pond and wasted away while staring at it | |
| **Nasrin** | Wild rose (Persian) | |
| **Natalia** | Birthday (Latin) | *Natalya, Natasha* |
| **Natalie** | French form of Natalia: birthday | *Nathalie* |
| **Natasha** | See **Natalia** | *Tash, Tasha* |
| **Nathalie** | [Nat-uh-lee] See **Natalie** | |
| **Natsuko** | Summer child (Japanese) | |
| **Natsumi** | Summer beauty (Japanese) | |
| **Naveen** | New (Sanskrit) | *Navita* |
| **Navita** | See **Naveen** | |
| **Navya** | New (Sanskrit) | |
| **Neala** | Female form of Niall: champion | |
| **Neelam** | Blue sapphire (Sanskrit) According to Hindu tradition, the stone is said to represent health, wealth, happiness and long life | |
| **Nell** | Short for Eleanor, Ellen, Helen or Helena | *Nellie, Nelly* |
| **Nerina** | Female form of Nereo; taken from Nereus, a Greek sea god | *Rina* |
| **Nerissa** | Sea sprite (Greek) | *Rissa* |
| **Neroli** | After the essential oil from the Seville orange tree | |
| **Nerys** | [Ner-iss] Lord (Welsh) | |
| **Nessa** | Short for Agnes or Vanessa | *Nessie* |
| **Nessie** | Short for Agnes or Vanessa… or a pet name for the Loch Ness Monster | |
| **Nesta** | Welsh pet form of Agnes | *Nest* |
| **Netta** | See **Nettie** | |
| **Nettie** | Short for Annette, Antoinette, Jeannette, Lynette, Mignonette, Minette, Nanette or Ninette | *Netta* |

| Name | Definition | Short forms/ Variations |
|------|-----------|-------------------------|
| **Neva** | Snow (Italian) | |
| **Nevaeh** | [Na-vay-uh] Heaven, spelled backwards | |
| **Neve** | English form of Niamh: brightness; beauty | |
| **Nevena** | Marigold (Bulgarian) | |
| **Ngaio** | [Ny-oh] Clever (Maori) | |
| **Ngaire** | [Ny-ree] Flaxen (Maori) | *Nyree* |
| **Nia** | Welsh form of Niamh: brightness; beauty | |
| **Niamh** | [Neev] Brightness; beauty (Gaelic) | *Neve* |
| **Nicky** | Short for Nicola | *Nic / Nicki, Nikki* |
| **Nico** | May have gained in popularity thanks to Andy Warhol's muse, the singer-songwriter Nico (born Christa Päffgen) | |
| **Nicola** | Female form of Nicholas: victorious people | *Nic, Nicki, Nicky, Nikki / Nichole, Nicole, Nicolette* |
| **Nicolette** | See **Nicola** | *Nic / Nicola* |
| **Nieves** | Snows (Spanish) | |
| **Nigella** | Female form of Nigel: black. Also the botanical name for the spice onion seed. | |
| **Nikeisha** | Combination of Nicola (victorious people) and Keisha (favourite daughter) | |
| **Nikita** | [Nik-ee-ta] Unconquerable (Greek) Originally a boy's name | *Nik* |
| **Nina** | [Nee-na] Originally short for Antonina | |
| **Ninette** | French pet form of Nina, short for Antonina: priceless | *Nettie* |

| Name | Definition | Short forms/ Variations |
|------|-----------|-------------------------|
| **Nisha** | Night (Sanskrit) | |
| **Nissa** | Sign (Hebrew) | |
| **Nita** | [Neet-a] Short for Anita, Benita, Bonita, Juanita or Sunita | *Neeta* |
| **Noelle** | [No-ell] Female form of Noel: Christmas | *Noella* |
| **Noirin** | Irish pet form of Nora | |
| **Nola** | Short for Finola: white shoulders | |
| **Nolene** | Female form of Nolan: originally an Irish surname, meaning descendant of a nobleman | *Noleen* |
| **Nona** | Ninth (Latin) | |
| **Nonie** | Pet form of Ione | |
| **Noor** | Light (Arabic) Also a boy's name | *Nur* |
| **Nora** | Short for Eleanora, Honora, Honoria or Leonora | *Norah, Noreen* |
| **Noreen** | See **Nora** | |
| **Noriko** | Child of principles (Japanese) | |
| **Norma** | Rule (Latin) | |
| **Normina** | Female form of Norman: Norseman | *Mina* |
| **Nova** | New (Latin) | |
| **Nuala** | [Noo-luh] Short for Fionnuala | |
| **Nur** | [Noor] Light (Arabic) Also a boy's name | |
| **Nyree** | English form of Ngaire: flaxen | |

| Name | Definition | Short forms/Variations |
|---|---|---|
| **Océane** | Ocean (French) | *Oceana* |
| **Octavia** | Female form of Octavius: eight | *Tavia, Tavie, Tavy* |
| **Odele** | Wealthy (Greek) | *Odelita* |
| **Odelita** | Pet form of Odele | |
| **Odette** | French form of Odile | *Odetta* |
| **Odile** | [O-deel] Prosperity (Germanic) | *Dillie, Dilly / Odette, Odila, Odilia, Ottilie* |
| **Oenone** | Wine woman (Greek) The associations are not positive. In Greek myth, Oenone was a nymph with the powers of prophecy and healing. She married the Trojan prince, Paris, but he left her for Helen. When he was mortally wounded, he begged her to heal him but she refused and he died. Wracked with guilt, she committed suicide | |
| **Olalla** | Spanish form of Eulalia: to talk well | |
| **Olga** | Prosperous, successful (Old Norse) | |

| Name | Definition | Short forms/Variations |
|------|-----------|------------------------|
| **Olivia** | Olive (Latin) Traditionally, an olive branch symbolises peace. The name is thought to have been invented by Shakespeare for an heiress in *Twelfth Night* | *Liv, Livia* |
| **Olwen** | Blessed footprint (Welsh) In Welsh folklore, flowers sprang up wherever Olwen trod | *Olwin* |
| **Oonagh** | [On-ya or Oo-nuh] See **Una** | *Oona* |
| **Ophelia** | Help (Greek) The associations are not positive. In Shakespeare's *Hamlet*, Ophelia loves Hamlet but goes mad and commits suicide | |
| **Ophira** | Gold (Hebrew) According to myth, a place called Ophir is the source of King Solomon's treasure, but sadly its whereabouts is unknown | *Phira* |
| **Ophrah** | Fawn (Hebrew) Also a boy's name | *Ofra, Ophra* |
| **Oprah** | See **Orpah** | |
| **Oreithyia** | In Greek myth, Oreithyia was the daughter of the King of Athens. When she spurned the advances of Boreas, the north wind, he abducted her | *Orithyia* |
| **Oriana** | [Orry-ah-na] Gold (Spanish) | *Orianna* |
| **Oriel** | See **Auriel** | *Aura, Auria, Aurial* |
| **Orinda** | Invented by 17th-century poet Katherine Philips | |
| **Orla** | Golden princess (Irish Gaelic) | |
| **Orlaith** | See **Orla** | *Orla* |
| **Orlanda** | Female form of Orlando: fame; land | |
| **Orna** | Female form of Oran: dark-haired | |
| **Ornella** | Flowering ash tree (Italian) | *Ornetta* |
| **Orpah** | Female deer (Hebrew) | *Oprah* |
| **Otthild** | Fortune in battle (Germanic) | |
| **Ottilie** | See **Odile** | *Ottoline* |
| **Ottoline** | French pet form of Ottilie | |
| **Owena** | Female form of Owen: born of the god Esos | |

girls'

O

names

| Name | Definition | Short forms/ Variations |
|------|------------|-------------------------|
| **Pacifica** | Peacemaker (Latin) | |
| **Paderau** | Rosary (Welsh) Also a boy's name | |
| **Padma** | Lotus (Sanskrit) The lotus chakra (one of the body's centres of spiritual energy) symbolises the link between the human and the divine. Also a boy's name | |
| **Page** | Originally a surname, meaning a page, a servant to a knight or lord. Also a boy's name | *Paige* |
| **Pallas** | Maiden (Greek) In Greek myth, Pallas was accidentally killed by her friend, the goddess Athena, who took her name in homage | |
| **Paloma** | Dove (Spanish) | |
| **Pam** | Short for Pamela | *Pammie, Pammy* |
| **Pamela** | Thought to have been invented by 16th-century poet Sir Philip Sidney | *Pam, Pammie, Pammy* |

| Name | Definition | Short forms/ Variations |
|------|-----------|------------------------|
| Pandora | Every gift (Greek) The associations are not positive. In Greek myth, Pandora was the first woman, created by the gods as a punishment for mankind. Pandora was given a box that she was forbidden to open. She opened it and unleashed great suffering on the world | |
| Panita | Admired (Sanskrit) | |
| Paola | Female version of Paolo: small | |
| Paolabella | Combination of Paolo (small) and Bella (beautiful) | |
| Parina | Like a fairy (Sanskrit) | |
| Parker | Originally a surname, meaning gamekeeper. Also a boy's name | |
| Parminder | The greatest god (Sikh) Also a boy's name | |
| Parmita | Intelligence (Sanskrit) | |
| Parnel | See **Petronel** | *Pernel, Petronella, Petronilla* |
| Parthenia | Maiden (Greek) | |
| Parvati | Daughter of the mountain (Sanskrit) | |
| Pascale | [Pas-kahl] Passover (Hebrew) | |
| Pasha | To pass over (Greek) Born at Easter. Also a boy's name | |
| Pat | Short for Patrice, Patricia, Patsy or Patty | |
| Patrice | Medieval French form of Patricia: patrician, belonging to the Roman nobility. Also a boy's name | *Pat, Patsy, Patti, Pattie, Patty* |
| Patricia | Female form of Patrick: patrician, belonging to the Roman nobility | *Pat, Patsy, Patti, Pattie, Patty, Tricia, Trisha / Patrice* |
| Patrina | Combination of Patricia (patrician) and Katrina (pure) | *Pat, Trina* |
| Patsy | Short for Patrice or Patricia | *Pat* |
| Patty | Short for Patrice or Patricia | *Pat / Patti, Pattie* |
| Paula | Female form of Paul: small | |
| Paulette | French female pet form of Paul: small | *Pauletta* |
| Paulina | Female form of Paul: small | *Pauline* |

| Name | Definition | Short forms/ Variations |
|------|-----------|------------------------|
| **Pax** | Peace (Latin) | |
| **Payton** | Originally an English surname, meaning soldier's town. Also a boy's name | *Peyton* |
| **Pearlie** | Pet form of Pearl | |
| **Peggoty** | Pet form of Margaret | *Peg, Peggy* |
| **Peggy** | Pet form of Margaret | *Peg / Peggoty* |
| **Penelope** | [Pen-ell-oh-pee] Duck (Greek) In Greek myth, Penelope was Odysseus's loyal wife, who waited twenty years for him to return from his travels, though many people assumed he was dead | *Penny* |
| **Peninnah** | Coral or pearl (Hebrew) | *Penny* |
| **Penny** | Short for Peninnah or Penelope | |
| **Perdie** | Short for Perdita | *Purdita* |
| **Perdita** | [Perditt-a] Lost (Latin) Invented by William Shakespeare for a character in *The Winter's Tale* | *Dita, Perdie, Purdie, Purdey / Purdita* |
| **Perla** | Pearl (Italian) | |
| **Pernilla** | Short for Petronel or Petronilla | |
| **Perpetua** | Everlasting (Latin) | |
| **Perrine** | Female form of Perrin: rock | |

| Name | Definition | Short forms/ Variations |
|------|-----------|------------------------|
| **Persephone** | [Per-sef-oh-nee] Dazzlingly bright (Greek) In Greek myth, Persephone is the daughter of Zeus and Demeter, goddess of the earth. She's abducted by Hades and although she's eventually rescued, she still has to spend several months each year in the Underworld. When Demeter and Persephone are together, the earth flourishes, but when they're apart, it's winter | |
| **Persis** | Persian woman (Greek) | |
| **Peta** | Female form of Peter: rock | |
| **Petra** | Rock (Greek, Latin) | *Petronia* |
| **Petrina** | Female form of Peter: rock | *Rina, Trina* |
| **Petronel** | From the Roman family name Petronius | *Pernilla / Parnel, Pernel, Petronella, Petronilla* |
| **Petronia** | See **Petra** | |
| **Petula** | To ask (Latin) | |
| **Peyton** | See **Payton** | |
| **Phaedra** | [Fed-ruh] Bright (Greek) In Greek myth, Phaedra fell in love with her stepson then committed suicide when he rejected her | |
| **Pherenike** | Bringer of victory (Greek) | |
| **Philippa** | Female form of Philip: lover of horses | *Pip, Pippa* |
| **Phillida** | See **Phyllis** | *Phyllida* |
| **Philomena** | Beloved (Greek) | |
| **Phira** | Short for Ophira | |
| **Phoebe** | [Fee-bee] Bright (Greek) The name of a Greek goddess | |
| **Phyllida** | See **Phyllis** | |
| **Phyllis** | Foliage (Greek) In Greek myth, Phyllis committed suicide for love and was turned into an almond tree | *Phillida, Phillis, Phyllida* |
| **Pia** | [Pee-uh] Pious (Latin) | |
| **Piera** | Italian female form of Peter: rock | |
| **Piper** | Originally a surname, meaning someone who plays the pipes | |
| **Pippa** | Short for Philippa | *Pip* |
| **Pirouette** | A movement in ballet where the dancer spins around | |

| Name | Definition | Short forms/ Variations |
|------|-----------|-------------------------|
| **Pixie** | In English folklore, pixies are a race of little people or fairies | |
| **Pleasance** | To please (Old French) | |
| **Pocahontas** | She is playful (Algonquin) The name of a 16th/17th-century Native American girl who married an Englishman | |
| **Polly** | Pet form of Mary | *Mollie, Molly* |
| **Pollyanna** | It became popular thanks to Eleanor Hodgman Porter's children's novel, *Pollyanna*, about a very sunny-natured child | |
| **Portia** | [Por-sha] Invented by William Shakespeare for the character of an heiress in *The Merchant of Venice* | |
| **Preeti** | Love; pleasure (Sanskrit) | *Priti* |
| **Prema** | Female form of Prem: love | |
| **Prima** | [Pree-mah] Female form of Primo: first | |
| **Prisca** | Short for Priscilla | *Prissie, Prissy* |
| **Priscilla** | [Priss-ill-a] Ancient (Latin) | *Cilla, Prisca, Prissie, Prissy* |
| **Prissie** | Short for Prisca or Priscilla | *Prissy* |
| **Priya** | Beloved (Sanskrit) | |
| **Prue** | Short for Prudence or Prunella | *Pru* |
| **Prunella** | Plum (Latin) | *Pru, Prue* |
| **Psyche** | [Sy-kee] Soul, spirit (Greek) | |
| **Punita** | Holy, pure (Hindi) | *Pun* |
| **Purdey** | Originally a surname. It may have gained in popularity thanks to Purdey, a high-kicking spy played by Joanna Lumley in 1970s British TV series *The New Avengers*. The character is apparently named after gun and rifle makers James Purdey & Sons | |

| Name | Definition | Short forms/ Variations |
|------|-----------|-------------------------|
| **Queenie** | In Victorian times this was sometimes used as a pet name for girls called Victoria. Perhaps now it could be a pet name for girls called Elizabeth | |
| **Questa** | Seek (Latin) | |
| **Quinn** | Originally an Irish surname, meaning descendant of Conn. Also a boy's name | |
| **Quintella** | Female pet form of Quentin: fifth | |
| **Quintina** | Female form of Quentin: fifth | *Quentina* |

| Name | Definition | Short forms/<br>Variations |
|------|-----------|---------------------------|
| **Rachel** | [Ray-shell] Ewe (Hebrew) | *Rachael* |
| **Racquel** | [Rak-ell] See **Raquel** | *Racquelle, Raquelle* |
| **Radha** | Vision (Irish Gaelic) | |
| **Rae** | Female form of Ray: wise protection | |
| **Rafaela** | Spanish female form of Raphael: God heals | *Raphaela* |
| **Rafferty** | Originally an Irish surname, meaning descendant of Rohartach. Also a boy's name | |
| **Ragna** | Advice (Old Norse) | |
| **Rahimah** | Graceful (Arabic) | |
| **Ramona** | Female form of Ramon: wise protection | |
| **Ramya** | Beautiful; elegant (Sanskrit) | |
| **Rana** | Beautiful (Arabic) | |
| **Rani** | Queen; princess (Sanskrit) | |
| **Ranya** | Loving gaze (Arabic) | |
| **Raphaela** | Female form of Raphael: God heals | *Rafaela* |
| **Raquel** | [Rak-ell] Spanish form of Rachel: ewe | *Racquel, Racquelle, Raquelle* |

| Name | Definition | Short forms/ Variations |
|------|-----------|-------------------------|
| **Rasa** | Dew (Lithuanian) | |
| **Raveena** | Sunny (Sanskrit) | |
| **Rea** | [Ree-uh] See **Rhea** | *Reah, Ria* |
| **Reagan** | [Ree-g'n] See **Regan** | |
| **Reba** | [Ree-buh] Short for Rebecca | |
| **Rebecca** | Captivator (Hebrew) | *Becca, Becky, Reba / Rebekah, Rivka* |
| **Reema** | Deer (Arabic) | |
| **Reena** | Pearl (Sanskrit) | |
| **Reenie** | Short for Irene | |
| **Reese** | Female form of Rhys: ardour | *Reece* |
| **Regan** | [Ree-g'n] Queen (Gaelic) In Shakespeare's *King Lear*, Regan is the king's cruel daughter, who turns him out into a storm. In the US, the name may be given in homage to former president Ronald Reagan | *Reagan* |
| **Regina** | [Ree-jigh-nuh] Queen (Latin) | |
| **Reisel** | Rose (Yiddish) | *Reisl* |
| **Remi** | Female form of Remy: oarsman | *Remie* |
| **Rena** | [Ree-na] Short for Serena | |
| **Renata** | [Reh-nah-tuh] Reborn (Latin) | |
| **Rene** | [Ree-nee] Short for Irene | *Reenie* |
| **Renée** | [Ren-ay] See **Renata** | |
| **Renita** | To struggle (Latin) | |
| **Reva** | See **Rivka** | |
| **Rhea** | [Ree-a] Stream (Greek) The mother of Romulus and Remus, founders of Rome | *Rea, Reah, Ria* |
| **Rheanna** | See **Rhian** | |
| **Rhian** | Maiden (Welsh) | *Rhianu* |
| **Rhianna** | See **Rhian** | |
| **Rhiannon** | [Ree-an-on] Great queen (Celtic) | |
| **Rhianydd** | See **Rhian** | |
| **Rhoda** | Roses (Greek) | |
| **Rhona** | Female form of Ronald: ruler's decision | *Rona* |
| **Rhonda** | Good lance (Welsh) | |
| **Rhonwen** | Fair or blessed lance (Welsh) | |

| Name | Definition | Short forms/ Variations |
|------|-----------|-------------------------|
| **Rhosyn** | Rose (Welsh) | |
| **Ria** | Short for Maria | |
| **Rica** | Short for Ricarda | |
| **Ricarda** | Female form of Richard: strong and powerful | *Rica, Richie* |
| **Richenda** | Female form of Richard: strong and powerful | *Richie* |
| **Richie** | Short for Ricarda or Richenda. Also a boy's name | |
| **Rika** | [Reek-a] Short for Ulrika | *Rike* |
| **Riley** | Originally a surname, meaning rye clearing. Traditionally a boy's name | |
| **Rilla** | Brook (German) | |
| **Rima** | White antelope (Arabic) | |
| **Rina** | [Ree-na] Short for Alexandrina, Carina, Katerina, Marina, Nerina, Petrina, Sabrina, Xandrina or Zarina | *Reena* |
| **Riona** | [Ree-oh-nuh] Queenly (Irish Gaelic) | *Rionach* |
| **Rionach** | See **Riona** | |
| **Ripley** | Originally an English surname. It may have gained in popularity thanks to Ellen Ripley, the heroic character played by Sigourney Weaver in the *Alien* films. Also a boy's name | |
| **Rissa** | Short for Clarissa, Larissa, Merissa or Nerissa | |
| **Rita** | [Ree-ta] Short for Margarita, Margeurite or Sarita. Sometimes given in homage to film star Rita Hayworth | |
| **Riva** | [Ree-va] Riverbank; shore (Hebrew, Latin) | |
| **Rivka** | Hebrew form of Rebecca: captivator | *Reva* |
| **Riya** | [Ree-yah] Singer (Sanskrit) | |
| **Roberta** | Female form of Robert: bright, shining fame | *Bobbi, Bobbie* |
| **Robina** | Unambiguously female form of Robin | |
| **Roche** | [Rosh] Short for Rochelle, Roshan or Rosheen | *Rosh* |
| **Rochelle** | Female form of Roch: rest | *Roche / Rosh* |
| **Rocio** | Dew (Spanish) | |
| **Roisin** | [Rosh-een] Irish form of Rose | *Rosheen* |
| **Roma** | A Roman goddess | |

names

r

girls'

| Name | Definition | Short forms/ Variations |
|---|---|---|
| **Romaine** | Roman (French) | *Romayne* |
| **Romilda** | Fame in battle (Germanic) | |
| **Romilla** | See **Romilly** | |
| **Romilly** | Originally an English surname | *Romy / Romilla* |
| **Romola** | Female form of Romulus: according to legend, one of the founders of Rome | *Romy* |
| **Romy** | Short for Romilly, Romola or Rosemary | |
| **Rona** | Female form of Ronald: ruler's decision | |
| **Ronnie** | Short for Veronica. Also a boy's name | *Roni, Ronny* |
| **Roo** | Pet form of Ruth. In AA Milne's children's book *Winnie-the-Pooh*, Roo is a joey (a baby kangaroo) | *Rue* |
| **Rosa** | Rose (Latin) | *Rosie / Rosalie, Rosalind, Rosamund, Rose, Rosina, Rosita* |
| **Rosabel** | English form of Rosabella: beautiful rose | |
| **Rosabella** | Beautiful rose (Italian) | *Rosabel, Rosabelle* |
| **Rosalba** | White rose (Latin) | |
| **Rosalie** | Rose (Latin) | *Ros, Rosa, Rose / Rosalia, Rosalin, Rosalind, Rosalyn, Rosie-Leigh* |
| **Rosalind** | Lovely rose (Latin) The heroine in Shakespeare's *As You Like It* | *Ros / Rosalie, Rosalinda, Rosaline, Rosalyn* |
| **Rosalita** | May have gained in popularity thanks to Bruce Springsteen's 1973 hit *Rosalita (Come Out Tonight)* | |

| Name | Definition | Short forms/ Variations |
|------|-----------|------------------------|
| **Rosamaria** | Combination of Rosa (rose) and Maria (sea) | |
| **Rosamund** | [Roz-uh-mund] Rose of the world (Latin) | Ros / Rosamond |
| **Rosario** | [Roze-uh-ree-oh] Rosary (Spanish) | |
| **Roseanne** | [Ro-zan] Combination of Rose and Ann (favoured by God) | Rosie / Rosanna, Rosanne, Roseanna |
| **Rosetta** | Italian pet form of Rosa: rose | Etta, Rose, Rosie |
| **Roshan** | Shining (Persian) Famous (Urdu) Also a boy's name | |
| **Rosheen** | English form of Roisin: rose | |
| **Roshni** | Light (Sanskrit) | |
| **Rosie** | Pet form of Rose | |
| **Rosina** | Italian pet form of Rosa: rose | |
| **Rosita** | Spanish pet form of Rosa: rose | Rosie |
| **Rou** | Gentle (Chinese) | |
| **Rowena** | Happy fame (Germanic) | |
| **Roxane** | [Rox-ahn or Rox-an] Dawn (Persian) | Roxie, Roxy / Roxana, Roxanna, Roxanne |
| **Roxy** | Short for Roxane | Roxie |
| **Roza** | Rose (Arabic) | |
| **Rue** | Pet form of Ruth | Roo |
| **Rufina** | Female form of Rufus: red or ruddy | Fina |
| **Ruhi** | Soul, spirit (Sanskrit) | |
| **Ruksana** | Radiant (Arabic) | |
| **Rumer** | Gypsy (Slavic) | |
| **Runa** | Rune (Old Norse) | |
| **Rupali** | Beautiful girl (Sanskrit) | Roopali |
| **Rupinder** | God of beauty (Sikh) Also a boy's name | |
| **Ruth** | Compassion (English) | Ruthie, Roo |
| **Ryder** | Originally a surname, meaning horse rider. Also a boy's name | |
| **Ryoko** | Good child (Japanese) | |

| Name | Definition | Short forms/ Variations |
|------|-----------|-------------------------|
| **Sabah** | Morning (Arabic) | |
| **Sabella** | Short for Isabella | |
| **Sabina** | Sabine woman (the Sabines were an ancient people) | *Sabine* |
| **Sable** | The heraldic term for black | |
| **Sabra** | Rest; or cactus (Hebrew) | *Sabrah* |
| **Sabrin** | See **Sabrina** | |
| **Sabrina** | An old name for the River Severn, the longest British river | *Breena, Brina, Rina / Sabrin* |
| **Sacha** | [Sash-uh] See **Sasha** | *Sascha, Sashura* |
| **Sachiko** | Happy child (Japanese) | |
| **Sadie** | Originally short for Sarah | *Zadie* |
| **Safa** | Purity; sincerity (Arabic) Also a boy's name | |
| **Saffy** | Short for Saffron | |
| **Safi** | Short for Safiyya | |
| **Safiyya** | Good friend (Arabic) | *Safi / Safiya* |
| **Saida** | Happy, lucky (Arabic) | |

| Name | Definition | Short forms/Variations |
|------|-----------|------------------------|
| **Sairah** | Traveller (Arabic) | |
| **Sajani** | Loved (Sanskrit) | |
| **Sakurah** | Cherry blossom (Japanese) | |
| **Salima** | Female form of Salim: safe | |
| **Salina** | See **Selena** | |
| **Sally** | Originally short for Sarah | *Sal / Sallie* |
| **Sally-Ann** | Combination of Sally (short for Sarah: princess) and Ann (favoured by God) | |
| **Salma** | Calm; peaceful (Arabic) | |
| **Salome** | [Sah-low-may] Peace (Aramaic) The associations are not positive. According to myth, Salome was the stepdaughter of King Herod, who was so captivated by her dancing that he offered her anything she wanted. She asked for the head of John the Baptist on a platter – and got it | |
| **Saloni** | Stunning (Arabic) | |
| **Salud** | Salvation (Spanish) | |
| **Salvadora** | Female form of Salvador: saviour | |
| **Samantha** | Female form of Samuel: asked of God | *Sam* |
| **Samara** | Mountain (Arabic) | |
| **Samina** | Healthy (Arabic) | |
| **Samiya** | Female form of Sami: sublime | *Samia* |
| **Samsara** | Passing through (Sanskrit) | |
| **Sana** | Radiance (Arabic) | |
| **Sanchia** | Holy (Latin) | *Sancha* |
| **Sandra** | Originally short for Alessandra or Alexandra | *Sandi, Sandy / Saundra, Xandra, Zandra* |
| **Sandy** | Short for Alessandra, Alexandra or Sandra | *Sandi* |
| **Sapphira** | Expanded form of Sapphire | |
| **Sara** | [Sah-rah] See **Sarah** | *Zara* |
| **Sarah** | [Sair-ah] Princess (Hebrew) | *Sadie, Sally, Sarina / Sara* |
| **Sarai** | Quarrelsome (Hebrew) | |
| **Sarala** | Honest (Sanskrit) | *Sarla* |
| **Saree** | Most noble (Arabic) | |

| Name | Definition | Short forms/ Variations |
|------|-----------|------------------------|
| **Sari** | Finnish form of Sarah: princess | |
| **Sarika** | Singing bird (Sanskrit) | |
| **Sarina** | Pet form of Sarah | |
| **Sarita** | Spanish pet form of Sara: princess | *Rita* |
| **Sasha** | Originally short for Alexandra | *Sacha, Sascha Sashura* |
| **Sashura** | Russian pet form of Sasha | *Shura* |
| **Saskia** | Saxon (Germanic) | |
| **Sassa** | Swedish short form of Astrid | |
| **Satine** | The name of the cabaret star played by Nicole Kidman in the 2001 film *Moulin Rouge* | |
| **Saundra** | Scottish Gaelic form of Sandra, short for Alexandra: protector | |
| **Savita** | The sun (Sanskrit) | |
| **Scout** | In Harper Lee's 1960 novel *To Kill a Mockingbird*, Scout is the nickname of the young narrator, Jean Louise Finch | |
| **Scully** | Town crier (Irish Gaelic) May have increased in popularity thanks to Dana Scully, the sceptical FBI agent played by Gillian Anderson in American TV drama *The X-Files*. Also a boy's name | |
| **Seana** | [Shawn-a] Female form of Sean: God is gracious | |
| **Seirian** | [Ser-en] Sparkling (Welsh) | |
| **Selena** | [Sel-ee-na] Greek goddess of the moon | *Salina, Selina* |
| **Selene** | [Sel-een] French form of Selena: Greek goddess of the moon | |
| **Selima** | [She-lee-mah] Peace (Arabic) Thought to have first been used by 18th-century writer and politician Horace Walpole, for his cat | |
| **Selma** | Peace (Arabic) | |
| **Senga** | Slender (Scottish Gaelic) | |
| **Seonag** | [Sho-na] Gaelic form of Joan: God is gracious | *Shona* |
| **Sequoia** | A species of tree, thought to be named after the Cherokee leader Sequoyah. Giant Sequoia, found in California, have been known to grow up to 93m in height | |

| Name | Definition | Short forms/ Variations |
| --- | --- | --- |
| **Seraphina** | Angel (Hebrew) | *Serafina* |
| **Seren** | Star (Welsh) | |
| **Serena** | [Seh-ree-nuh] Serene, calm (Latin) | *Rena* |
| **Shae** | [Shay] See **Shea** | *Shay, Shaye* |
| **Shahira** | Famous (Arabic) | |
| **Shaila** | One who lives in the mountains (Sanskrit) | |
| **Shakira** | Thankful (Arabic) | *Shaira* |
| **Shan** | Mountain (Chinese) Also a boy's name | |
| **Shana** | See **Sian** | *Shanae* |
| **Shanae** | Female form of Sean: God is gracious | |
| **Shandy** | From the drink | *Shandie* |
| **Shanee** | [Shah-nee] English form of Siani: God is gracious | |
| **Shania** | [Shah-nee-uh] See **Sian** | |
| **Shanna** | See **Shannagh** | |
| **Shannagh** | [Shan-uh] Originally an Irish surname | *Shanna* |
| **Shannon** | A river in Ireland | |
| **Shanta** | Spiritually calmed (Sanskrit) | |
| **Shanti** | [Shont-ee] Peace, tranquillity (Sanskrit) | |
| **Sharon** | A place mentioned in the Biblical *Song of Solomon* | *Sharron* |
| **Shatha** | Fragrance (Arabic) | |
| **Shauna** | [Shawn-uh] Female form of Sean: God is gracious | *Shawna* |
| **Shayla** | See **Sheila** | *Shaela, Sheelagh, Sheelah, Shelagh Shyla* |
| **Shea** | [Shay] Originally an Irish surname. Also a boy's name | *Shae, Shay, Shaye* |
| **Sheba** | Originally short for Bathsheba | |
| **Sheela** | Good character; piety (Sanskrit) | |
| **Sheena** | See **Síne** | *Sheenagh* |
| **Sheila** | English form of Síle, the Irish form of Cecily: clever. In Australia, Sheila is the slang word for a woman | *Shaela, Shayla, Sheelagh, Sheelah, Shelagh, Shyla* |
| **Shelby** | Originally an English surname. Also a boy's name | |

| Name | Definition | Short forms/Variations |
|------|-----------|------------------------|
| **Shelley** | Originally a surname, meaning a wood on a slope. Sometimes given in homage to the Romantic poet Percy Bysshe Shelley | |
| **Sheridan** | Originally an Irish surname, meaning to seek. Also a boy's name | *Sheri, Sherie, Sherri, Sherrie, Sherry* |
| **Sherilyn** | Combination of Sheryl and Lyn. May have increased in popularity thanks to American actress Sherilyn Fenn (born Sheryl Ann Fenn) | |
| **Sherry** | From the drink | *Sheri, Sherie, Sherri, Sherrie* |
| **Sheryl** | See **Cheryl** | *Cherith, Cheryth* |
| **Shevaun** | English form of Siobhan: God is gracious | |
| **Shifra** | Beauty, grace (Hebrew) | *Shifrah* |
| **Shiloh** | [Shy-lo] He who is to be sent (Hebrew) In the Bible, this may refer to the Messiah. Traditionally a boy's name but occasionally used for girls | |
| **Shira** | Poetry (Hebrew) | |
| **Shirin** | Sweet, charming (Persian) | |
| **Shirley** | Originally a surname, meaning bright wood. Although it was traditionally a boy's name, it's now used only for girls. It gained in popularity thanks to child film star Shirley Temple | |
| **Shona** | See **Seonag** | |
| **Shoshannah** | Hebrew form of Susanna: lily | *Shoshana, Shoshanna* |
| **Shu** | Fair (Chinese) | |
| **Shula** | Short for Shulamit | |
| **Shulamit** | Peacefulness (Hebrew) | *Shula / Shulamite* |
| **Shura** | Short for Sashura | |
| **Shyla** | See **Sheila** | |
| **Sian** | [Sharn] Welsh form of Jane: God is gracious | *Siani, Sianie / Shana, Shanae, Shanee* |
| **Sibyl** | Prophetess (Greek) | *Sibella, Sybil, Sybilla, Sybille* |
| **Sidney** | Originally an aristocratic surname, meaning wide meadow. Traditionally a boy's name | *Sydney* |
| **Sidonia** | See **Sidony** | |

names
S
girls'

| Name | Definition | Short forms/ Variations |
|------|-----------|------------------------|
| **Sidony** | Person from Sidon | *Sidonia, Sidonie* |
| **Sidra** | Star born (Latin) | |
| **Siegrun** | Magic victory (Germanic) | *Sigi / Sigrun* |
| **Sighile** | Gaelic form of Cecily: clever | *Sile* |
| **Sigi** | Short for Sigrid or Siegrun | |
| **Signy** | New victory (Old Norse) | *Signe, Signi* |
| **Sigourney** | Conqueror (Scandinavian) Also a boy's name | |
| **Sigrid** | Beautiful victory (Old Norse) | *Sigi, Siri* |
| **Sigrun** | Secret victory (Old Norse) | |
| **Síle** | [She-luh] Gaelic form of Cecily: clever | |
| **Silvana** | Female form of Silvano: wood | |
| **Silvestra** | Female form of Silvester: of the woods | *Silvie* |
| **Silvia** | Wood (Latin) | *Silvie, Sylvia, Sylvie* |
| **Simcha** | Joy (Hebrew) Also a boy's name | |
| **Simone** | [Simm-on or Simm-oan] Female form of Simon: hearkening | *Simona* |
| **Simran** | God's gift (Sanskrit) | |
| **Sinai** | [Sine-ay-eye] From Mount Sinai. In the Bible, this is the place where God gave Moses the Ten Commandments. Also a boy's name | |
| **Sindy** | Short for Cynthia or Lucinda | *Cindie, Cindy, Sindie* |
| **Síne** | [Shee-na] Gaelic form of Jane: God is gracious | *Sheena, Sheenagh* |
| **Sinead** | [Shin-ade] Gaelic form of Janet: God is gracious | |
| **Siobhan** | [Shiv-awn] Gaelic form of Joan: God is gracious | |
| **Siren** | In Greek myth, sirens were sea nymphs who lived on cliffs and rocks. Their enchanting singing caused sailors to sail too close and drown | |
| **Siri** | Short for Sigrid | |
| **Sisley** | English form of Cecily: clever | |
| **Sissie** | Short for Cecilia or Cecily | *Sissy* |
| **Sistine** | From the Sistine Chapel in Vatican City, Rome | *Sistene* |
| **Siv** | Bride (Old Norse) In Norse myth, Siv was the wife of Thor, god of thunder | |

| Name | Definition | Short forms/ Variations |
|------|-----------|------------------------|
| **Siwan** | Welsh form of Joan, a female form of John: God is gracious | |
| **Sloane** | Originally an Irish surname. Now associated with upper-class women from the exclusive Sloane Square area of London | |
| **Sly** | Short for Sylvia or Sylvie | |
| **Sofya** | Russian form of Sophia: wisdom | |
| **Sol** | Sun (Latin) Also a boy's name | |
| **Solange** | Solemn; religious (Latin) | *Solène* |
| **Soledad** | [Sol-eh-dad] Solitude (Spanish) | |
| **Soleil** | [Sol-ay] Sun (French) | *Sol, Sunny* |
| **Solène** | See **Solange** | |
| **Sonia** | Pet name for Sofya, the Russian form of Sophia | *Sonja, Sonya* |
| **Sonnet** | A type of poem (English) | |
| **Soo** | Long life (Korean) | |
| **Sophia** | Wisdom (Greek) | *Sofia, Sofya, Sophie, Zofia* |
| **Sophie** | French form of Sophia: wisdom | *Sofie, Sophy* |
| **Soraya** | See **Suraya** | |
| **Sorcha** | [Sorr-ka] Brightness (Celtic) | |
| **Stacey** | Originally a boy's name, short for Eustace (fruitful). Now more common as a girl's name | *Stacie, Stacy* |
| **Starla** | From Star | |
| **Stasia** | [Stay-zee-uh] Short for Anastasia | *Stacia* |
| **Stefanie** | See **Stephanie** | |
| **Steffi** | Short for Stefanie | *Stephi* |
| **Stella** | Star (Latin) | |
| **Stephanie** | Female form of Stephen: crown | *Steffi, Steph, Stevie / Stefanie* |
| **Stevie** | Short for Stephanie. May be given in homage to the 19th-century English poet and novelist Stevie Smith (born Florence Margaret). Also a boy's name | |
| **Stockard** | Originally an English surname, meaning tree stump. Also a boy's name | |

| Name | Definition | Short forms/ Variations |
|------|-----------|------------------------|
| **Sue** | Short for Susan, Susanna, Suzanne or Suzette | |
| **Suha** | Star (Arabic) | |
| **Sukie** | Short for Susan | *Sukey, Suki, Suky* |
| **Sula** | Sun (Icelandic) | |
| **Sumati** | Good mind; prayer (Sanskrit) | |
| **Sumiko** | Pure child (Japanese) | |
| **Sunita** | Righteous (Sanskrit) | *Neeta, Nita* |
| **Sunniva** | Sun's gift (Old English) | *Sunny* |
| **Suraya** | Many stars (Arabic) | *Soraya, Thuraya, Thurayya* |
| **Susan** | See **Susanna** | *Sue, Sukey, Suki, Sukie, Suky, Susie Suzie, Suzy* |
| **Susanna** | Lily (Hebrew) | *Sue, Susie, Suzie Suzy, Zanna, Zannah / Susannah, Suzanna, Suzannah, Zsuzsanna* |
| **Susie** | Short for Susan or Susanna | *Suzie, Suzy* |
| **Suvarna** | Golden (Sanskrit) | |
| **Suzanne** | French form of Susanna: lily | *Sue, Suzie, Suzy / Susanne, Suzette* |
| **Suzette** | See **Suzanne** | *Sue, Suzie, Suzy* |
| **Suzie** | Short for Susan, Susanna, Suzanne or Suzette | *Sue / Suzy* |
| **Svanhild** | Beautiful swan (Saxon) | |
| **Svetlana** | Light (Slavic) | *Lana* |
| **Sybil** | See **Sibyl** | *Sibella, Sybilla, Sybille* |
| **Sydney** | See **Sidney** | |
| **Sylpha** | See **Sylphide** | |
| **Sylphide** | [Sil-feed] Spirit (Latin) | *Sylpha* |
| **Sylvie** | French form of Silvia: wood | *Sly / Silvia, Silvie, Sylvia* |
| **Symphony** | A piece of classical music played by an orchestra (English) | |
| **Syrie** | Female form of Cyril: lord | |

| Name | Definition | Short forms/ Variations |
|------|-----------|------------------------|
| **Tabitha** | Doe, a female deer (Aramaic) | |
| **Taffeta** | From the fabric, often used for party dresses | |
| **Takara** | Treasure (Japanese) | |
| **Talia** | See **Thalia** | |
| **Talitha** | Little girl (Aramaic) | *Tallie, Tally* |
| **Tallie** | Short for Talitha | *Tally* |
| **Tallula** | English form of Tuilelaith | *Lula / Tallulah, Talula* |
| **Talya** | Dew from God (Hebrew) | *Talia* |
| **Tamar** | See **Tamara** | |
| **Tamara** | Date tree (Hebrew) | *Tammie, Tammy* |
| **Tamay** | In the centre (Quechua – a Native American language) | |
| **Tamika** | Sweet (Swahili) | |
| **Tamiko** | Child of abundance (Japanese) | |
| **Tammy** | Short for Tamara or Tamsin | *Tammie* |
| **Tamsin** | See **Thomasina** | *Tammie, Tammy / Tamzin* |

| Name | Definition | Short forms/ Variations |
|------|-----------|-------------------------|
| **Tandie** | Fire (Old Norse) | *Tandy* |
| **Tania** | See **Tanya** | |
| **Tanisha** | Ambition (Sanskrit) | |
| **Tanith** | A Phoenician goddess | |
| **Tanvi** | Slender; beautiful; young (Sanskrit) | |
| **Tanvir** | Illuminating (Arabic) Also a boy's name | |
| **Tanya** | Short for Tatiana | *Tania* |
| **Tara** | Star (Sanskrit) Also the name of Scarlett O'Hara's family estate in Margaret Mitchell's novel *Gone with the Wind*. This was named after a place in Meath, Ireland, meaning hill | |
| **Tarana** | Song (Sanskrit) | |
| **Taree** | Fig tree (Aboriginal) | |
| **Tarika** | One who belongs to the stars (Sanskrit) | |
| **Tasha** | Short for Natasha | *Tash / Tashie* |
| **Tate** | Originally an English surname, meaning cheerful. Also a boy's name | |
| **Tatiana** | [Tat-yah-na] Female form of Tatianus, an old Roman family name | *Tania, Tanya, Tiana / Tatyana* |
| **Tatum** | Originally an English surname, meaning Tate's homestead. Also a boy's name | |
| **Tavia** | Short for Octavia | |
| **Tavy** | Short for Octavia | *Tavie* |
| **Taylor** | Originally a surname, meaning tailor. Also a boy's name | |
| **Teague** | [Teeg] English form of Tadhg: poet or philosopher. Also a boy's name | *Teigue* |
| **Tegan** | [Tee-gan] Irish form of Tegwen: lovely and fair or blessed | *Teagan, Teigan, Tiegan* |
| **Tegwen** | Lovely and fair or blessed (Welsh) | |
| **Tempe** | [Temp-ee] A valley in eastern Greece. In Greek myth, it was the home of the Muses | |
| **Teone** | See **Theone** | *Teoni, Theoni* |
| **Teresa** | To harvest (Greek) Sometimes given in homage to Mother Teresa | *Teri, Terri, Terry, Tess, Tessa, Tessie / Terese, Theresa* |

| Name | Definition | Short forms/ Variations |
|------|-----------|------------------------|
| **Terese** | Basque form of Teresa: to harvest | *Teri, Terri, Terry, Tess, Tessa, Tessie / Therese* |
| **Teri** | Short for Theresa | *Terri, Terry* |
| **Tess** | Short for Theresa. It may have gained in popularity thanks to the tragic heroine of Thomas Hardy's 19th-century novel, *Tess of the d'Urbervilles* | *Tessa, Tessie* |
| **Thalia** | [Tah-lee-uh] To bloom (Greek) | *Talia* |
| **Thana** | Praise (Arabic) | |
| **Thandiwe** | Loving one (African) | |
| **Thea** | Short for Alethea, Althea or Dorothea | |
| **Thecla** | God's glory (Greek) | |
| **Theda** | Short for Theodora or Theodosia | |
| **Thelma** | Wish (Greek) | |
| **Theodora** | Female form of Theodore: gift from God | *Dora, Thea, Theda* |
| **Theodosia** | God's giving (Greek) | *Thea, Theda* |
| **Theone** | God's name (Greek) | *Teone, Teoni, Theoni* |
| **Theresa** | See **Teresa** | *Teri, Terri, Terry, Tess, Tessa, Tessie / Terese* |
| **Thessa** | Short for Thessaly | |
| **Thessaly** | A region in east-central Greece | *Thessa* |
| **Thirza** | Cypress tree (Hebrew) | *Thirzah, Thyrza, Tirzah* |
| **Thomasina** | Female form of Thomas: twin | *Tommie* |
| **Thora** | Female form of Thor, the Norse god of thunder | |
| **Thuraya** | See **Suraya** | *Thurayya* |
| **Tia** | Princess (Greek) | |
| **Tiana** | Short for Christiana or Tatiana | |
| **Tiara** | A small crown (English) | |
| **Tibbie** | Short for Isabel | *Tib / Tibby* |
| **Tierney** | Originally an Irish surname, meaning kingly. Also a boy's name | |
| **Tierra** | Land, earth (Spanish) | |

| Name | Definition | Short forms/ Variations |
|---|---|---|
| **Tiffany** | Epiphany (Greek) Sometimes given to girls born on January 6, the feast of the Epiphany. These days, it's more usually connected with the New York jewellers and the 1961 film *Breakfast at Tiffany's*, starring Audrey Hepburn | |
| **Tiggy** | Pet form of Antigone | |
| **Tikvah** | Hope (Hebrew) | *Tikva* |
| **Tilda** | Short for Matilda | *Tillie, Tilly* |
| **Tillie** | Short for Matilda | *Tilly* |
| **Tina** | Short for Albertina, Bettina, Christina, Clementina, Ernestina, Ernestine, Martina or Valentina | *Teena* |
| **Ting** | Graceful (Chinese) | |
| **Tippi** | Pet name for Tupsa: sweetheart. May have gained in popularity thanks to American actress Tippi (born Nathalie) Hedren. Her father, who was Swedish, gave her Tippi as a nickname | |
| **Tirion** | Kind, gentle (Welsh) | |
| **Tirzah** | Delight (Hebrew) | *Tirza* |
| **Tisha** | Short for Laetitia or Latisha | *Tish* |
| **Toinette** | [Twon-et] Short for Antoinette | *Nettie, Toni* |
| **Toltse** | [Tolt-see] Yiddish form of Dulcie: sweet | |
| **Tomeka** | Female form of Tomek: twin | |
| **Tomiko** | Child of wealth (Japanese) | |
| **Tommie** | Short for Thomasina. Also a boy's name | |
| **Toni** | Short for Antoinette, Antonia or Antonina | |
| **Tonia** | [Ton-yah] Short for Antonia | |
| **Topsy** | Thought to have first been used as a name for a young slave girl in Harriet Beecher Stowe's 19th-century novel *Uncle Tom's Cabin*. The phrase 'topsy-turvy' means upside down or chaotic | *Topsie* |
| **Torren** | Originally a surname, meaning hill | |
| **Tory** | Short for Victoria | *Tori* |
| **Tova** | Beautiful Thor, the god of thunder (Old Norse) | *Tuva* |
| **Tovah** | Good (Hebrew) | |

| Name | Definition | Short forms/ Variations |
|------|-----------|------------------------|
| **Toyah** | A small town in Texas. Also a boy's name | |
| **Tracy** | Originally a French surname and traditionally a boy's name. It's now almost exclusively a girl's name – probably thanks to the influence of the 1956 film *High Society*, in which Grace Kelly starred as heiress Tracy Samantha Lord | *Tracey, Tracie* |
| **Treasa** | Strength (Irish Gaelic) | |
| **Treena** | See **Trina** | |
| **Tricia** | Short for Patricia | *Trish / Trisha* |
| **Triffy** | Short for Tryphena | *Triffie* |
| **Trilby** | Thought to have first been used as a name for the main character in George du Maurier's 19th-century novel, *Trilby*. It's also a type of hat | *Trilbie* |
| **Trina** | Short for Catrina, Catriona, Katrina, Katriona, Patrina or Petrina | *Treena* |
| **Trinity** | The Father, Son and Holy Spirit of the Christian God | *Trinnie, Trinny* |
| **Trisha** | See **Tricia** | *Trish* |
| **Trissie** | Short for Beatrice | *Trissy* |
| **Trixie** | Short for Beatrice or Beatrix | *Trixi* |
| **Trixiebelle** | Combination of Trixie (short for Beatrix: bringer of joy) and Belle (beautiful) | |
| **Trude** | Short for Ermintrude or Gertrude | *Trudi, Trudie, Trudy* |
| **Tryphena** | [Trif-eh-nuh] Dainty girl (Greek) | *Triffie, Triffy / Tryphaena* |
| **Tuathla** | Princess of the people (Irish Gaelic) | |
| **Tuilelaith** | [Til-a-la] Abundant lady (Gaelic) | |
| **Tupsa** | Sweetheart (Swedish) | *Tippi* |
| **Twiggy** | May have gained in popularity thanks to the 1960s supermodel born Lesley Hornby but named Twiggy for her waif-like appearance | |
| **Tyler** | Originally a surname, meaning roof tiler. In the US, it may be given in homage to a former president, John Tyler. Also a boy's name. | |
| **Tyra** | Female form of Tyr. In Old Norse myth, Tyr was god of war and justice | |

girls'

t

names

| Name | Definition | Short forms/ Variations |
|------|-----------|------------------------|
| **Ulanda** | Female form of Uland: noble country | |
| **Uliana** | Russian form of Juliana, from the Roman family name Julius | |
| **Ulla** | Short for Ulrika | |
| **Ulrika** | Female form of Ulric: wolf power | *Rika, Ulla / Ulrike* |
| **Ulyssia** | Female form of Ulysses, Latin form of Odysseus: the wandering hero in Homer's ancient Greek epic poem *The Odyssey* | |
| **Uma** | Light, brightness (Sanskrit) | |
| **Una** | [Yu-nah or Oo-nah] Lamb (Irish) | *Oona, Oonagh* |
| **Urmila** | Enchanter (Sanskrit) | |
| **Ursie** | Short for Ursula | *Ursy* |
| **Ursula** | Female bear (Latin) | *Ursie, Ursy* |
| **Usha** | Dawn (Sanskrit) | |
| **Ute** | Heritage (Germanic) | |
| **Uzma** | Greatest (Arabic) | |

| Name | Definition | Short forms/ Variations |
| --- | --- | --- |
| **Vada** | Rose (Hebrew) Also a boy's name | |
| **Vaishali** | The noble one (Sanskrit) | |
| **Valda** | Combination of Valerie (healthy; strong) and Linda (pretty) | |
| **Valeda** | Healthy; strong (Latin) | |
| **Valentina** | Female form of Valentine: healthy; strong. The feast of St Valentine is celebrated on 14 February, which coincided with a pagan fertility festival – hence the modern St Valentine's Day | *Tina, Val* |
| **Valerie** | Healthy; strong (Latin) | *Val / Valeria* |
| **Vandana** | Worship (Sanskrit) | |
| **Vanessa** | Invented by the 17th/18th-century writer Jonathan Swift for a female friend | *Nessa, Nessie* |
| **Vania** | See **Vanya** | |
| **Vanna** | Golden (Khmer) Also a boy's name | |
| **Vanora** | White wave (Celtic) | |

| Name | Definition | Short forms/ Variations |
|------|-----------|------------------------|
| **Vanya** | Usually a boy's name, the pet form of Ivan: God is gracious | *Vania* |
| **Varada** | One who grants wishes; a river (Sanskrit) | |
| **Varda** | Pet form of Vered | |
| **Varija** | Born in water (Sanskrit) | |
| **Vashti** | Star (Persian) | |
| **Veda** | See **Vida** | |
| **Vega** | Taken from Las Vegas | |
| **Velma** | See **Wilma** | |
| **Velvet** | From the luxurious fabric | |
| **Venetia** | [Ven-eesh-a] Blessed (Celtic) Also a region of north-eastern Italy | |
| **Ventura** | Good fortune (Spanish) | |
| **Venus** | Roman goddess of love | |
| **Venya** | Lovable (Sanskrit) | |
| **Vera** | Faith (Russian) True (Latin) | *Verena* |
| **Vered** | Rose (Hebrew) | *Varda* |
| **Verena** | See **Vera** | *Verina* |
| **Veronica** | True image (Latin) | *Roni, Ronnie / Veronique* |
| **Veronique** | French form of Veronica: true image | *Roni, Ronnie* |
| **Vesper** | Evening (Latin) Sometimes used to refer to the evening star. The name may have gained in popularity thanks to the first 'Bond girl', Vesper Lynd, in Ian Fleming's novel *Casino Royale* | |

| Name | Definition | Short forms/ Variations |
|------|-----------|-------------------------|
| **Vesta** | Roman goddess of the hearth | |
| **Veva** | Short for Genevieve | |
| **Vianne** | Short form of Vivianne | *Vienne* |
| **Vicky** | Short for Victoria | *Vicki, Vickie, Vikki* |
| **Victoria** | Victory (Latin) | *Vicki, Vickie, Vicky, Vikki, Tori, Tory* |
| **Vida** | [Vee-dah] Spanish form of Vita: life | *Veda* |
| **Viennay** | Originally a French surname. Sometimes given by Roman Catholics in homage to St Jean Viennay, the patron saint of parish priests | |
| **Viola** | [Vee-oh-luh] Violet (Latin) The aristocratic heroine of William Shakespeare's *Twelfth Night* | |
| **Violetta** | [Vee-oh-leh-tuh] Italian pet form of Violet | *Violette* |
| **Virginia** | From the Roman family name Virginius | *Ginger, Ginnie, Ginny* |
| **Vita** | [Vee-tuh] Life (Latin) | *Vida* |
| **Viva** | [Vee-vuh] Full of life (Latin) | |
| **Vivi** | [Vih-vee] Short for Vivien | *Viv* |
| **Vivien** | Alive (Latin) Sometimes given in homage to *Gone with the Wind* actress Vivien Leigh | *Vianne, Vienne, Viv, Vivi / Vivian, Viviana, Vivianne, Vivienne, Vivyan* |

| Name | Definition | Short forms/ Variations |
|------|-----------|------------------------|
| **Wakeeta** | Beautiful flower (Sanskrit) | |
| **Walburga** | Powerful protector (Anglo Saxon) | *Waldburga* |
| **Walda** | Female form of Waldo: rule | |
| **Wanda** | The name of a princess in Polish folk tales | *Vanda, Wenda* |
| **Wendla** | Wanderer (Teutonic) | |
| **Wendy** | Invented by playwright and author JM Barrie for his play *Peter Pan* | *Wenda* |
| **Whitney** | Originally an English surname, meaning white island. Also a boy's name | |
| **Whoopi** | [Woo-pee] May have increased in popularity thanks to the American actress and comedian Whoopi Goldberg. Born Caryn Elaine Johnson, she says she chose her stage name from a whoopee cushion, because 'if you get a little gassy, you've got to let it go' | *Whoopee* |
| **Wilda** | Willow tree (Germanic) | |
| **Wilhelmina** | Female form of Wilhelm: protector | *Mina, Minna, Minnie, Wilma* |

| Name | Definition | Short forms/ Variations |
|---|---|---|
| **Willa** | Female form of Will, short for William: protector | |
| **Wilma** | Short for Wilhelmina | *Velma* |
| **Winfred** | Joy and peace (Old English) | *Fred, Freddie, Win, Winnie, Wyn, Wynne* |
| **Winifred** | English form of Gwenfrewi: fair or blessed reconciliation | *Fred, Freddie, Win, Winnie, Wyn, Wynne / Winifrid* |
| **Winnie** | Short for Winfred or Winifred | |
| **Winona** | A place in Minnesota, USA | |
| **Wynn** | Fair or blessed (Welsh) | *Wynnie / Win, Winne Wyn, Wynne* |

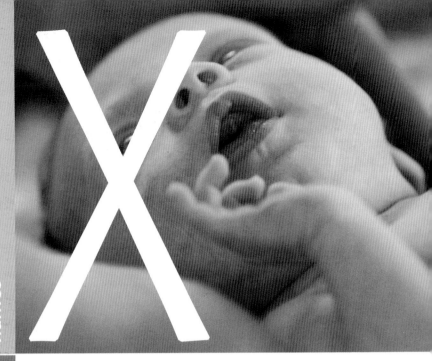

| Name | Definition | Short forms/ Variations |
|------|-----------|-------------------------|
| **Xanadu** | [Zan-a-doo] The summer capital of Kublai Khan's Mongol Empire | *Zanadu* |
| **Xandra** | [Zan-dra or Zahn-dra] Short for Alexandra or Alexandrina | *Sandra, Zandra* |
| **Xandrina** | [Zahn-dree-nuh] Short for Alexandrina | *Rina* |
| **Xanthe** | [Zanth-ee] Yellow, bright (Greek) | |
| **Xena** | [Zee-nuh] Stranger (Greek) | *Zena* |
| **Xenia** | [Zee-nee-uh] Hospitality (Greek) | *Xeniah, Zenia, Zeniah* |
| **Xia** | [Zee-uh] Rosy clouds (Chinese) | |
| **Xiulan** | Graceful orchid (Chinese) | |
| **Xue** | Snow (Chinese) | |
| **Xylene** | [Zeye-leen] See **Xylia** | |
| **Xylia** | [Zyl-ee-uh] Of the forest (Greek) | *Xylene* |

| Name | Definition | Short forms/ Variations |
|------|-----------|------------------------|
| **Yael** | [Yale] Female wild goat (Hebrew) In the Bible, Yael helps deliver Israel from the troops of King Jabin by killing the head of Jabin's army (she hammered a tent peg through his head while he slept) | *Jael* |
| **Yana** | Bulgarian female form of John: God is gracious | |
| **Yasmin** | Jasmine (Persian) | *Mina / Yasmina, Yasmine, Yazmin, Yazmine* |
| **Yelena** | Russian form of Helen: sunbeam | |
| **Yentl** | Yiddish form of Gentille: kind | |
| **Ygrayne** | See **Igraine** | |
| **Yoko** | Positive child (Japanese) | |
| **Yolanda** | Violet flower (Greek) | *Jolanda, Jolande, Yolande* |
| **Yoshi** | Good (Japanese) Also a boy's name | |
| **Yoshiko** | Good child (Japanese) | |
| **Yseult** | Medieval French form of Isolde: an Irish princess in Arthurian myth | *Issie, Issy, Izzie, Izzy / Iseult, Yseulte, Ysolt* |

| Name | Definition | Short forms/<br>Variations |
|---|---|---|
| **Yuriko** | Pleasant child (Japanese) | |
| **Yvette** | [Ee-vet] Female form of Yves: yew | |
| **Yvonne** | [Ee-von] Female form of Yvain: yew | *Ivonne* |

| Name | Definition | Short forms/ Variations |
|------|-----------|-------------------------|
| **Zadie** | [Zay-dee] See **Sadie** | |
| **Zahira** | Radiant (Arabic) | |
| **Zahra** | Shining; flower (Arabic) | |
| **Zaida** | Female form of Zayd: growth | |
| **Zaina** | See **Zayna** | Zaynia |
| **Zaira** | Rose (Arabic) | |
| **Zan** | Praise, support (Chinese) | |
| **Zana** | Well fed (Hebrew) | |
| **Zanadu** | [Zan-a-doo] See **Xanadu** | |
| **Zandra** | Short for Alexandra or Alexandrina | Sandra, Xandra |
| **Zanna** | Short for Susanna | Zannah |
| **Zara** | [Zah-rah] Flower (Arabic) | |
| **Zarina** | Golden (Persian) | Rina |
| **Zayna** | Female form of Zayn: good looks; grace | Zaina, Zaynia |
| **Zaynab** | A fragrant, flowering plant (Arabic) | Zainab |
| **Zeena** | Intelligence (Arabic) | |

| Name | Definition | Short forms/ Variations |
|------|-----------|------------------------|
| **Zelah** | A place mentioned in the Bible: one of the fourteen cities of the tribe of Benjamin | |
| **Zelda** | Short for Griselda | |
| **Zelie** | Ardent (French) | |
| **Zena** | See **Xena** | |
| **Zenia** | See **Xenia** | *Xeniah, Zeniah* |
| **Zenith** | The highest point in the heavens, or the time when someone or something is most successful (English) | |
| **Zephyr** | [Zef-eer] West wind (Greek) | |
| **Zeta** | [Zee-tuh] See **Zita** | |
| **Zhi** | Ambition; wisdom (Chinese) Also a boy's name | |
| **Zia** | [Zee-uh] Splendour; light (Arabic). Also a boy's name | *Ziya* |
| **Zillah** | Shadow (Hebrew) | |
| **Zina** | [Zih-nuh] Short for Zinovia | |
| **Zinovia** | [Zih-no-vee-uh] Life of Zeus (Greek) | *Zina* |
| **Zita** | [Zee-tuh] Girl (Italian) | *Zeta* |
| **Zoe** | [Zoh-ee] Life (Greek) | *Zola* |
| **Zofia** | Polish form of Sophia: wisdom | |
| **Zola** | See **Zoe** | |
| **Zona** | Girdle (Greek) | |
| **Zooey** | Originally a boy's name, invented by novelist JD Salinger for Franny's brother in his cult 1961 book *Franny and Zooey*. In the book, it's short for Zachary: God has remembered | |
| **Zora** | Dawn (Arabic) | |
| **Zsa Zsa** | Pet name for Zsuzsanna, the Hungarian form of Susanna: lily. May have gained in popularity thanks to Hungarian-born actress Zsa Zsa Gabor | |
| **Zsuzsanna** | Hungarian form of Susanna (lily) | *Zsa Zsa* |
| **Zula** | From the Zulu people of Southern Africa | |

# Boys' Names
## A–Z

My Notes

| Name | Definition | Short forms/ Variations |
|------|-----------|------------------------|
| **Aaron** | [Air-on] Mountain of strength (Hebrew) | *Aron, Arron* |
| Abban | St Abban was an Irish hermit who lived in Abingdon, Oxfordshire | |
| **Abbas** | Austere (Arabic) | |
| Abdon | St Abdon was a Persian nobleman who was martyred in Rome. He was put in an arena full of wild animals but they left him unharmed so gladiators were sent in to finish him off | |
| **Abdul** | Short for Abdullah | |
| Abdullah | Servant of Allah (Arabic) | *Abdul* |
| **Abe** | Short for Abel or Abraham | |
| Abel | Breath (Hebrew) | *Abe* |
| **Abelard** | [Abl-ard] Firm (Germanic) | |
| Abhay | Fearless (Sanskrit) | |
| **Abiel** | My father is God (Hebrew) | |
| Abner | Father of light (Hebrew) | |

| Name | Definition | Short forms/ Variations |
|---|---|---|
| **Abraham** | Father of nations (Hebrew) In the US, sometimes given in homage to President Abraham Lincoln | *Abe, Bram / Abram, Ibrahim* |
| Abraxas | Bright (Spanish) | |
| **Absalom** | Father of peace (Hebrew) | *Axel* |
| Abu | Father (Arabic) | |
| **Ace** | Short for Asa | *Acer* |
| Achille | [Ah-kil] French form of Achilles | |
| **Achilles** | [Ah-kil-eez] In Greek myth, Achilles was the son of a sea nymph and a mortal. He was eventually killed in battle after being wounded in the heel – the one vulnerable part of his body | |
| Acton | Originally an English surname, meaning town or village by an oak tree | |
| **Adair** | [Add-air] Negotiator (Scottish) Sometimes used for girls | |
| Adam | Earth (Hebrew) In the Bible, the first man | |
| **Adamson** | Originally a surname, meaning son of Adam | |
| Adarsh | Principles (Sanskrit) | |
| **Addison** | Originally a surname, meaning Addie's son. Also a girl's name | |
| Adel | Royal (Germanic) | |
| **Adelard** | [Adl-ard] Noble and strong (Germanic) | |
| Adesh | Command (Sanskrit) | |
| **Adil** | Just, fair (Arabic) | |
| Adlai | God is just (Hebrew) | |
| **Adler** | Eagle-eyed (Germanic) | |
| Adolph | See **Adolphus.** Now rarely used, due to its connection with Nazi dictator Adolf Hitler | *Adolf* |
| **Adolphus** | Noble wolf (Teutonic) | *Adolf, Adolph* |
| Adrian | Man from Hadria, a town in northern Italy (Latin) | *Ade / Hadrian* |
| **Adriel** | God's follower (Hebrew) | |
| Aedan | See Aidan | *Aiden, Edan* |
| **Aeneas** | To praise (Greek) In legend, Aeneas was a Trojan prince who settled in Italy and became the ancestor of the Roman people | *Aineas* |

| Name | Definition | Short forms/Variations |
|---|---|---|
| Afon | River (Welsh) Also a girl's name | |
| **Ahmed** | Commendable (Arabic) | *Ahmad* |
| Aidan | Fire (Irish Gaelic) | *Aedan, Aiden, Edan* |
| **Aiken** | Originally an English surname | |
| Aineas | See **Aeneas** | |
| **Ainsley** | Originally a surname, meaning meadow | *Ainslie* |
| Airlie | Originally an aristocratic Scottish name | |
| **Ajax** | Daring (Greek) | |
| Ajay | Invincible (Sanskrit) | *Ajit* |
| **Ajit** | See Ajay | |
| Akash | Sky (Sanskrit) | |
| **Akhil** | Complete (Sanskrit) | |
| Aki | Autumn; bright (Japanese) Also a girl's name | |
| **Akim** | Believer in Allah (Arabic) Also the Russian form of Joachim: appointed by God | |
| Akio | Bright man (Japanese) | |
| **Akira** | Bright; dawn (Japanese) Also a girl's name | |
| Akshay | Immortal (Sanskrit) | |
| **Alain** | French form of Alan: rock | |
| Alan | Rock (Celtic) | *Al / Alain, Allan, Allen, Alun* |
| **Alaric** | Powerful stranger (Germanic) | *Al* |
| Alasdair | Scottish form of Alexander: to defend | *Al, Ali, Aly / Alastair Alaster, Alisdair, Alistair, Alister* |
| **Alban** | See **Albion** | *Albie, Alby* |
| Albert | Noble knight (Old German) | *Albie, Alby, Bert, Bertie / Alberto* |
| **Alberto** | Italian form of Albert: noble knight | |
| Albie | Short for Alban, Albert or Albion | *Alby* |
| **Albion** | White (Latin) A poetic name for Britain | *Albie, Alby / Alban* |
| Albirich | Elf ruler (Germanic) | |
| **Aldo** | Noble (Germanic) | |
| Aldous | [Awl-dus] Old (Germanic) | *Aldis* |
| **Alec** | Short for Alexander | |

| Name | Definition | Short forms/ Variations |
|------|------------|--------------------------|
| Aled | Child (Welsh) | |
| **Alek** | Short for Aleksei | |
| Aleksei | Russian form of Alexis: to defend | *Alek* |
| **Alex** | Short for Alexander. Also a girl's name | *Alec* |
| Alexander | To defend (Greek) | *Alec, Alex, Alick, Lex, Sanders, Sandy, Sasha, Saunders, Xander* |
| **Alexis** | To defend (Greek) Also a girl's name | |
| Alfie | Short for Alfred | *Alf* |
| **Alfonso** | See **Alphonso** | *Al, Fonzie* |
| Alfred | Elf counsel (Old English) | *Alf, Alfie, Fred, Freddie, Freddy / Avery* |
| **Algernon** | With whiskers (French) | *Algie* |
| Algie | Short for Algernon | |
| **Ali** | Excellent (Arabic) | |
| Alick | Short for Alexander | *Alec, Alex* |
| **Alistair** | See **Alasdair** | *Al, Ali, Aly / Alastair, Alaster, Alisdair, Alister* |
| Allan | See **Alan** | *Al / Alain, Allen, Alun* |
| **Almerick** | Work ruler (Teutonic) | *Rick / Almeric* |
| Aloysius | [Al-oo-ish-uss] See **Louis** | *Al, Lou, Louie, Louis / Aloisius* |
| **Alphonso** | Noble and ready (Teutonic) | *Al, Fonzie / Alfonso* |
| Alrick | Leader (Germanic) | |
| **Alroy** | Red (Irish Gaelic) | |
| Alton | Originally a surname, meaning town or village near the source of a river | |
| **Alun** | See **Alan** | *Al / Alain, Allan, Allen* |
| Alva | Intelligent; dear friend (Hebrew) | |
| **Alvar** | Elf warrior (Old English) | *Al* |
| Alvin | Elf friend (Old English) | |
| **Alwyn** | See **Aylwin** | |
| Amadeus | [Ah-mah-day-us] God-loving (Latin) | |

| Name | Definition | Short forms/ Variations |
|---|---|---|
| **Amado** | Beloved (Latin) | *Amador, Amato* |
| Amal | Hope (Arabic) Also a girl's name | |
| **Amar** | Immortal (Sanskrit) | |
| Ambrose | Immortal (Greek) | *Brush / Emrys* |
| **Amerigo** | Sometimes given in homage to explorer Amerigo Vespucci, who gave his name to the continent of America | |
| Amias | Originally a surname, meaning from Amiens, northern France | |
| **Amiel** | My people's God (Hebrew) | |
| Amin | Honest (Arabic) | |
| **Amir** | Ruler (Arabic) | |
| Amish | Sincere (Sanskrit) | |
| **Amit** | Infinite (Sanskrit) | |
| Amiti | Eternal friend (Japanese) | |
| **Amor** | Love (French) Also a girl's name | |
| Amos | To carry (Hebrew) | |
| **Amrit** | Immortal (Sanskrit) Nectar (Sikh) Also a girl's name | |
| Amyot | Originally a French surname | |
| **Anand** | Happiness (Sanskrit) | |
| Anatole | Sunrise (Greek) | |
| **Anders** | Scandinavian form of Andreas: warrior | |
| André | [On-dray] French form of Andreas: warrior | *Andy* |
| **Andreas** | [An-dray-us] Warrior (Greek) | *Andy, Dries / Anders, André, Andrei* |
| Andrew | See **Andreas**. St Andrew is the patron saint of Scotland | *Andy, Drew* |
| **Andy** | Short for André, Andreas or Andrew. Also a girl's name | |
| Aneirin | Noble; modest (Old Welsh) | *Nye / Aneurin* |
| **Angel** | Angel (Greek) Also a girl's name | |
| Angelo | Angel (Greek) | |
| **Angus** | One choice (Celtic) | *Gus / Aonghas, Aonghus* |
| Anish | Supreme (Sanskrit) Also another name for Lord Vishnu | |

| Name | Definition | Short forms/<br>Variations |
|------|-----------|----------------------------|
| **Ansel** | Creative (French) | |
| Anselm | Divine helmet (Teutonic) | *Anzelm* |
| **Anthony** | Of inestimable worth (Latin) | *Ant, Tony /*<br>*Antoine, Anton,*<br>*Antonius, Antony* |
| Antoine | [An-twon] French form of Anthony: of inestimable worth | *Ant, Tony* |
| **Anton** | European form of Anthony: of inestimable worth | |
| Antonius | See **Anthony** | *Ant, Tony /*<br>*Antoine, Anton,*<br>*Antony* |
| **Antrim** | From County Antrim in Northern Ireland | |
| Anwar | Clear, bright (Arabic) | |
| **Anzelm** | Polish form of Anselm: divine helmet | |
| Aonghus | See **Angus** | *Gus / Aonghas* |
| **Aram** | Height (Hebrew) | |
| Archer | Originally a surname, meaning bowman. Also a girl's name | *Archie, Archy* |
| **Archibald** | Bold; genuine (Germanic) | *Archie, Archy* |
| Archie | Short for Archer or Archibald | *Archy* |
| **Ardal** | Great courage (Irish Gaelic) | |
| Ardan | High aspiration (Irish Gaelic) | |
| **Argus** | Shining (Greek) In Greek legend, Argus was the builder of the *Argo* – the ship Jason and the Argonauts used in their quest for the Golden Fleece. Argus was also the name of a giant with a hundred eyes | |

| Name | Definition | Short forms/ Variations |
| --- | --- | --- |
| Ariel | God's lion (Hebrew) A spirit of the air in Shakespeare's *The Tempest*. Also a girl's name | |
| Aries | [Air-eez] In astrology, the ram, first sign of the Zodiac | |
| Aristotle | May be given in homage to the Ancient Greek philosopher | |
| Arjun | Made of silver (Sanskrit) | |
| Armitage | Originally a surname, meaning safe haven | |
| Armon | Strong as a fortress (Hebrew) | |
| Armstrong | Originally a surname, meaning strong | |
| Arne | Eagle (Old Norse) | |
| Arnie | Short for Arnold | |
| Arnold | Eagle power (Old German) | Arnie |
| Aron | Generous (Hebrew) | |
| Arron | See **Aaron** | Aron |
| Art | Bear (Celtic) Also short for Artemas or Arthur | Artie |
| Artemas | Male form of Artemis, Greek goddess of the moon and hunting | Art, Artie / Artemus |
| Arthur | Strong as a bear (Celtic) May be given in homage to the legendary King Arthur | Art, Artie |
| Arun | Sun (Sanskrit) | |
| Arvid | Eagle tree (Old Norse) | |
| Arwel | Wept over (Welsh) | |
| Ary | Fierce as a lion (Hebrew) | |
| Aryan | Noble (Sanskrit) | |
| Asa | God heals (Hebrew) | Ace |
| Asad | Happy, lucky (Arabic) | |
| Ash | Short for Asher, Ashley or Ashton | |
| Ashby | Brash (Scandinavian) Also a girl's name | |
| Asher | Lucky; happy (Hebrew) | Ash |
| Ashish | Blessing (Sanskrit) | |
| Ashley | Originally an English surname, meaning ash wood. Also a girl's name | Ash |
| Ashton | Originally a surname, meaning town or village by an ash tree. Also a girl's name | Ash |
| Ashwin | Horse rider (Sanskrit) | |

| Name | Definition | Short forms/ Variations |
|------|-----------|------------------------|
| **Asim** | Protector (Arabic) | |
| Astley | Originally a surname, meaning eastern wood. Also a girl's name | |
| **Aston** | Originally a surname, meaning eastern town or village. Also a girl's name | |
| Atholl | From a district in Perthshire, Scotland | *Athol* |
| **Atif** | Compassionate (Arabic) | |
| Atlas | In Greek myth, Atlas was the Titan god of daring, condemned to carry the heavens on his shoulders | |
| **Atticus** | Atticus Finch is the honourable lawyer in Harper Lee's novel *To Kill a Mockingbird* | |
| Atul | Incomparable (Sanskrit) | |
| **Auberon** | [Or-ber-on] Noble bear (Germanic) | *Bron / Oberon* |
| Aubin | [Or-bin] Elfin (French) | |
| **Aubrey** | [Or-bree] Elf ruler (Germanic) | |
| Auden | [Or-dn] Originally a surname, meaning old friend | |
| **Audley** | [Ord-lee] Originally a surname | |
| Augustine | See **Augustus**. Also a girl's name | *Gus / Augustin, Austin* |
| **Augustus** | Magnificent (Latin) | *Gus / Augustine* |
| Aurelius | Golden son (Latin) | |
| **Austin** | English form of Augustine | *Austen* |
| Averill | April (French) | |
| **Avery** | See Alfred | *Avey, Avie, Avy* |
| Avey | Short for Avery | *Avie, Avy* |
| **Avon** | River (Welsh) | |
| Axel | Danish form of Absalom | *Axey, Axie, Axy* |
| **Aylmer** | [Ail-mer] Nobly famous (Anglo Saxon) | |
| Aylwin | [Al-win] Noble friend (Germanic) | *Alwyn* |
| **Ayo** | Happy (African) | |
| Azael | Loved by God (Spanish) | |
| **Aziz** | [Az-eez] Cherished (Arabic) | |
| Azriel | [Az-ree-el] God helps (Hebrew) | |

boys' a names

| Name | Definition | Short forms/ Variations |
|------|-----------|------------------------|
| Bach | [Bahk] May be given in homage to German composer Johann Sebastian Bach | |
| Baha | Splendour (Arabic) | |
| Bailey | Originally a surname, meaning bailiff. Also a girl's name | *Bay / Bayley* |
| Baird | Singer; poet (Irish) | |
| Bakari | Promising (African) | |
| Bakr | Young camel (Arabic) | |
| Bakul | Flowering tree (Sanskrit) | |
| Baldemar | Spanish form of Balthasar | |
| Balthasar | In Christian tradition, Balthasar was one of the three Wise Men | |
| Baptiste | From John the Baptist (French) | |
| Barclay | Originally a surname, meaning birch wood | *Berkeley* |
| Barindra | Sea (Sikh) Also a girl's name | |
| Barnabas | Son of consolation (Aramaic) | *Barney, Barny / Barnaby* |
| Barnard | See Bernhard | *Barnett, Bernard* |

| Name | Definition | Short forms/ Variations |
|------|-----------|------------------------|
| Barnes | Powerful bear (Old English) | |
| Barney | Short for Barnabas or Barnaby | *Barny* |
| Barra | Fair-haired (Irish Gaelic) | |
| Barrett | Strong like a bear (Germanic) | |
| Barrington | Originally an aristocratic English surname | |
| Barry | Spear (Celtic) | *Barrie* |
| Bart | Short for Bartholomew, Bartlemy or Bartram | *Bartey, Bartie, Barty* |
| Bartholomew | Son of Talmai (Aramaic) | *Bart, Bartey, Bartie, Barty, Tolly / Bartlemy, Bartley* |
| Bartle | Short for Bartlemy | |
| Bartlemy | English form of Bartholomew | *Bart, Bartie, Bartle* |
| Bartley | Irish form of Bartholomew | |
| Bartram | See Bertram | *Bart, Bartie, Bartle / Barthram, Bertrand* |
| Baruch | Blessed (Hebrew) | |
| Barun | Lord of the sea (Sanskrit) | |
| Basil | [Bazl] Kingly (Greek) | |
| Basim | Smiling (Arabic) | |
| Bastie | Short for Sebastian | *Basty* |
| Baxter | Originally a surname, meaning baker | |
| Bay | Short for Bailey | |
| Bayley | See Bailey | *Bay* |
| Baylon | Originally an English surname, meaning from the bay | |
| Beathan | Life (Gaelic) | |
| Beau | [Bo] Handsome (French) Also a girl's name | |
| Becket | Originally a surname. It may be given in homage to Thomas Becket, 12th-century Archbishop of Canterbury who was assassinated in Canterbury Cathedral | *Beckett* |
| Bede | [Beed] Prayer (Old English) | |
| Belmont | Gracious (French) | |
| Ben | Short for Benedictine, Benito, Benjamin, Bennet, Benno, Benoit or Benson | |
| Benedict | See Benedictine | |

boys'

b

names

| Name | Definition | Short forms/ Variations |
| --- | --- | --- |
| Benedictine | Blessed (Latin) | *Ben, Bennet / Benedict* |
| **Benicio** | Adventurous (Spanish) | |
| Benito | Spanish form of Benedictine: blessed | *Ben* |
| **Benjamin** | Son of the south (Hebrew) | *Ben, Benjie, Benjy, Bennie, Benny* |
| Benjy | Short for Benjamin | *Benjie* |
| **Bennet** | Short for Benedict | *Ben* |
| Benno | Short for Bernhard | *Ben* |
| **Benoit** | French form of Benedict | *Ben* |
| Benson | Originally a surname, meaning Benedict's son | *Ben* |
| **Bentley** | Originally an English surname, meaning meadow of bent grass. Also linked to the luxury cars | |
| Benton | Formidable (Old English) | |
| **Beppe** | [Beppy] Short for Giuseppe | *Beppo* |
| Beppo | Short for Giuseppe | *Beppe* |
| **Berkeley** | [Bar-klee] Originally an English surname, meaning birch wood | |
| Bernhard | Strong bear (Germanic) | *Benno / Barnard, Barnett, Bernard* |
| **Bertie** | Short for Albert, Bertram, Bertrand, Cuthbert, Egbert, Herbert or Norbert. Bertie (Bertram) Wooster is the foppish aristocrat in PG Wodehouse's Jeeves and Wooster novels. Also a girl's name | *Bert* |
| Bertram | Famous raven (Germanic) | *Bert, Bertie / Barthram, Bartram, Bertrand* |
| **Berwyn** | Fair head (Welsh) | |
| Bevan | Originally a surname, meaning son of Evan | |
| **Bevis** | Fair view (French) | |
| Bharat | India (Sanskrit) | |
| **Bhaskar** | Sun (Sanskrit) Also another name for Lord Shiva | |
| Bhavesh | Someone who exists everywhere (Sanskrit) Also another name for Lord Shiva | |
| **Bhupinder** | Looked after by God (Sikh) Also a girl's name | |
| Billy | Short for William | *Bill* |

| Name | Definition | Short forms/ Variations |
|---|---|---|
| **Bing** | May be given in homage to American actor and singer Bing Crosby (born Harry Lillis Crosby) | |
| Birkett | Originally an English surname, meaning birches | |
| **Bjorn** | [B'yorn] Bear (Old Norse) | |
| Blaine | Yellow (Gaelic) | *Blain, Blane* |
| **Blair** | Originally a surname, meaning field. Also a girl's name | |
| Blaise | Stuttering (Latin) Also a girl's name | |
| **Blake** | Originally a surname, meaning black | |
| Blaze | Fire (English) | |
| **Bleddyn** | [Bleth-in] Wolf; hero (Welsh) | |
| Blondell | Little fair-haired one (Old English). Also a girl's name | |
| **Bo** | To dwell (Old Norse) | |
| Boaz | [Bo-az] In him is strength (Hebrew) | |
| **Bobby** | Short for Robert | *Bob* |
| Bogart | May be given in homage to American movie star Humphrey Bogart | |
| **Bonifacio** | Good fate (Latin) | *Boniface* |
| Bono | Good (Spanish) | |

157

| Name | Definition | Short forms/ Variations |
|------|------------|-------------------------|
| **Booker** | Originally an English surname, meaning scribe or bookbinder | |
| Booth | Protective (Germanic) | |
| **Boris** | To fight (Slavonic) | |
| Boscoe | Originally an English surname, meaning woodsman | |
| **Boswell** | Originally an English surname, meaning a well near woods | |
| Boyd | Yellow (Celtic) | |
| **Brad** | Short for Bradley | |
| Braden | Salmon (Irish Gaelic) Also a girl's name | *Bradey, Bradie, Brady / Brayden, Brydon* |
| **Bradley** | Originally an English surname, meaning broad wood | *Brad* |
| Bradshaw | Originally an English surname | |
| **Brady** | Short for Braden | *Bradey, Bradie* |
| Bram | Short for Abraham or Bramwell. It may have gained in popularity thanks to *Dracula* author Bram Stoker | |
| **Bramwell** | Originally an English surname, meaning bramble well | *Bram / Branwell* |
| Bran | Raven (Welsh) | |
| **Brand** | Blade (Scandinavian) | |
| Brando | May be given in homage to American movie star Marlon Brando | |
| **Brandon** | Originally a surname, meaning gorse hill | *Branden* |
| Branko | Peaceful protection (Serbian) | |
| **Brannon** | Bright (Irish) | |
| Brayden | See Braden. Also a girl's name | *Bradey, Bradie, Brady / Brydon* |
| **Brendan** | Prince (Celtic) | *Brendon* |
| Brennan | Originally a surname, meaning drop of water. Also a girl's name | |
| **Brent** | Originally a surname, meaning hill | |
| Brett | Originally a surname, meaning Breton | *Bret* |
| **Brewster** | Originally an English surname, meaning brewer | |

| Name | Definition | Short forms/ Variations |
|------|------------|-------------------------|
| Brian | Noble (Celtic) | *Brien, Brion, Bryan* |
| **Brice** | Speckled (Welsh) | |
| Brigham | [Brig-ham] Originally an English surname, meaning settlement by a bridge | |
| **Brock** | Badger (Old English) | |
| Broder | Brother (Old Norse) | *Bror* |
| **Broderick** | Brother (Norse) | |
| Brodie | Originally a Scottish surname, meaning muddy place. Also a girl's name | *Brodey, Brody* |
| **Brogan** | English form of the Irish surname, meaning shoe. Also a girl's name | |
| Bron | Short for Auberon or Oberon | |
| **Brooklyn** | One of the five boroughs of New York City. Used by footballer David Beckham for his first son. | |
| Bronson | Originally an English surname, meaning Brown's son | |
| **Bruce** | Originally a Scottish surname. Sometimes given in homage to Robert the Bruce, the Scottish king who defeated the English at the Battle of Bannockburn | |
| Bruno | Brown (Germanic) | |
| **Brush** | Short for Ambrose | |
| Bryan | See Brian | *Brien, Brion* |
| **Bryce** | Originally a Scottish surname | |
| Brydon | See Braden | |
| **Bryn** | Hill (Welsh) | *Brynn* |
| Brynmor | Large hill (Welsh) | *Bryn* |
| **Buckley** | Originally a surname, meaning deer meadow | |
| Burton | Originally a surname, meaning fortified town or village | *Burt* |
| **Byrne** | [Burn] Brook (Old English) | |
| Byron | Originally a surname, meaning at the cattle byres. Sometimes given in homage to the poet Lord Byron | |

boys'

b

names

| Name | Definition | Short forms/ Variations |
|------|-----------|------------------------|
| **Cade** | Short for Caden | *Kade* |
| Cadell | Battle (Welsh) | |
| **Caden** | Originally a surname | *Cade / Cayden, Kaden, Kayden* |
| Cadfael | [Cad-vile] Prince of battle (Welsh) | |
| **Cadfan** | [Cad-van] Battle; peak (Welsh) | |
| Cadmus | Prince (Greek) | |
| **Cadoc** | Battle (Welsh) | |
| Cadogan | Battle glory (Welsh) | *Cadwgan* |
| **Cadwallader** | Battle arranger (Welsh) | |
| Cadwallon | Lord of battle (Welsh) | |
| **Caesar** | [See-zer] Emperor (Latin) | |
| Cai | See **Kai** | |
| **Cain** | Acquired (Hebrew) In the Bible, the elder son of Adam and Eve, who killed his brother, Abel | *Cane, Kain, Kane* |
| Cal | Short for Caleb, Calvert or Calvin | |

| Name | Definition | Short forms/ Variations |
|---|---|---|
| **Calder** | Stream (Old English) | |
| Caldwell | Cold well (Old English) | |
| **Cale** | See Cathal | |
| Caleb | Dog (Hebrew) | *Cal, Cale* |
| **Calhoun** | From the narrow woods (Irish) | |
| Callahan | Spiritual (Irish) | |
| **Calum** | Gaelic form of Columba: dove | *Callum, Colm, Colum* |
| Calvary | The English form of Golgotha, the hill outside Jerusalem where Jesus was crucified | |
| **Calvert** | Originally an English surname, meaning 'calf herder' | *Cal* |
| Calvin | Little bald one (French) Its popularity may be thanks to the fashion designer Calvin Klein | *Cal* |
| **Cam** | Short for Cameron or Campbell | |
| Cameron | Originally a surname, meaning crooked nose. Also a girl's name | *Cam / Camron* |
| **Campbell** | [Kam-bl] Originally a surname, meaning crooked mouth | *Cam* |
| Canaan | [Kay-nan] An ancient name for the region covering present-day Israel, the West Bank and Gaza | |
| **Canute** | [K'noot] Knot (Old Norse) Canute the Great was an 11th-century Danish king | *Knut* |
| Caradoc | Love (Welsh) | *Caradog, Craddock, Cradock* |
| **Cardan** | Crafty (Old English) | |
| Cardwell | Craftsman (Old English) | |
| **Carey** | See Cary. Also a girl's name | |
| Carl | See Karl | *Charles* |
| **Carlo** | Italian form of Charles: free man | |
| Carlos | Spanish form of Charles: free man | |
| **Carlson** | Originally an English surname, meaning son of Carl | |
| Carlton | Originally an English surname, meaning Carl's town | |
| **Carmichael** | Friend of Michael, the Archangel (Celtic) | |
| Carmody | [Car-mo-dee] Manly (French) | |

boys'

c

names

| Name | Definition | Short forms/ Variations |
|------|-----------|------------------------|
| **Carney** | Winner (Irish) | |
| Carr | Originally a Scandinavian surname, meaning swampy place | *Kerr* |
| **Carrick** | Rock (Gaelic) | |
| Carson | Originally a surname. Also a girl's name | |
| **Carter** | Originally a surname, meaning cart-driver | |
| Cartwright | Originally an English surname, meaning cart-mender | |
| **Caruso** | Musical (Italian) | |
| Carwyn | Holy love (Welsh) | |
| **Cary** | Originally a surname, meaning pleasant stream. It may have gained in popularity thanks to film star Cary Grant. Also a girl's name | *Carey* |
| Casey | Vigilant in war (Irish Gaelic) In the US, it's sometimes given in homage to 19th-century folk hero Casey Jones, a train driver who saved the lives of his passengers but sacrificed his own. However, his name was a nickname taken from his birthplace, Cayce in Kentucky. Also a girl's name | *Kasey* |
| **Cash** | Originally short for Cassius. It may have increased in popularity thanks to American singer/songwriter Johnny Cash | |
| Caspar | Imperial (German) According to legend, Caspar was one of the three Wise Men who brought gifts to the baby Jesus | *Casper* |
| **Cassidy** | Originally an Irish surname, meaning curly-haired. Also a girl's name | |
| Cassius | Hollow (Latin) | *Cash* |
| **Castor** | Beaver (Greek) The twins Castor and Pollux of Greek myth became the astrological Gemini | |
| Cathal | Strong in battle (Irish Gaelic) | *Cale* |
| **Cathan** | Battle (Irish) | *Kane* |
| Cato | Cato the Elder and Cato the Younger were both Roman politicians | |
| **Cavan** | Attractive man (Irish) | |
| Cavance | Handsome (Irish) | |
| **Caxton** | Originally an English surname | |

names

c

boys'

| Name | Definition | Short forms/ Variations |
|---|---|---|
| Ceallach | Bright head (Irish) | *Kelly* |
| Cecil | [Sess-ill] Blind (Latin) | |
| Cedric | [Sed-rik] Thought to have been invented by Sir Walter Scott for a character in his 19th-century novel *Ivanhoe* | *Cerdic* |
| Celso | [Sel-so] Tall (Latin) | |
| Chadwick | Originally an English surname, meaning dairy farm | |
| Chai | Life (Hebrew) Also a girl's name | |
| Chance | Good fortune (Anglo-Norman) | |
| Chandan | Sandalwood (Sanskrit) | |
| Chandler | Originally a surname, meaning candle maker. Also a girl's name | |
| Chandra | Moon (Sanskrit) Also a girl's name | *Chandran* |
| Channing | Originally a surname, meaning church official. Also a girl's name | |
| Charles | See **Karl** | *Charley, Charlie / Carl, Carlo, Carlos* |
| Charlie | Short for Charles. Also a girl's name | *Charley* |
| Charlton | Originally a surname, meaning town of the free peasants | |
| Chase | Originally a surname, meaning huntsman. Also a girl's name | |
| Chauncey | Originally a French surname | *Chauncy* |
| Che | [Chay] May be given in homage to the Argentine-born revolutionary Ernesto 'Che' Guevara. In Spanish, the word is an interjection meaning 'man' or 'hey' | |
| Chell | See **Kjell** | |
| Cheng | Accomplished (Chinese) | |
| Chesney | Originally an English surname, meaning camp. Also a girl's name | |
| Chet | Short for Chester. Occasionally used for girls | |
| Chevy | Short for Chevrolet, a brand of car often seen as particularly American – partly thanks to the line in Don McLean's 1971 hit *American Pie*, 'Drove my Chevy to the levee/But the levee was dry'. Also a girl's name | |
| Chris | Short for Christian or Christopher | *Kris* |

| Name | Definition | Short forms/ Variations |
|---|---|---|
| **Christer** | Swedish form of Christian: follower of Christ | |
| Christian | Follower of Christ (Latin) | *Chris / Kristian* |
| **Christopher** | To carry Christ (Greek) In legend, St Christopher carried the Christ child over a stream | *Chris, Christy, Kit, Kyd / Christos* |
| Christos | Greek form of Christopher: to carry Christ | |
| **Christy** | Short for Christopher | |
| Cian | Ancient (Irish) | *Keane, Kian* |
| **Ciaran** | [Keer-an] Black (Irish) | *Keiran, Keiron, Kieran, Kieron* |
| Cicero | [Siss-er-oh] Sometimes given in homage to the great Roman orator and writer | |
| **Cillian** | [Sil-ee-an] Church (Irish) | |
| Cipriano | Man from Cyprus (Latin) | *Ciprian, Cyprian* |
| **Ciro** | Italian form of Cyrus: lord | |
| Clancy | Originally an Irish surname, meaning red-headed fighter | |
| **Clarence** | Of Clare (Latin) | *Clary* |
| Clark | Originally a surname, meaning clerk. It may have gained in popularity thanks to the film star Clark Gable and Superman's alter ego, Clark Kent | *Clarke* |
| **Clary** | Short for Clarence | |
| Claude | Lame (Latin) | *Claud, Claudian* |
| **Claus** | Short for Nicholas | *Klaus* |
| Claxton | Originally an English surname, meaning Clark's town | |
| **Clay** | Short for Clayton | |
| Clayton | Originally a surname, meaning town or village built on clay | *Clay* |
| **Cleary** | Originally an Irish surname, meaning scholar or minstrel | |
| Clem | Short for Clement | *Clemmie, Clemmy* |
| **Clement** | Merciful (Latin) | *Clem / Clemence* |
| Cliff | Short for Clifford or Clifton | |
| **Clifford** | Originally an aristocratic surname, meaning ford near a cliff | *Cliff* |

| Name | Definition | Short forms/ Variations |
|------|-----------|------------------------|
| Clifton | Originally a surname, meaning town or village near a cliff | *Cliff* |
| Clint | Short for Clinton. It may have gained in popularity thanks to American actor, producer and director Clint (Clinton) Eastwood | |
| Clinton | Originally a surname, meaning town or village near a hill | *Clint* |
| Clive | Originally a surname, meaning cliff | |
| Clooney | Originally an Irish surname, meaning meadow | |
| Clovis | Famous warrior (German) | |
| Clyde | The name of a Scottish river. It may have gained in popularity thanks to the 1967 film *Bonnie and Clyde*, about bank robber Clyde Barrow | *Clydell* |
| Clydell | See Clyde | |
| Cody | Originally an Irish surname, meaning prosperous. Its popularity in the US may be thanks to Buffalo Bill, the showman William Cody. Also a girl's name | |
| Col | Short for Colbert, Colborn, Colin, Columba or Nicholas | |
| Colan | Dove (Cornish) | |
| Colbert | Cool brightness (Teutonic) | *Col* |
| Colborn | Black bear (Teutonic) | *Col* |
| Colby | Originally a surname, meaning Cole's settlement | |
| Cole | Originally a surname, meaning swarthy or coal-black. Sometimes given in homage to songwriter Cole Porter | |

| Name | Definition | Short forms/<br>Variations |
|------|-----------|---------------------------|
| **Colin** | See Nicholas | *Col* |
| Collier | Originally an English surname, meaning miner | |
| **Colm** | See **Calum** | *Callum* |
| Colman | Little dove (Latin) | |
| **Columba** | Dove (Latin) | *Col / Callum, Calum,*<br>*Colm* |
| Columbus | May be given in homage to explorer<br>Christopher Columbus | |
| **Comanche** | [Kom-an-chee] A native American tribe | |
| Conall | Strong as a wolf (Celtic) | *Con / Conal, Conel,*<br>*Conell, Connal,*<br>*Connall, Connel,*<br>*Connell* |
| **Conan** | Wolf (Irish) May have become more popular<br>thanks to Sherlock Holmes creator Sir Arthur<br>Conan Doyle | |
| Conn | Chief; wisdom (Irish) | |
| **Connaire** | Gaelic form of Connor: high will, high courage | |
| Connery | Originally a surname. It may have increased<br>in popularity thanks to Scottish James Bond<br>actor Sean Connery | |
| **Connor** | High will, high courage (Irish) | *Connaire, Conor* |
| Conrad | See **Konrad** | *Corrado* |
| **Constantine** | Constant (Latin) | *Con, Dinos* |
| Conway | Originally a surname | *Con* |
| **Cooke** | Originally a surname, meaning cook | |
| Cooper | Originally a surname, meaning barrel maker | |
| **Corbin** | Crow (Anglo-Norman) | |
| Corcoran | Ruddy (Irish) | |
| **Corey** | Originally an Irish surname, meaning spear.<br>Also a girl's name | *Cory* |
| Corin | Spear (Latin) | *Corey* |
| **Cormac** | Charioteer (Gaelic) | *Mac / Cormack,*<br>*Cormick* |
| Cormick | See **Cormac** | *Mick / Cormack* |
| **Cornelius** | Hero (Latin) | *Cornell* |
| Cornell | See **Cornelius** | |

| Name | Definition | Short forms/ Variations |
|------|-----------|------------------------|
| **Corrado** | Italian form of Conrad: bold counsel | |
| Corrigan | Originally an Irish surname, meaning spear | |
| **Cosmo** | Order, beauty (Greek) | *Cosimo* |
| Costas | Constant (Greek) | |
| **Craig** | Rock (Gaelic) | |
| Crawford | Originally a surname, meaning crow ford | |
| **Crispin** | Curly-haired (Latin) | *Crispian* |
| Cruz | [Crooth] Christ's cross (Spanish) Usually a girl's name, although it was used by footballer David Beckham for his third son | |
| **Curran** | Hero (Irish Gaelic) | |
| Curt | Short for Curtis | |
| **Curtis** | Courteous (Old French) | *Curt* |
| Cuthbert | Famous splendour (Anglo Saxon) | *Bert, Bertie* |
| **Cyprian** | [Sip-ree-an] Man from Cyprus (Latin) | |
| Cyrano | [See-rah-no] From Cyrene (Greek) May have gained in popularity thanks to Cyrano de Bergerac, a 17th-century French dramatist and duellist whose life was made into a play and, later, a film | |
| **Cyril** | [Sir-ill] Lord (Greek) | *Kiril, Kirill* |
| Cyrus | [Sigh-rus] Lord (Greek) | *Cy / Ciro* |

| Name | Definition | Short forms/ Variations |
|------|------------|-------------------------|
| Dacre | [Day-ker] Originally a surname, meaning trickling stream | |
| **Dafydd** | [Dav-ith] Welsh form of David: darling | *Taff, Taffy / Dafod* |
| Dai | [Die] To shine (Celtic) | *Day* |
| **Dakarai** | Happy (African) | |
| Daksh | Capable (Sanskrit) | |
| **Dakshesh** | Talented (Sanskrit) Also another name for Lord Shiva | |
| Daley | Assembly (Irish Gaelic) | |
| **Dalton** | Originally an English surname, meaning town in the valley | *Delton* |
| Damian | See **Damon** | *Damien* |
| **Damon** | To tame (Greek) | *Damian, Damien* |
| Dan | He judged (Hebrew) | *Danny* |
| **Dane** | Originally a surname, meaning Danish | |
| Daniel | God is my judge (Hebrew) In the Bible, Daniel was thrown into a lions' den, but God protected him | *Dan, Danny* |

| Name | Definition | Short forms/ Variations |
|------|-----------|------------------------|
| **Danno** | Field gathering (Japanese) | |
| Danny | Short for Daniel | *Dan* |
| **Danon** | Remembered (French) | |
| Dante | [Dan-tay] Steadfast (Latin) | |
| **Danvir** | Charitable (Sanskrit) | |
| Dara | Pearl of wisdom (Hebrew) Wise; compassionate (Sikh) Also a girl's name | |
| **Darby** | English form of Diarmaid: without envy | |
| Darcy | Originally a surname, meaning from the fortress. Sometimes given in homage to the hero of Jane Austen's 19th-century novel *Pride and Prejudice* | *D'Arcy* |
| **Darian** | See **Darius** | |
| Darin | See **Darius** | |
| **Dario** | Italian form of Darius: he who upholds the good | |
| Darion | See **Darius** | |
| **Darius** | He who upholds the good (Greek) | *Darian, Darin, Dario, Darion, Darren, Deron* |
| Darnell | Originally an English surname, meaning hidden place | |
| **Darpan** | Self-reflective (Sanskrit) | |
| Darragh | [Dar-ah] Oak (Gaelic) | |
| **Darrell** | Originally a surname, meaning from Airelle, Calvados, north-west France. Also a girl's name | *Darrel, Darryl, Daryl* |
| Darren | See **Darius** | *Darin* |
| **Darsh** | Worth looking at (Sanskrit) Also another name for Lord Krishna | |
| Darshan | Vision (Sanskrit) | |
| **Darwin** | Dear friend (Old English) Sometimes given in homage to the 19th-century evolutionist Charles Darwin | |
| Daryl | Originally a surname, meaning from Airielle, Calvados, north-west France. Also a girl's name | *Darrel, Darrell, Darryl* |
| **Dash** | Sprint; style and confidence (English) | |
| Dasher | See **Dash**. According to the 19th-century poem *A Visit from St Nicholas*, it's also the name of one of Santa's reindeer | |

| Name | Definition | Short forms/ Variations |
|------|-----------|------------------------|
| **David** | Darling (Hebrew) In the Bible, the young David killed Goliath with his sling. He became king of Israel. St David is the patron saint of Wales. | *Dai, Dave, Davey, Davie, Davy / Dewi* |
| Davie | Short for David or Davis. Also a girl's name | *Dave / Davey, Davy* |
| **Davis** | Originally a surname | *Dave, Davey, Davie, Davy* |
| Dawson | Originally a surname, meaning son of David | |
| **Dax** | A Roman spa town in the region of Aquitaine, France | |
| Day | English form of Dai: to shine | |
| **Deacon** | Servant (Greek) | |
| Dean | Originally a surname, meaning someone who lives in a valley, or a dean in a church | *Dino* |
| **Declan** | Man of prayer; light (Irish) | *Dec* |
| Deepak | Light (Sanskrit) | |
| **Delaney** | [D'lane-ee] Dark challenger (Irish Gaelic) Also a girl's name | |
| Delano | [D'lahn-oh] See **Delaney** | |
| **Delmore** | From the sea (French) | |
| Delroy | Royal (French) | |
| **Delton** | Originally an English surname, meaning town in the valley | *Dalton* |
| Demetrius | [D'mit-ree-us] Follower of Demeter, Greek goddess of fertility | *Demetrios, Demitri, Dmitri* |
| **Demitri** | [D'mit-ree] See **Dmitri** | |
| Dempsey | Proud (Irish Gaelic) | |
| **Denim** | A rugged cotton developed in Nimes ('de Nimes'), southern France | |
| Dennis | Follower of the Greek god Dionysos | *Den / Denis* |
| **Denzil** | Originally an English surname, meaning stronghold | *Densil, Denzel* |
| Depp | Originally a surname, possibly meaning the town of Dieppe in northern France. May have increased in popularity thanks to American movie star Johnny Depp | |
| **Derek** | Ruler (Old German) | *Derrick* |
| Dermot | English form of Diarmaid: without envy; free man | |

names

d

boys'

| Name | Definition | Short forms/ Variations |
|------|-----------|-------------------------|
| **Deron** | See **Darius** | |
| Derry | Originally an Irish surname, meaning descendant of the red-head | |
| **Desmond** | Originally an Irish surname, meaning man from South Munster | *Des* |
| Destry | Originally a surname. In the 1939 Western *Destry Rides Again*, James Stewart plays Tom Destry, an easy-going deputy sheriff trying to clean up a corrupt frontier town. Occasionally used as a girl's name | |
| **Dev** | Divinity (Sanskrit) | |
| Deven | Chief of the gods (Sanskrit) | |
| **Devendra** | Chief of the gods (Sikh) Also a girl's name | |
| Devin | Poet (Irish Gaelic) | *Devyn* |
| **Devlin** | Brave (Irish) | |
| Dewey | [Dew-ee] See **Dewi** | |
| **Dewi** | [Deh-wee] Welsh form of David: darling | *Dewey* |
| Dex | Short for Dexter | |
| **Dexter** | Originally a surname, meaning right-handed, skilful | *Dex* |
| Dharmesh | Lord of religion (Sanskrit) | |
| **Dhu** | Swarthy, black (Celtic) | |
| Diarmaid | Without envy; free man (Irish) | *Darby, Dermot, Diarmad, Diarmait, Diarmid* |
| **Diaz** | Originally a surname, meaning son of Diego | |
| Dick | Short for Richard or Dickon | |
| **Dickon** | Short for Richard | *Dick / Diccon* |
| Didier | Longing (Latin) | |
| **Diego** | [Dee-ay-go] Spanish form of James: supplanter | |
| Dieter | [Dee-ter] Warrior race (Old German) | |
| **Digby** | Originally a surname, meaning settlement by a ditch | |
| Diggory | Lost (French) | *Digory* |
| **Dillon** | Irish form of Dylan: sea | |
| Dimitri | [D'mit-ree] See **Dmitri** | |
| **Dinesh** | [D'nesh] Sun (Sanskrit) | |

| Name | Definition | Short forms/ Variations |
|------|-----------|-------------------------|
| Dino | [Dee-no] Pet form of Dean | |
| **Dinos** | [Dee-noss] Short for Constantine | |
| Dion | [Dee-on] From Zeus, king of the gods in Greek legend | |
| **Dirk** | Dutch form of Derek: ruler. Its popularity may have increased thanks to actor Dirk Bogarde | |
| Dizzy | Giddy (English) May be given in homage to jazz musician 'Dizzy' Gillespie (born John Birks Gillespie) | |
| **Dmitri** | Russian form of Demetrius: follower of Demeter, Greek goddess of fertility | *Demitri, Dimitri* |
| Domingo | Born on a Sunday (Spanish) | |
| **Dominic** | Lord (Latin) | *Dom / Dominick* |
| Domino | Lord, master (Latin) Also a girl's name | |
| **Don** | Short for Donald, Donnell or Donoghue | |
| Donahue | See **Donoghue** | *Donohoe* |
| **Donald** | World rule (Old Celtic) | *Don, Donnie, Donny / Donal, Donnell, Donnelly* |
| Donato | Given by God (Latin) | |
| **Donnell** | See **Donald** | *Don, Donnie, Donny* |
| Donnelly | See **Donald** | |
| **Donnie** | Short for Donald, Donnell or Donoghue | *Don / Donny* |
| Donoghue | Brown chieftain (Celtic) | *Don, Donnie, Donny / Donahue* |
| **Donovan** | Dark-haired warrior (Irish) | |
| Dorian | Invented by 19th-century writer Oscar Wilde for his novel *The Portrait of Dorian Gray*. In the novel, Dorian lives a bad and dissolute life but never seems to age; however, in his attic his portrait ages on his behalf | *Dory / Dorien* |
| **Doron** | Gift (Greek) | *Dory / Doran* |
| Dory | Short for Dorian or Doron | |
| **Doug** | Short for Dougal or Douglas | *Dougie* |
| Dougal | Dark stranger (Scottish Gaelic) | *Doug, Dougie / Dhugal, Dowal, Dugald* |
| **Douglas** | From the dark stream (Celtic) | *Doug, Dougie* |

| Name | Definition | Short forms/ Variations |
|------|-----------|-------------------------|
| Dowal | Irish form of Dougal: dark stranger | |
| Doyle | Originally an Irish surname, meaning dark stranger | |
| Drake | Originally an English surname, meaning male duck. It may have gained in popularity thanks to English explorer Sir Francis Drake | |
| Drew | Short for Andrew. Also a girl's name | |
| Dries | Dutch short form of Andreas: warrior | |
| Drogo | Dear (Slavic) | |
| Drummond | Originally a Scottish surname, meaning ridge | |
| Dryden | Originally an English surname, meaning dry valley. May be given in homage to 17th-century poet and playwright John Dryden | |
| Drystan | Welsh form of Tristan: sad | |
| Duane | [Dwane] Originally a surname, meaning descendant of the dark-haired man (Irish) | |
| Duff | Dark (Gaelic) | |
| Dugald | See Dougal | |
| Duke | A man with a very high social position. May be given in homage to jazz musician 'Duke' Ellington (born Edward Kennedy Ellington) | |
| Dunbar | Castle headland (Irish Gaelic) | |
| Duncan | Brown chief (Gaelic) | |
| Dunstan | Stony hill (Old English) | |
| Durant | [Dew-rant] Enduring (Latin) | |
| Dustin | Originally a surname, meaning Thor's stone. It may have gained in popularity thanks to actor Dustin Hoffman | *Dusty* |
| Dusty | Short for Dustin. Also a girl's name | |
| Duval | [Dew-val] From the valley (French) | |
| Dwight | White; fair-haired (Flemish) | |
| Dwyer | Dark wisdom (Irish) | |
| Dylan | Sea (Celtic) Sometimes given in homage to Welsh poet Dylan Thomas or American singer Bob Dylan | *Dillon* |

boys'

d

names

| Name | Definition | Short forms/Variations |
|------|-----------|------------------------|
| Eachan | Horse (Celtic) | *Eachaid* |
| **Eamon** | [Ay-mon] Irish form of Edmund: rich protector | *Eaman, Eamann, Eamonn* |
| Ean | Manx form of John: God is gracious | |
| **Earl** | Warrior; nobleman (Old English) | *Earle* |
| Eashan | Wish (Sanskrit) Also another name for Lord Vishnu | |
| **Easton** | Originally an English surname, meaning eastern town or village | |
| Eaton | Originally an English surname, meaning town or village on an island | |
| **Ebenezer** | [Eb-er-nee-zuh] Stone of help (Hebrew) | |
| Edan | See Aidan | |
| **Eddie** | Short for Edgar, Edmund, Edric, Edward or Edwin | *Ed / Eddy* |
| Eden | Place of pleasure (Hebrew) From the Biblical Garden of Eden. Also a girl's name | |
| **Edgar** | Rich; spear (Old English) | *Ed, Eddie, Eddy* |

| Name | Definition | Short forms/Variations |
|------|-----------|------------------------|
| Edmund | Rich protector (Old English) | Ed, Eddie, Eddy / Edmond |
| Edom | Red (Hebrew) | |
| Edric | Rich and powerful (Old English) | Ed, Eddie, Eddy |
| Eduardo | [Ed-wardo] Spanish form of Edward: guard; wealth | |
| Edward | Guard; wealth (Old English) | Ed, Eddie, Eddy, Ned, Ted, Teddie, Teddy, Woody / Eduardo |
| Edwin | Wealthy friend (Old English) | Ed, Eddie, Eddy, Ned, Ted, Teddie, Teddy / Edwyn |
| Egan | [Ee-gan] Little flame (Irish Gaelic) | |
| Egbert | Bright edge (Anglo Saxon) | Bert, Bertie |
| Egmont | Sword protection (Anglo Saxon) | Monty |
| Einar | Lone warrior (Old Norse) | |
| Elan | Finesse (French) | |
| Elder | Older sibling (English) | |
| Eldon | Originally an English surname, meaning Ella's hill | |
| Eldred | Old counsel (Old English) | Eldridge |
| Eldridge | See **Eldred** | |
| Elford | Originally a surname, meaning Ella's ford | |
| Elgin | Noble; white (Old English) | |
| Eli | [Eel-eye] Height (Hebrew) | Ely |
| Elian | Spirited (Spanish) | |
| Elias | [El-eye-ass] See **Elijah** | Ellis |
| Elihu | Jehovah is God (Hebrew) | |
| Elijah | Yahweh is God (Hebrew) | Elias, Elliot, Ilya |
| Elisud | Kind (Welsh) | Ellis |
| Elkan | Possessed by God (Hebrew) | |
| Ellery | Originally a surname. Ellery Queen is a fictional American detective in a series of novels by Frederic Dannay and Manfred Bennington Lee. Also a girl's name | |
| Elliot | See **Elijah** | Eliot, Eliott, Elliott |
| Ellis | See **Elias** or **Elisud** | |

| Name | Definition | Short forms/ Variations |
|---|---|---|
| **Elman** | Noble man (Old English) | |
| Elmer | Originally an English surname, meaning noble and famous | *Elmar* |
| **Elmo** | Helmet (Germanic) | |
| Elmore | Originally an English surname, meaning moor with elm trees | |
| **Eloy** | To choose (Latin) | |
| Elroy | See **Leroy** | |
| **Elton** | Originally an English surname, meaning old town or village | |
| Elvis | All wise (Scandinavian) May be given in homage to American musician Elvis Presley | |
| **Elwyn** | Holy (Welsh) | *Elwin* |
| Ely | [Eel-eye] See **Eli** | |
| **Emerson** | Son of Emery | |
| Emery | Brave and powerful (Germanic) | *Emerson, Emmery* |
| **Emil** | [Em-eel] Rival (Latin) | *Emile, Émile, Emlyn* |
| Emilio | [Em-eel-ee-oh] Rival (Latin) | |
| **Emlyn** | Welsh form of Emil: rival | |
| Emmanuel | God is with us (Hebrew) | *Emuel / Emanuel, Immanuel* |
| **Emmet** | Male form of Emma: entire. In Ireland, it's sometimes given in homage to Robert Emmet, an 18th-century Irish nationalist who led an unsuccessful uprising against the British | *Emmett, Emmot, Emmott, Emott* |
| Emrys | Welsh form of Ambrose: immortal | |
| **Emuel** | Short for Emmanuel | |
| Emyr | Ruler (Welsh) | |
| **Engelbert** | Angel-bright (German) | |
| Ennis | See **Innis**. Also a girl's name | |
| **Enoch** | [Ee-nok] Dedicated (Hebrew) | |
| Enos | [Ee-nos] Mankind (Hebrew) | |
| **Enrico** | [On-ree-ko] Italian form of Henry: home ruler | |
| Enrique | [On-ree-kay] Spanish form of Henry: home ruler | |
| **Enzo** | Italian form of Henry: home ruler | |

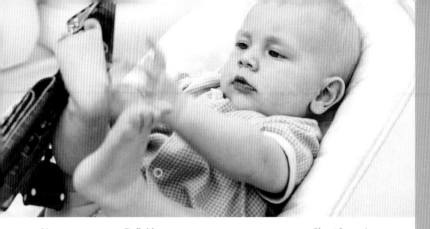

| Name | Definition | Short forms/ Variations |
| --- | --- | --- |
| Eoin | Irish form of John: God is gracious | |
| **Ephraim** | [Ee-frame] Fruitful (Hebrew) | |
| Erasmus | I love (Greek) | |
| **Eric** | One ruler (Old Norse) | *Erick, Erik* |
| Ermin | From the name of a Teutonic demi-god | |
| **Ernest** | Determined (German) May have gained in popularity thanks to Oscar Wilde's 19th-century play *The Importance of Being Earnest* | *Ernie* |
| Ernesto | Spanish form of Ernest: determined | |
| **Ernie** | Short for Ernest | |
| Errol | Originally a Scottish surname. It may have gained in popularity thanks to actor Errol Flynn | *Erroll* |
| **Esau** | [Ee-saw] Hairy (Hebrew) In the Bible, Esau's cunning younger twin, Jacob, persuaded him to part with his birthright in exchange for a bowl of soup | |
| Esmond | Divine protection (Old English) | |
| **Estéban** | Spanish form of Stephen: crown | |
| Etash | Bright, shining (Sanskrit) | |
| **Ethan** | Long-lived (Hebrew) | |
| Ethelred | Noble speech or counsel (Anglo Saxon) | |
| **Étienne** | French form of Stephen: crown | |
| Euan | [Yu-an] Yew tree (Gaelic) | *Evan, Ewan, Ewen* |
| **Eugene** | [Yu-jheen] Well-born, noble (Greek) | *Gene, Gino / Yevgeni* |
| Eustace | [Yu-stis] Fruitful (Greek) | *Stacey, Stacy* |

| Name | Definition | Short forms/ Variations |
|------|-----------|-------------------------|
| **Evan** | See Euan | *Ewan, Ewen* |
| Evander | Good man (Greek) | *Evan* |
| **Evelyn** | [Ev-lyn] Living (Hebrew) Also a girl's name | |
| Everard | Strong and brave as a wild boar (Old English) | *Everett, Ewart* |
| **Everett** | See Everard | *Evett* |
| Evett | Short for Everett | |
| **Evon** | Welsh form of Evan: yew tree | |
| Evron | Yiddish form of Ephraim: fruitful | |
| **Ewan** | [Yu-an] See Euan | *Evan, Ewen* |
| Ewart | See Everard | |
| **Ezekiel** | [Iz-eek-ee-el] God strengthens (Hebrew) | *Zeke* |
| Ezra | Help (Hebrew) | *Ezzie* |
| **Ezzie** | Short for Ezra | |

| Name | Definition | Short forms/ Variations |
|------|-----------|------------------------|
| Fa | Setting off (Chinese) | |
| **Faber** | See Fabian | |
| Fabian | Bean (Latin) | *Faber* |
| **Fabio** | [Fab-ee-oh] Italian, Portuguese and Spanish form of Fabian: bean | |
| Fabrice | [Fab-rees] Works with the hands (French) | |
| **Fabrizio** | [Fab-ritz-ee-oh] Italian form of Fabrice: works with the hands | |
| Fahd | Panther or leopard (Arabic) | |
| **Fairfax** | Originally a surname, meaning beautiful hair | |
| Falak | Heaven (Sanskrit) | |
| **Fareed** | Unique (Arabic) | *Farid* |
| Fargo | A place in North Dakota, USA | |
| **Farhan** | Joyful (Arabic) | |
| Farnham | Originally an English surname, meaning settlement with ferns | |
| **Farr** | Voyager (Old English) | |

| Name | Definition | Short forms/ Variations |
| --- | --- | --- |
| Farrar | Distinguished (French) | |
| **Farrell** | English form of Fearghal: brave man | |
| Farris | Strong as iron (Old English) | *Ferris* |
| **Fearghal** | Brave man (Irish) | *Farrell, Fergal* |
| Fearghas | Vigorous man (Irish) | *Fergus* |
| **Felix** | Happy, lucky (Latin) | |
| Fenn | Short for Fenton | |
| **Fenton** | Originally a surname, meaning town or village by a fen (a flat, marshy area) | *Fenn* |
| Ferdie | Short for Ferdinand | *Ferdey, Ferdy* |
| **Ferdinand** | Ready for the journey (Germanic) | *Ferdey, Ferdie, Ferdy* |
| Fergal | English form of Fearghal: brave man | |
| **Fergus** | English form of Fearghas: strong man | |
| Ferguson | Originally a surname, meaning son of Fergus | |
| **Fernando** | Spanish form of Ferdinand: ready for the journey | |
| Ferrer | Blacksmith (Catalan) | |
| **Ferris** | See Farris | |
| Festus | Steadfast (Latin) | |
| **Fiachra** | Raven (Irish Gaelic) Fiachra is the patron saint of travellers and gardeners | |
| Fidelis | [Fid-ay-liss] Faithful (Latin) | *Fidel* |
| **Fielding** | Originally an English surname, meaning field. May be given in homage to 18th-century novelist and playwright Henry Fielding, author of *Tom Jones* | |
| Fillan | Wolf (Irish) | |
| **Filmore** | Famous (Old English) | |
| Finbar | English form of Fionnbarr: fair-haired | *Finbarr* |
| **Fingal** | Fair-haired stranger (Celtic) | |
| Finian | Fair (Irish Gaelic) | *Finnian, Phinean, Phinian, Phinnian* |
| **Finlay** | Fair hero (Gaelic) | *Finn / Findlay, Findley, Finley* |
| Finn | Fair (Irish) | *Finnegan* |
| **Finnegan** | Pet form of Finn | |
| Finton | Originally a surname, meaning Finn's town | |

| Name | Definition | Short forms/ Variations |
|---|---|---|
| **Fionnbarr** | [Fin-bar] Fair head (Irish) | |
| Firdos | Paradise (Arabic) | |
| **Fitz** | Short for Fitzgerald or Fitzroy | |
| Fitzgerald | Originally a surname, meaning son of Gerald | *Fitz* |
| **Fitzroy** | Originally a surname, meaning son of Roy – or, occasionally, an illegitimate son of the king | *Fitz* |
| Flavian | [Flay-vee-an] Blond (Latin) | *Flavio* |
| **Flavio** | [Flay-vee-oh] See Flavian | |
| Fletcher | Originally a surname, meaning arrow maker | |
| **Flin** | Short for Flinders | |
| Flinders | Man from Flanders | *Flin* |
| **Florian** | Flourishing (Latin) | |
| Floyd | See Lloyd | |
| **Flynn** | Red, ruddy (Gaelic) Sometimes used for girls | |
| Fonzie | Short for Alphonso | *Fonz* |
| **Forbes** | Originally a Scottish surname, meaning field | |
| Ford | Originally an English surname, meaning from the ford | |

| Name | Definition | Short forms/ Variations |
|---|---|---|
| **Foster** | Originally a surname, meaning forester | |
| Fran | Short for Francesco, Francis, Francisco or Franklin. Also a girl's name | |
| **Francesco** | [Fran-chess-ko] Frenchman (Latin) | *Fran, Franco, Frank, Frankie* |
| Francis | Frenchman (Germanic) | *Fran, Frank, Frankie / Francisco* |
| **Francisco** | [Fran-chiss-ko] Spanish form of Francis: Frenchman | *Fran, Frank, Frankie, Frisco, Paco* |
| Franco | Short for Francesco | |
| **Francois** | [Fran-swahz] Frenchman (French) | |
| Frank | Frenchman (Germanic) | *Frankie* |
| **Frankie** | Short for Francesco, Francis, Francisco, Frank or Franklin. Also a girl's name | |
| Franklin | Originally a surname, meaning free man. In the US, it's sometimes given in homage to President Franklin D Roosevelt | *Fran, Frank, Frankie / Franklyn* |
| **Fraser** | Originally a Scottish surname | *Frasier, Frazer, Frazier* |
| Fred | Short for Alfred, Frederick, Manfred or Wilfred | *Freddie, Freddy* |
| **Freddie** | Short for Alfred, Frederick or Wilfred. Also a girl's name | *Fred / Freddy* |
| Frederick | Peaceful ruler (Germanic) | *Fred, Freddie, Freddy, Frederic, Fredric, Friedrich* |
| **Freeman** | Originally a surname, meaning free man | |
| Friedrich | German form of Frederick: peaceful ruler | *Fritz* |
| **Frisco** | Short for Francisco | |
| Fritz | Short for Friedrich, the German form of Frederick | |
| **Fulbert** | Incredibly bright (Teutonic) | |
| Fulbright | See **Fulbert** | |
| **Fulco** | One of the people (Germanic) | |
| Fulton | Originally a Scottish surname | |

| Name | Definition | Short forms/ Variations |
|------|-----------|------------------------|
| **Gabe** | Short for Gabriel | |
| Gabriel | Man of God (Hebrew) In the Bible, the angel Gabriel appeared to the Virgin Mary to tell her she would give birth to Christ | Gabe |
| **Gage** | Pledge (Old French) | |
| Galen | Healer (Greek) | Jalen |
| **Gamaliel** | Benefit of God (Hebrew) | |
| Garcia | [Gar-see'uh] Strong (Spanish) | |
| **Gardner** | Originally an English surname, meaning gardener | |
| Gareth | Gentle (Welsh) | Garry, Garth, Gary |
| **Garner** | Originally an English surname, meaning gatherer of grain | |
| Garrett | Spear-brave (Old English) | Garret, Jarret, Jarrett |
| **Garrick** | Originally a French surname, meaning limestone country | |
| Garron | Gelding (Irish Gaelic) | Garin, Garon |
| **Garth** | Originally a surname, meaning enclosure | Garret, Garrett |

| Name | Definition | Short forms/ Variations |
|---|---|---|
| Gary | Spear (Germanic) | *Garry* |
| Gavin | White hawk (Welsh) In Arthurian legend, Gavin, or Gawain, was one of the knights of the Round Table | *Gawain, Gawaine, Gawen, Gwalchmai* |
| Gawain | See **Gavin** | *Gawaine, Gawen* |
| Gene | [Jeen] Short for Eugene | |
| Geoff | [Jef] Short for Geoffrey | |
| Geoffrey | See **Godfrey** | *Geoff / Jeffery, Jeffrey* |
| Geordie | Short for George | |
| George | Farmer (Greek) St George is the patron saint of England | *Geordie, Georgie / Yuri* |
| Geraint | Old man (Greek) A popular name in Wales | |
| Gerald | Spear; rule (Germanic) | *Gerry, Jerry / Jarrold* |
| Gerard | Spear; brave (Germanic) | *Gerry, Jerry / Gerhard* |
| Gerhard | [Gehr-hart] See **Gerard** | |
| Germain | [Jer-mane] Brother (Latin) | *Germaine, Jermaine, Jermyn* |
| Geronimo | [Jer-on-ee-mo] Italian form of Jerome: holy name | *Gerry* |
| Gerry | Short for Gerald, Gerard or Geronimo | *Jerry* |
| Gervaise | See **Jarvis** | *Gervase, Jarvis, Jervis* |
| Gerwyn | Fair love (Welsh) | *Gerwen* |
| Gethin | Swarthy (Welsh) | *Gethen* |
| Giacomo | [Jee-ah-ko-mo] Italian form of James: supplanter | |
| Gianni | [Jee-an-ee] Short for Giovanni | |
| Giannino | [Jee-an-een-o] Pet form of Giovanni | |
| Gideon | He who cuts down (Hebrew) | |
| Gil | Short for Gilbert, Gilchrist, Gillespie, Gilmour or Gilroy | |
| Gilbert | Pledge; bright, famous (Germanic) | *Gil* |
| Gilchrist | Servant of Christ (Celtic) | *Gil* |
| Giles | [Jiles] Kid, a young goat (Greek) | *Gillis* |
| Gillespie | Bishop's servant (Gaelic) | *Gil* |
| Gillis | See **Giles** | |
| Gilmour | Servant of Mary (Celtic) | *Gil / Gilmore* |

boys' | g | names

| Name | Definition | Short forms/ Variations |
|------|-----------|------------------------|
| **Gilroy** | Red-haired lad (Gaelic) | *Gil* |
| Gino | [Jee-no] Short for Eugene | |
| **Giorgio** | [Jee-or-jee-o] Italian form of George: farmer | |
| Giovanni | [Jee-o-van-ee] Italian form of John: God is gracious | *Gianni, Giannino* |
| **Giri** | Mountain (Sanskrit) | |
| Girik | A person who lives on a mountain (Sanskrit) Also another name for Lord Shiva | |
| **Giuseppe** | [Jee-sep-ee] Italian form of Joseph: God shall add | *Beppe, Beppo* |
| Gladstone | Originally a Scottish surname, meaning rock where the kites live | |
| **Glaw** | Rain (Welsh) Also a girl's name | |
| Glendower | English form of Glyndwr: sometimes given in homage to medieval Welsh patriot Owain Glyndwr (in English, Owen Glendower) | |
| **Glyn** | Valley (Welsh) | *Glen, Glenn, Glynn* |
| Glyndwr | Sometimes given in homage to medieval Welsh patriot Owain Glyndwr (in English, Owen Glendower) | *Glendower* |
| **Goddard** | Strong in God (Germanic) | |
| Godfrey | God's peace (Germanic) | *Geoffrey* |
| **Goodwin** | Good friend (Old English) | *Godwin* |
| Goral | Lovable (Sanskrit) | |

| Name | Definition | Short forms/Variations |
|------|-----------|------------------------|
| **Gordon** | Originally a surname | |
| Graham | Originally a surname, meaning gravelly homestead | *Graeme* |
| **Grant** | Originally a Scottish surname, meaning large. In the US, it's sometimes given in homage to the Civil War general and president, Ulysses S Grant | |
| Granville | Originally a French surname, meaning large town | |
| **Grayden** | Combination of Gray (the colour) and Hayden (heathen) | *Graydon* |
| Greg | Short for Gregor or Gregory | *Gregg, Greig* |
| **Gregor** | Scottish form of Gregory: vigilant | *Greg* |
| Gregory | Vigilant (Greek) | *Greg / Gregor* |
| **Greville** | Originally a Norman surname; taken from Gréville in La Manche, north-west France | |
| Griff | Short for Griffin or Griffith | |
| **Griffin** | See Griffith | *Griff* |
| Griffith | English form of Gruffudd: lord | *Griff / Griffin* |
| **Grover** | Originally an English surname, meaning someone who lives near a grove of trees | |
| Gruffudd | [Griff-ith] Lord (Welsh) | *Griffidd, Griffith, Gruffydd* |
| **Guido** | [Gwee-doh] Italian form of Guy: wood | |
| Gunn | Short for Gunnar or Gunther | |
| **Gunnar** | Scandinavian form of Gunther: battle; warrior | *Gunn* |
| Gunther | [Guhn-ter] Battle; warrior (Germanic) | *Gunn* |
| **Gus** | Short for Augustine, Augustus, Angus or Gustav | |
| Gustav | [Goo-stahv] Goth's staff (Old Norse) | *Gus / Gustaf, Gustavus* |
| **Guthrie** | [Guh-three] Windy place (Irish Gaelic) May be given in homage to American folk singer Woody Guthrie | |
| Guy | [Gigh] Wood (Germanic) | |
| **Gwalchmai** | Welsh form of Gavin: white hawk | |
| Gwilym | [Gwill-im] Welsh form of William: protector | |

boys' | names | g

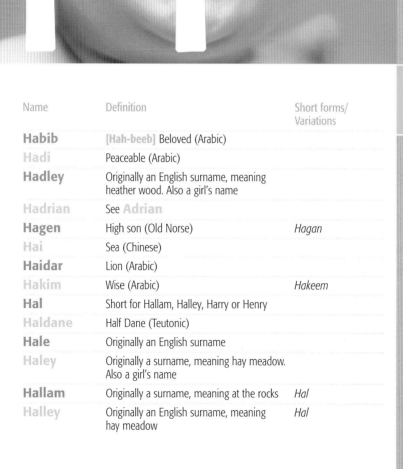

| Name | Definition | Short forms/ Variations |
|------|-----------|-------------------------|
| **Habib** | [Hah-beeb] Beloved (Arabic) | |
| Hadi | Peaceable (Arabic) | |
| **Hadley** | Originally an English surname, meaning heather wood. Also a girl's name | |
| Hadrian | See Adrian | |
| **Hagen** | High son (Old Norse) | *Hagan* |
| Hai | Sea (Chinese) | |
| **Haidar** | Lion (Arabic) | |
| Hakim | Wise (Arabic) | *Hakeem* |
| **Hal** | Short for Hallam, Halley, Harry or Henry | |
| Haldane | Half Dane (Teutonic) | |
| **Hale** | Originally an English surname | |
| Haley | Originally a surname, meaning hay meadow. Also a girl's name | |
| **Hallam** | Originally a surname, meaning at the rocks | *Hal* |
| Halley | Originally an English surname, meaning hay meadow | *Hal* |

| Name | Definition | Short forms/ Variations |
|---|---|---|
| **Halmer** | Robust (Old English) | |
| Halwell | Originally an English surname, meaning holy well | *Haliwell* |
| **Ham** | Short for Hamilton or Hamish | |
| Hamil | See **Hamilton** | |
| **Hamilton** | Originally a Scottish surname, meaning flat-topped hill | *Ham / Hamil* |
| Hamish | English form of Seumas: supplanter | *Ham* |
| **Hamlet** | Small village (Old English) Hamlet is the complex and tragic prince of Denmark in Shakespeare's play of the same name | |
| Hamza | Lion (Arabic) | |
| **Handel** | Sometimes given in homage to the German-born composer George Frideric Handel | |
| Hani | Happy (Arabic) | |
| **Hank** | Short for Henry | |
| Hannibal | Grace of Baal (Phoenician) | |
| **Hanno** | Grace (Phoenician) A traditional Cornish name | |
| Hans | German form of John: God is gracious | |
| **Hanshal** | Like a swan (Sanskrit) | |
| Harding | Hardy (Old English) | |
| **Harinder** | Lord (Sikh) Also a girl's name | |
| Harish | Alternative names for Lord Shiva and Lord Vishnu (Sanskrit) | |
| **Harith** | Provider (Arabic) Green (Sanskrit) | |
| Harlan | Originally an English surname, meaning rocky land | *Harland* |
| **Harley** | Originally a surname, meaning hare wood. Sometimes used in reference to the Harley Davidson motorbikes. Also a girl's name | |
| Harold | Ruler of an army (Old English) | *Harry / Harald* |
| **Harper** | Originally a surname, meaning someone who plays the harp. Also a girl's name | |
| Harpo | See **Harper**. May be given in homage to entertainer and comedian 'Harpo' Marx (born Adoph Arthur Marx), so called because he played the harp | |
| **Harris** | Originally a surname, meaning Harry's son | |

| Name | Definition | Short forms/ Variations |
|------|-----------|------------------------|
| Harrison | Harry's son | *Harry* |
| **Harry** | Short for Harold, Harrison or Henry. It has become very popular in its own right since the publication of JK Rowling's *Harry Potter* novels | *Hal* |
| Hart | Stag (Old English) | |
| **Hartley** | Originally a surname, meaning stag wood | |
| Harvey | Battle-worthy (Breton) | |
| **Harvir** | Brave Lord (Sikh) Also a girl's name | |
| Hasan | Laughter (Sanskrit) | |
| **Hasim** | Decisive (Arabic) | |
| Hassan | Good; handsome (Arabic) | *Hasan* |
| **Haul** | Sun (Welsh) | |
| Haven | Sanctuary (English) | |
| **Hayden** | Heathen (Germanic) | *Haydn, Haydon* |
| Heathcliff | May be given in homage to the brooding romantic hero of Emily Bronte's 19th-century novel *Wuthering Heights* | |
| **Heaton** | Originally an English surname, meaning town or village on a heath | |
| Hector | To restrain (Greek) In classical legend, Hector was a Trojan champion | |
| **Heddwyn** | Blessed peace (Welsh) | |
| Hedley | Originally a surname, meaning heather clearing | |
| **Hefin** | Summer (Welsh) | |
| Helmut | Brave (Germanic) | |

| Name | Definition | Short forms/ Variations |
| --- | --- | --- |
| **Hemming** | Werewolf, shape-shifter (Old Norse) | *Heming* |
| Henderson | Originally a surname, meaning son of Henry | |
| **Heng** | Eternal (Chinese) | |
| Henry | Home ruler (Germanic) | *Hal, Hank, Harry / Heinrich, Henri* |
| **Herbert** | Army bright (Old German) | *Herb, Herbie* |
| Herbie | Short for Herbert | *Herb* |
| Hercules | [Her-kue-leez] Glory of Hera, a Greek goddess. In Greek legend, Hercules was the son of Zeus, king of the gods, and a mortal woman. After completing twelve tasks he was made a god himself | |
| **Herman** | Soldier (Old German) May have increased in popularity thanks to 19th-century American writer Herman Melville, author of *Moby Dick* | |
| Heskel | Yiddish form of Ezekiel: God strengthens | |
| **Hilary** | Cheerful (Latin) Also a girl's name | |
| Hildebrand | [Hild-uh-brand] Battle sword (Germanic) | |
| **Hiram** | [High-ram] Most noble (Hebrew) | |
| Hiro | [He-ro] Abundant (Japanese) Also a girl's name | |
| **Hiroki** | [He-ro-kee] Abundant joy (Japanese) | |
| Hitchcock | May be given in homage to English-born film director Sir Alfred Hitchcock | |
| **Hogan** | Youth (Irish Gaelic) | |
| Holbrook | Originally an English surname, meaning stream near a hollow | |
| **Holden** | Originally a surname, meaning deep valley. Holden Caulfield is the teenage narrator of JD Salinger's cult 1951 novel *The Catcher in the Rye* | |
| Homer | The name of the Greek poet | |
| **Horace** | [Hor-iss] From Horatians, a noble clan in Ancient Rome | |
| Horatio | [Hor-ay-shee-oh] See **Horace**. Sometimes given in homage to Britain's greatest naval hero, Admiral Horatio Nelson | *Horace* |
| **Horatius** | [Hor-ay-shee-us] See **Horace** | *Horace, Horatio* |

names

h

boys'

| Name | Definition | Short forms/ Variations |
|---|---|---|
| Howard | Originally an aristocratic surname, meaning high guardian | |
| **Howell** | English form of Hywel: eminent | *Howel* |
| Huan | Happiness (Chinese) Also a girl's name | |
| **Hubert** | Bright heart, mind, spirit (Germanic) | *Hubie, Hugh, Huw / Hobart* |
| Hubie | Short for Hubert | |
| **Huck** | Short for Huckleberry or Huxley | |
| Huckleberry | Huckleberry Finn is the straight-talking, free-spirited young hero of Mark Twain's 19th-century novel *The Adventures of Huckleberry Finn* | *Huck* |
| **Hudson** | Originally a surname | |
| Hugh | Heart, mind, spirit (Germanic) | *Hewie, Huey, Hughie, Huwie / Hew, Hu, Huw* |
| **Hughie** | Pet form of Hugh | |
| Hugo | Heart, mind, spirit (Germanic) | *Hew, Hugh, Huw* |
| **Humbert** | Bright giant (Teutonic) | |
| Humphrey | Peaceful giant (Old German) Sometimes given in homage to American actor Humphrey Bogart | *Humfrey* |
| **Hunter** | Originally a surname. Also a girl's name | |
| Hussein | [Hoo-sane] Handsome (Arabic) | *Hussain* |
| **Huw** | Welsh form of Hugh | *Huwie* |
| Hux | Short for Huxley | |
| **Huxley** | Originally a surname, meaning Hucc's wood | *Huck, Hux* |
| Hywel | Eminent (Welsh) | *Howell, Hywell* |

boys'

h

names

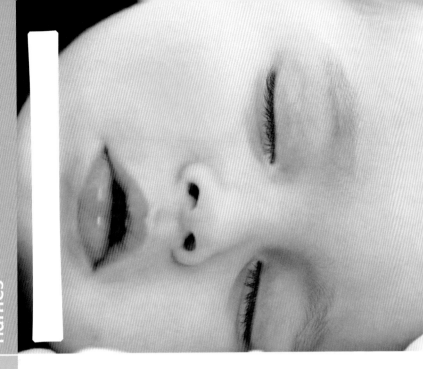

| Name | Definition | Short forms/Variations |
|------|-----------|------------------------|
| **Iago** | [Ee-ah-go] Spanish form of James: supplanter. Iago is the name of the villain in Shakespeare's tragedy *Othello* | |
| Ian | Scottish form of John: God is gracious | *Ean, Iain* |
| **Ibrahim** | Arabic form of Abraham: father of nations | |
| Icarus | [Ik-uh-russ] In Greek myth, Icarus and his father escaped from a tower in Crete by constructing artificial wings out of feathers and wax. Icarus's father instructed him not to fly too near the sun, but he did. The wax melted and Icarus fell into the sea and drowned | *Ikaros, Ikarus* |
| **Ichabod** | [Ik-uh-bod] The glory is gone (Hebrew) May have increased in popularity thanks to the character of Ichabod Crane in Washington Irving's 19th-century short story *The Legend of Sleepy Hollow*, later made into a film starring Johnny Depp | |
| Ichiro | First son (Japanese) | |
| **Idris** | [Id-riss] Ardent lord (Welsh) | |

| Name | Definition | Short forms/Variations |
|------|-----------|------------------------|
| Ieuan | [Yew-an] Welsh form of John: God is gracious | |
| **Ifor** | [Eye-vor] Lord (Welsh) | *Ivor* |
| Iggy | Short for Ignatius | |
| **Ignatius** | [Ig-nay-shus] Fire (Latin) | *Iggy* |
| Igor | [Ee-gor] Russian form of Ivor: yew; army | |
| **Ike** | Short for Isaac | |
| Ikram | Honour; respect (Arabic) | |
| **Ikshan** | Vision (Sanskrit) | |
| Ilan | Tree (Hebrew) | |
| **Illarian** | Cheerful (Greek) | |
| Ilya | Russian form of Elijah: Yahweh is God | |
| **Iman** | [Ee-mahn] Faith (Arabic) Also a girl's name | |
| Immanuel | See Emmanuel | *Emanuel* |
| **Imran** | Strong; long-lived (Arabic) | |
| Indra | Possessing drops of rain (Sanskrit) Indra is the Hindu warrior god of the sky and rain. Also a girl's name | |
| **Inesh** | King (Sanskrit) Also another name for Lord Vishnu | |
| Inge | [In-ga] Taken from Ing, the Old Norse fertility god. Also a girl's name | |
| **Ingmar** | Taken from Ing, the Old Norse fertility god. May have gained in popularity thanks to Swedish film director Ingmar Bergman | *Ingemar* |
| Ingram | Raven (Norman) | |
| **Ingwar** | Protector of the god Ing (Viking) | |
| Inigo | [In-ee-go] Fire (Latin) | |
| **Innis** | Originally a Scottish surname, meaning island. Also a girl's name | *Ennis* |
| Ioan | Welsh form of John: God is gracious | |
| **Iolo** | Welsh form of Julius: originally a Roman family name | |
| Ira | [Eye-ra] Watchful (Hebrew) Sometimes given in homage to the lyricist Ira Gershwin | |
| **Iravan** | King of the ocean (Sanskrit) | |
| Irving | Originally a Scottish surname, meaning fresh water. Sometimes given in homage to the songwriter Irving Berlin | *Irvine* |

| **Irwin** | Boar; friend (Old English) | |
| Isaac | [Eye-zak] To laugh (Hebrew) In the Bible, Abraham was prepared to sacrifice his son, Isaac, on God's command. At the very last moment God told him to sacrifice a ram instead | *Ike, Zac, Zach, Zack / Izaak* |
| **Isadore** | See Isidore | |
| Isaiah | [Eye-zi-uh] God is salvation (Hebrew) | |
| **Isambard** | [Iz-am-bard] May be given in homage to Isambard Kingdom Brunel, the pioneering 19th-century engineer | |
| Ishan | Lord of wealth (Sanskrit) | |
| **Ishmael** | To hear God (Hebrew) May have gained in popularity thanks to Herman Melville's 19th-century novel *Moby Dick*; Ishmael is the narrator | *Ismail* |
| Isidore | Gift from the Egyptian goddess Isis (Greek) | *Issie, Issy, Izzie, Izzy / Isadore, Isidro* |
| **Isidro** | See Isidore | |
| Ismail | See **Ishmael** | |
| **Issachar** | Hired man (Hebrew) | *Issie, Issy* |
| Issy | Short for Isidore or Issachar | *Issie* |
| **Ithel** | Generous lord (Welsh) | |
| Ivan | Russian form of John: God is gracious | *Vanya* |
| **Ivo** | See Yves | |
| Ivor | Yew; army (Old Norse) | *Ifor, Igor* |
| **Izaak** | Polish form of Isaac: to laugh | |
| Izzy | Short for Isidore | *Izzie* |

| Name | Definition | Short forms/Variations |
|------|-----------|------------------------|
| **Jabez** | [Jay-bez] Tall (Hebrew) | |
| Jacek | [Yaht-zek] Lily (Polish) | |
| **Jacinto** | [Ha-seen-toe] Hyacinth (Spanish) | |
| Jack | Short for John or Jackson | *Jackie, Jacky* |
| **Jackson** | Originally a surname, meaning son of Jack | *Jack, Jackie, Jacky, Jax* |
| Jacob | Supplanter (Hebrew) | *Jake* |
| **Jacques** | French form of Jacob: supplanter | |
| Jadon | He will judge (Hebrew) Occasionally used as a girl's name | *Jade, Jay / Jaden, Jayden, Jaydon* |
| **Jaeger** | [Jay-gr] Hunter (Germanic) | |
| Jael | Mountain goat (Hebrew) | *Yael* |
| **Jafar** | Small river (Arabic) | |
| Jafe | Short for Japheth | |
| **Jagan** | See **Jago** | |
| Jagger | Originally an English surname, meaning carter. May have gained in popularity thanks to rock singer Mick Jagger | |

| Name | Definition | Short forms/ Variations |
|------|-----------|-------------------------|
| **Jago** | Cornish form of James: supplanter | *Jay* |
| Jai | Victory (Sanskrit) | *Jay* |
| **Jaiman** | Victorious (Sanskrit) | |
| Jaime | Spanish form of James. Also a girl's name | *Jamey, Jamie* |
| **Jairo** | [High-ro] Jehovah enlightens (Spanish) | |
| Jaivant | Long-lived (Sanskrit) | |
| **Jakar** | From Jakarta, capital city of Indonesia | |
| Jake | Short for Jacob | |
| **Jalen** | See Galen | |
| Jamal | Good looks (Arabic) | |
| **Jameel** | Courteous (Arabic) | |
| James | Supplanter (Hebrew) | *Jamey, Jamie, Jazz, Jem, Jim, Jimmie, Jimmy* |
| **Jameson** | James's son | *Jamey, Jamie / Jamieson* |
| Jamie | Short for Jaime, James or Jameson. Also a girl's name | *Jim / Jamey* |
| **Jamil** | Handsome, graceful (Arabic) | |
| Jan | Dutch form of John: God is gracious | |
| **Janak** | Father (Sanskrit) Also another name for Lord Buddha | |
| Janesh | King of men (Sanskrit) | |
| **Jankin** | Medieval pet form of John | *Jenkin, Jenkins* |
| Janson | Son of Jan | |
| **Japheth** | Expansion (Hebrew) | *Jafe* |
| Jarah | [Jay-rah] God gives sweetness (Hebrew) | *Jareth* |
| **Jared** | Descent (Hebrew) | *Jed / Jarod, Jarred, Jarrod, Jerod* |
| Jarek | Spring (Slavik) | |
| **Jareth** | See Jarah | |
| Jarrett | See Garrett | *Garret, Jarret* |
| **Jarrold** | See **Gerald** | |
| Jarvis | Originally a surname, meaning spear | *Jarvie / Gervaise, Gervase, Jervis* |

| Name | Definition | Short forms/<br>Variations |
|---|---|---|
| **Jashith** | Protector (Sanskrit) | |
| Jasminder | Lord's glory (Sikh) Also a girl's name | |
| **Jason** | To heal (Greek) In Greek mythology, Jason was a hero, leader of the Argonauts | |
| Jasper | Treasurer (Persian) | *Jazz* |
| **Jaswant** | Admirable; victorious (Sikh) Also a girl's name | |
| Javan | Wine (Hebrew) | |
| **Javier** | See **Xavier** | |
| Javon | Hopeful (Hebrew) | |
| **Jax** | Short for Jackson | |
| Jay | See Jai | |
| **Jayant** | Ultimately victorious (Sanskrit) | |
| Jaydon | See Jadon | *Jade, Jay / Jayden* |
| **Jayesh** | Lord of victory (Sanskrit) | |
| Jazz | Short for James or Jasper | |
| **Jean** | [Jon] French form of John: God is gracious | |
| Jean-Paul | Combination of Jean (God is gracious) and Paul (small) | |
| **Jean-Pierre** | Combination of Jean (God is gracious) and Pierre (rock) | |
| Jeavon | Young man (Latin) | |
| **Jeb** | Short for Jebediah | |
| Jebediah | See **Jedidiah** | *Jeb* |
| **Jed** | Short for Jared, Jediah or Jedidiah | |
| Jediah | Short for Jedidiah | *Jed* |
| **Jedidiah** | Lover of God (Hebrew) | *Jed, Jediah /*<br>*Jebediah, Jedediah* |
| Jeevan | Life (Sanskrit) | *Jevan* |
| **Jeff** | Short for Jefferson or Jeffrey | |

| --- | --- | --- |
| Jefferson | Jeffrey's son. In the US, it's sometimes given in homage to Thomas Jefferson, president and principal author of the Declaration of Independence | Jeff |
| Jeffrey | See Geoffrey | Jeff; Jeffery |
| Jem | Short for James or Jeremy | |
| Jenkins | See Jankin | |
| Jenson | Jan's son | |
| Jeremiah | Appointed by God (Hebrew) | Jerry / Jeremy |
| Jeremy | English form of Jeremiah | Jem, Jerry |
| Jermaine | See Germain | Jermyn |
| Jerod | See Jared | |
| Jerome | Holy name (Greek) | Jerry / Geronimo |
| Jerry | Short for Gerald, Gerard, Jeremiah, Jeremy or Jerome | |
| Jesse | [Jess-ee] Gift (Hebrew) Also a girl's name | Jess / Jessie |
| Jesus | [Hay-zuss] Aramaic form of Joshua: God is salvation. Commonly given as an expression of Christian faith in Spanish-speaking countries | |
| Jethro | Excellence (Hebrew) | |
| Jevan | See Jeevan | |
| Jevon | Young (French) | |
| Jian | Healthy (Chinese) | |
| Jim | Short for James | Jimmie, Jimmy |
| Jinan | Paradise (Arabic) Also a girl's name | |
| Jiro | Second son (Japanese) | |
| Joab | [Jo-ab] Praise Jehovah (Hebrew) | |
| Joachim | [Wah-keem] Appointed by God (Hebrew) | Joaquin |
| Joaquin | [Wah-keen] See Joachim | |
| Job | [Jobe] Persecuted (Hebrew) | Jobe |
| Jocelyn | [Joss-lin] Taken from the Gauts, a Germanic tribe. Also a girl's name | Joss / Jocelin, Joselyn, Joslyn |
| Jock | Scottish pet form of John | |
| Jody | Pet form of Jude. Also a girl's name | |
| Joe | Short for Jolyon, Jonah, Jonas, Joseph or Josiah | Joey / Jo |

names

boys' J

| Name | Definition | Short forms/Variations |
|---|---|---|
| Joel | Yahweh is God (Hebrew) | |
| **Joey** | Short for Joseph | |
| John | God is gracious (Hebrew) | *Jack, Jankin, Jenkin, Jock, Johnnie, Johnny / Jon, Juan, Sion* |
| **Joly** | Short for Jolyon | *Jolly* |
| Jolyon | See Julian | *Jo, Joe, Joly, Jolly* |
| **Jon** | Short for Jonathan | *Jonnie, Jonny* |
| Jonah | Dove (Hebrew) In the Bible, Jonah was thrown off a ship and swallowed by a whale after disobeying God's command | *Jo, Joe / Jonas* |
| **Jonas** | See Jonah | *Jo, Joe* |
| Jonathan | God has given (Hebrew) | *Jon, Jonnie, Jonny / Jonathon* |
| **Jordan** | Going down (Hebrew) | *Jordy, Judd* |
| Jordy | Short for Jordan | |
| **Joren** | Dutch form of George: farmer | *Jory* |
| Jorge | [Hoch-hay] Spanish form of George: farmer | |
| **Jory** | Short for Joren | |
| José | [Ho-say] Spanish form of Joseph: God shall add | |
| **Josef** | See Joseph | |
| Joseph | God shall add (Hebrew) | *Jo, Joe, Joey / José, Josef, Yosef, Yusuf* |
| **Josh** | Short for Joshua | |
| Joshua | God is salvation (Hebrew) In the Bible, after Moses' death, Joshua led the Children of Israel to take possession of the Promised Land | *Josh* |

| Name | Definition | Short forms/ Variations |
|---|---|---|
| **Josiah** | God heals (Hebrew) | *Jo, Joe* |
| Joss | Short for Jocelyn. Also a girl's name | |
| **Jove** | English form of Jupiter: in Roman myth, the most powerful of the gods | |
| Juan | [Wahn] Spanish form of John: God is gracious | |
| **Jubal** | Sound (Hebrew) In the Bible, Jubal is the first musician | |
| Judah | Praised (Hebrew) | *Jude / Judas* |
| **Judd** | Short for Jordan | |
| Jude | Short for Judah or Judas. The name of the unfortunate hero in Thomas Hardy's 19th-century novel *Jude the Obscure* | *Jody* |
| **Jules** | Short for Julian or Julius. Also a girl's name | *Jools* |
| Julian | See Julius. Occasionally a girl's name | *Jules* |
| **Julio** | [Hoo-lee-oh] Spanish form of Julius | |
| Julius | Originally a Roman family name | *Jules / Iolo, Julio* |
| **Junior** | Son (English) | |
| Jupiter | In Roman myth, Jupiter was the most powerful of the gods. Also the name of a planet | |
| **Jurgen** | Scandinavian form of George: farmer | *Jorgen* |
| Justin | See **Justus** | |
| **Justus** | Just and fair (Latin) | *Justin* |

| Name | Definition | Short forms/ Variations |
|------|-----------|-------------------------|
| **Kade** | See **Cade** | |
| Kaden | See **Caden** | *Cayden, Kayden* |
| **Kai** | The sea (Hawaiian) | *Cai* |
| Kailash | A mountain in the Himalayas where, according to Hindu tradition, Lord Shiva lives | |
| **Kain** | See **Cain** | *Cane, Kane* |
| Kairav | Born in water (Sanskrit) | |
| **Kalpesh** | Perfection (Sanskrit) | |
| Kamal | Perfection (Arabic) Red (Sanskrit) | |
| **Kanak** | Gold (Sanskrit) | |
| Kane | English form of Cathan: battle | |
| **Kano** | A city in Nigeria | |
| Karam | Generosity (Arabic) Also a girl's name | *Karim* |
| **Karl** | Free man (Germanic) | *Carl, Charles* |
| Kasey | See Casey | |
| **Kaspar** | Scandinavian form of Caspar: one of the three Wise Men who brought gifts to the baby Jesus | |

| Name | Definition | Short forms/ Variations |
|------|-----------|-------------------------|
| Kavi | Poet (Sanskrit) | |
| **Kavish** | King of poets (Sanskrit) | |
| Kay | Originally short for any name beginning with K. Also a girl's name | |
| **Keane** | [Keen] English form of Cian: ancient | |
| Keanu | [Kee-ah-nu] Cool breeze blowing from the mountains (Hawaiian) | |
| **Kearney** | Warrior (Celtic) | |
| Keaton | Originally a surname, meaning hawk town or village. May be given in homage to American silent movie actor 'Buster' Keaton (born Joseph Frank Keaton Jr) | |
| **Keats** | May be given in homage to the English Romantic poet John Keats | |
| Keegan | Small flame; ardent (Irish Gaelic) | |
| **Keeley** | Good looking (Irish Gaelic) Also a girl's name | |
| Keenan | Descendant of Cian | |
| **Keir** | Swarthy (Gaelic) | |
| Keiron | See **Ciaran** | *Keiran, Kieran, Kieron* |
| **Keith** | Originally a Scottish surname, meaning wood | |
| Kelly | English form of Ceallach: bright head. Also a girl's name | |
| **Kelsey** | Originally an English surname, meaning ship's victory. Also a girl's name | |
| Kelvin | The name of a Scottish river | |
| **Kemp** | Originally an English surname, meaning athlete or wrestler | |
| Ken | Short for Kendall, Kendrick, Kenelm, Kennard, Kennedy or Kenneth | *Kenny* |
| **Kendall** | Originally an English surname, meaning valley of the River Kent | *Ken, Kenny* |
| Kendrick | Originally a surname, meaning chief man | *Ken, Kenny* |
| **Kenelm** | Bold; helmet (Old English) | *Ken, Kenny* |
| Kennard | Royal and brave (Middle English) | *Ken, Kenny* |
| **Kennedy** | Originally a surname. It's sometimes given in homage to the assassinated American president John F Kennedy. Also a girl's name | *Ken, Kenny* |
| Kenneth | Born of fire; handsome (Gaelic) | *Ken, Kenny* |

| Name | Definition | Short forms/ Variations |
|---|---|---|
| **Kentigern** | [Ken-tee-gern] Head chief (Welsh) | *Kent* |
| Kenton | Originally a surname, meaning royal manor | *Kent* |
| **Kerr** | Originally a surname, meaning marsh | |
| Kerry | From the Irish county. Also a girl's name | |
| **Kes** | Short for Kester | |
| Kester | Medieval Scottish form of Christopher: to carry Christ | *Kes* |
| **Kevin** | Beloved (Irish) | |
| Khalil | Dear friend (Arabic) | |
| **Khan** | Prince (Arabic) | |
| Kian | See Cian | |
| **Kiefer** | [Kee-fer] Barrel maker (German) | |
| Kieran | [Kee-ran] See **Ciaran** | *Keiran, Keiron, Kieron* |
| **Killian** | Warlike (Gaelic) | |
| Kim | Short for Kimball or Kimberley | |
| **Kimball** | Kimball O'Hara is the Irish hero of Rudyard Kipling's 1901 novel *Kim* | *Kim* |
| Kimberley | From a town in South Africa, besieged by the Boers during the Boer War. Also a girl's name | *Kim* |
| **Kingsley** | Originally an English surname, meaning king's wood | |
| Kipling | Originally a surname, meaning small hill. May be given in homage to English writer Rudyard Kipling, author of the 19th-century children's novel *The Jungle Book* | |

| Name | Definition | Short forms/Variations |
|------|-----------|------------------------|
| **Kipps** | Originally a surname, meaning small hill | |
| Kiran | Ray of light (Sanskrit) Occasionally used for girls | |
| **Kirill** | Russian form of Cyril: lord | *Kiril* |
| Kirin | Poet, author (Sanskrit) | |
| **Kirit** | Crown (Sanskrit) | |
| Kirk | Originally a northern English and Scottish surname, meaning church | |
| **Kirpal** | Kind; merciful (Sikh) Also a girl's name | |
| Kishan | Dark-skinned (Sanskrit) Also another name for Lord Krishna | |
| **Kit** | Short for Christopher | |
| Kiyoshi | Pure, saintly (Japanese) | |
| **Kjell** | [Chell] Sacrificial cauldron (Old Norse) | *Chell* |
| Klaus | See **Claus** | |
| **Knox** | Round-top hill (Old English) | |
| Knut | See **Canute** | |
| **Koji** | Happy second son (Japanese) | |
| Kolya | Short for Nikolai | |
| **Konrad** | Bold counsel (Germanic) | *Conrad, Kurt* |
| Krishna | Dark-skinned (Sanskrit) | |
| **Kristian** | Scandinavian form of Christian: follower of Christ | |
| Kristo | Short for Kristopher | |
| **Kristopher** | Scandinavian form of Christopher: to carry Christ | *Kris, Kristo* |
| Kulvinder | Hero of the family (Sikh) Also a girl's name | |
| **Kumar** | [Koo-mar] Son (Sanskrit) | |
| Kunal | [Koo-nal] Bird (Sanskrit) | |
| **Kurt** | See **Konrad** | |
| Kushad | Talented (Sanskrit) | |
| **Kwame** | [Kwah-mee] Saturday's child (Ghanaian) | |
| Kwan | [K-wahn] Strong (Korean) | |
| **Kyd** | [Kid] Short for Christopher | *Kidd, Kydd* |
| Kyle | Narrow channel (Scottish) | |

l

names

| Name | Definition | Short forms/ Variations |
|------|-----------|-------------------------|
| **Lachlan** | Norwegian man (Gaelic) | *Lachlann* |
| Lahar | Wave (Sanskrit) | |
| **Laird** | Lord (Scottish) | |
| Lambert | Originally a surname, meaning famous land | |
| **Lance** | A weapon (Old French) | |
| Lancelot | In Arthurian myth, Lancelot is a knight, who became the lover of Queen Guinevere | *Lance, Launce / Launcelot* |
| **Langham** | Originally an English surname, meaning long settlement | |
| Langley | Originally an English surname, meaning long meadow | |
| **Larry** | Short for Laurence | |
| Lars | Scandinavian form of Laurence: man from Laurentum | |
| **Latif** | [Lah-teef] Kind; friendly (Arabic) | |
| Laurence | Man from Laurentum (Latin) May have gained in popularity thanks to actor Sir Laurence Olivier | *Larry, Laurie, Lawrie / Laurens, Laurent, Lawrence, Lorenzo, Lorne* |

| Name | Definition | Short forms/ Variations |
| --- | --- | --- |
| **Laurens** | Scandinavian form of Laurence: man from Laurentum | |
| Laurent | French form of Laurence: man from Laurentum | |
| **Laurie** | Short for Laurence or Lorimer | *Lawrie* |
| Lawrence | See Laurence | |
| **Lawson** | Originally a surname, meaning son of Lawrence | |
| Lazarus | God assists (Hebrew) In the Bible, Jesus brings Lazarus back to life after he has been dead for four days | |
| **Lea** | Short for Leander | |
| Leander | Lion man (Greek) Also a girl's name | *Lea, Lee / Leandro* |
| **Lear** | Joyful (Teutonic) In Shakespeare's tragedy *King Lear*, the king's misjudgment of his daughters' characters leads to his downfall | |
| Lee | Originally a surname, meaning wood or clearing | |
| **Lei** | Thunder (Chinese) | |
| Leif | Heir (Old Norse) | |
| **Leighton** | Herb garden (Old English) | |
| Lemar | From the sea (French) | |
| **Lemuel** | Devoted to God (Hebrew) | |
| Len | Short for Lennon, Lennox or Leonard | *Lennie, Lenny* |
| **Lennon** | Sometimes given in homage to musician John Lennon | *Len, Lennie, Lenny* |
| Lennox | Originally a Scottish surname | *Len, Lennie, Lenny* |
| **Lenny** | Short for Lennon, Lennox or Leonard | *Len / Lennie* |
| Leo | Lion (Latin) May be given to a child born under the star sign of Leo, from 24 July to 23 August | *Leon* |
| **Leon** | See Leo | *Levon* |
| Leonard | Brave lion (Germanic) | *Len, Lennie, Lenny* |
| **Leonardo** | Italian, Spanish and Portuguese form of Leonard: brave lion. Sometimes given in homage to Renaissance genius Leonardo da Vinci | *Leo* |
| Leonzio | Lion (Latin) | |

| Name | Definition | Short forms/Variations |
|------|------------|------------------------|
| **Leopold** | Brave people (Germanic) | *Leo* |
| Leroy | [Lee-roy] The king (French) | *Elroy* |
| **Leslie** | Originally a Scottish surname, meaning garden of holly trees | |
| Lev | Lion (Russian) | |
| **Levi** | [Lee-vigh] Joined (Hebrew) Occasionally used for girls | |
| Levon | Armenian form of Leon: lion | |
| **Lew** | Short for Lewin, Lewis or Llewelyn | |
| Lewin | Dear friend (Old English) | *Lew* |
| **Lewis** | English form of Louis: fame in war | *Lew* |
| Lex | Short for Alexander | |
| **Li** | [Lee] Strength (Chinese) Also a girl's name | |
| Liam | Short for William | |
| **Liang** | [Lee-ang] Bright (Chinese) | |
| Linden | Lime tree (Old English) | |
| **Lindsay** | Originally a surname. Also a girl's name | *Lindsey, Linsay, Linsey* |
| Linford | Originally a surname, meaning lime tree by a ford | *Lynford* |
| **Linley** | Originally an English surname, meaning flax field | |
| Linus | In Greek legend, Linus was a musician. He's now better known as the boy with the security blanket in the Peanuts cartoons | |
| **Lionel** | Little lion (Greek) | |
| Lior | My light (Hebrew) | |
| **Livingstone** | May be given in homage to Scottish explorer and missionary David Livingstone | |
| Lleu | [Lew or Clew] Bright, shining (Welsh) | |
| **Llewelyn** | [Lew-ell-in or Clew-ell-in] Lion (Welsh) | *Lew, Llew / Llewellyn* |
| Lloyd | Originally a Welsh surname, meaning grey-haired | *Floyd* |
| **Loarn** | In about 500AD, Loarn and his two brothers, Angus and Fergus, led the migration from Ireland to Scotland | *Lorn, Lorne* |
| Loch Lainn | Migrant from Norway, land of the lochs (Irish) | *Lochlan* |

| Name | Definition | Short forms/Variations |
|------|-----------|------------------------|
| **Lochan** | Bright eyes (Sanskrit) | |
| Lochlan | See Loch Lainn | *Lochlain* |
| **Lockhart** | Originally an English surname, meaning sheep-herder | *Lockie* |
| Lockie | Short for Lockhart | |
| **Logan** | Originally a Scottish surname. Also a girl's name | *Logie* |
| Logie | Short for Logan | |
| **Lokesh** | King of all people (Sanskrit) Also another name for Lord Brahma | |
| Lonan | Blackbird (Irish) | |
| **Lorcan** | Fierce (Irish) | |
| Lorenzo | Spanish form of Laurence: man from Laurentum | |
| **Lori** | Short for Lorimer. Also a girl's name | |
| Lorimer | Originally a surname, meaning someone who made spurs. Also a girl's name | *Lori / Laurie, Lawrie* |
| **Lorne** | See Laurence | |
| Lothar | Famous warrior (Frankish) | *Lothair, Lothario, Lowther* |
| **Lothario** | See Lothar | |
| Lou | Short for Aloysius, Louie, Louis or Ludovic. Also a girl's name | |
| **Loughlin** | English form of Loch Lainn: migrant from Norway | |

| Name | Definition | Short forms/ Variations |
|------|------------|-------------------------|
| Louie | [Loo-ee] See **Louis** | Lou |
| **Louis** | [Loo-ee] Fame in war (Germanic) | Lou / Aloysius, Louie, Luigi, Luis |
| Lovell | Wolf cub (Old French) | Lowell |
| **Lowell** | See Lovell | |
| Lowry | May be given in homage to English industrial artist LS Lowry | |
| **Lowther** | See Lothar | Lothair |
| Luc | French form of Lucas: man from Lucania | |
| **Luca** | Italian form of Lucas: man from Lucania | |
| Lucas | Man from Lucania (Greek) Luke was the writer of one of the Gospels in the New Testament. May also have gained in popularity thanks to the character Luke Skywalker in the 1977 film *Star Wars* | Luc, Luca, Lukas, Luke |
| **Lucian** | [Loo-see-an] See Lucius | Luc, Luke / Lucien |
| Luciano | [Loo-chah-no] See Lucius | Lucio |
| **Lucio** | [Loo-chee-o] Short for Luciano | |
| Lucius | [Loo-see-us] Light (Latin) | Luc, Luke / Lucian, Lucien |
| **Ludo** | Short for Ludovic | |
| Ludovic | Latin form of Ludwig: famous fighter | Lou, Ludo / Ludovick |
| **Ludwig** | Famous fighter (Germanic) | |
| Luigi | Italian form of Louis: fame in war | |
| **Luis** | Spanish form of Louis: fame in war | |
| Luke | See Lucas | Luc, Luca |
| **Luther** | People; army (Germanic) Sometimes given in homage to medieval theologian Martin Luther or 20th-century civil rights leader Martin Luther King | |
| Lux | Light (Latin) Also a girl's name | |
| **Lyall** | Wolf (Old Norse) | |
| Lyle | Originally a Scottish surname, meaning from the island | |
| **Lysander** | Free (Greek) One of the lovers in Shakespeare's *A Midsummer Night's Dream* | |

boys' names

l

| Name | Definition | Short forms/ Variations |
|------|-----------|------------------------|
| Mac | Short for Cormac or any name beginning with Mac or Mc | *Mack* |
| Macauley | Righteous (Scottish) | |
| Mackenzie | Originally a Scottish clan name and surname. Also a girl's name | *Mac, Mack* |
| Macy | Short for Mason | *Macey* |
| Maddox | Benefactor's son (Welsh) Occasionally used for girls | |
| Madison | Originally a surname. Often connected with the famous New York locations, Madison Avenue and Madison Square. In the US, it may be given in homage to former president James Madison. Also a girl's name | *Maddison* |
| Madoc | Fire (Celtic) | *Madog* |
| Magdi | Praiseworthy (Arabic) | |
| Magen | Protector (Hebrew) | |
| Magnus | Great (Latin) | |
| Maguire | Originally an Irish surname | |
| Mahin | Bringer of joy (Sanskrit) | |

| Name | Definition | Short forms/ Variations |
|---|---|---|
| Mahir | Skilled (Sanskrit) | |
| Mahmoud | Someone who is praised (Arabic) | *Mahmud* |
| Maitland | Originally a French surname, meaning bad temper. Also a girl's name | |
| Majid | Glorious (Arabic) | |
| Makoto | True (Japanese) | |
| Malachy | [Mal-uh-kee] My messenger (Hebrew) | *Mal / Malachi* |
| Malcolm | Devotee of St Columba | *Mal, Malc* |
| Malik | King (Arabic) | |
| Mallory | Originally a French surname, meaning bad temper. Also a girl's name | |
| Maloney | [Mah-low-nee] Devotee of St John (Irish Gaelic) | *Malone* |
| Mandar | Determined (Sanskrit) | |
| Mandeep | Light of the mind (Sikh) Also a girl's name | |
| Manfred | Man of peace (Germanic) | *Fred, Freddie, Freddy* |
| Mannan | Thought (Sanskrit) | |
| Manolo | Spanish form of Emmanuel: God is with us | |
| Mansur | Victorious (Arabic) | |
| Manuel | [Man-well] Spanish form of Emmanuel: God is with us | |
| Marc | French form of Mark: taken from Mars, the Roman god of war | |
| Marc-Anthony | Combination of Marc (taken from Mars, the Roman god of war) and Anthony (of inestimable worth). Marcus Antonius – known in English as Mark Antony – was a Roman politician and general. He committed suicide along with his lover, Cleopatra, Queen of Egypt | |
| Marcel | [Mar-sell] See Marcus | *Marcelo* |
| Marcellus | [Mar-sell-us] French pet form of Marcus | |
| Marcin | [Mar-cheen] Polish form of Martin; taken from Mars, the Roman god of war | |
| Marco | Italian form of Mark: taken from Mars, the Roman god of war | |
| Marcos | Spanish form of Marcus: taken from Mars, the Roman god of war | |

| Name | Definition | Short forms/ Variations |
|------|------------|-------------------------|
| Marcus | Taken from Mars, the Roman god of war | Marcel, Marcellus, Marcius, Marco, Marcos, Marius, Mark |
| **Mario** | See **Marius** | |
| Marion | Unlikely as it may seem, the real name of the actor John Wayne. More often used as a girl's name | |
| **Marius** | See Marcus | |
| Mark | See Marcus | Marco |
| **Marley** | Originally an English surname, meaning pleasant wood. Sometimes given in homage to musician Bob Marley | |
| Marlon | May have gained in popularity thanks to actor Marlon Brandon | |
| **Marlowe** | A town in Buckinghamshire, England. May be given in homage to 16th-century English dramatist Christopher Marlowe or Raymond Chandler's fictional 'hardboiled' LA detective Philip Marlowe | |
| Marmaduke | Devotee of Maedoc, an Irish saint | |
| **Mars** | The Roman god of war | |
| Marshall | Originally a surname, meaning someone who looked after horses | |
| **Martin** | Taken from Mars, the Roman god of war | Marty / Martyn |
| Marty | Short for Martin | |
| **Marvin** | See Mervin | Mervyn |
| Mason | Originally a surname, meaning stone mason | Macy, Macey |
| **Masoud** | Happy; lucky (Arabic) | |
| Massimo | Greatest (Latin) | Max |
| **Masud** | See **Masoud** | Musad |
| Matt | Short for Matteo, Matthew or Matthias | Matty |
| **Matteo** | [Mah-tay-oh] Italian form of Matthew: gift from God | Matt, Matty |
| Matthew | Gift from God (Hebrew) | Matt, Matty / Mathew, Mathias, Mattheo |
| **Matthias** | [Math-eye-us] See Matthew | Matt, Matty / Mathias |
| Maurice | [Mor-ees] Moorish (Latin) | Maurizio, Morrice, Morris |

| Name | Definition | Short forms/ Variations |
|---|---|---|
| **Maurizio** | [Mor-itz-ee-oh] Spanish or Italian form of Maurice: Moorish | |
| Max | Short for Massimo, Maxim, Maximilian, Maximus or Maxwell | |
| **Maxim** | See **Maximus** | *Max* |
| Maximilian | See **Maximus** | *Max, Maxim / Maximilien, Maximillian* |
| **Maximus** | Greatest (Latin) | *Max, Maxim / Maximillian* |
| Maxwell | Originally a surname, meaning Mack's stream | *Max* |
| **Maynard** | Originally a surname, meaning brave and strong | |
| Meirion | See **Marcus** | *Merrion* |
| **Mel** | Short for Melville or Melvin | |
| Melchior | [Mel-kee-or] King; city (Persian) In medieval tradition, Melchior was one of the three Wise Men who brought gifts to the baby Jesus | |
| **Melville** | Originally a French surname | *Mel / Melvin* |
| Melvin | See **Melville** | *Mel* |
| **Mendel** | Comforter (Hebrew) | |
| Menzies | [Min-giss] Originally a Scottish surname, meaning clemency | |
| **Meredith** | Lord (Old Welsh) Also a girl's name | |
| Merioth | Rebellious (Hebrew) Also a girl's name | |
| **Merle** | [Murl] Blackbird (Old French) Also a girl's name | |
| Merlin | Sea; fort (Welsh) In legend, Merlin is a magician who guides King Arthur. A merlin is also a small falcon | |
| **Merrill** | Originally a surname. Also a girl's name | *Merry* |
| Merry | Short for Merrill | |
| **Merton** | Originally a surname, meaning town or village by a lake | |
| Mervin | Famous friend (Anglo Saxon) | *Merv / Marvin, Mervyn* |
| **Meyrick** | Work-ruler (Teutonic) | |
| Micah | [My-kah] Who is like Yahweh (God) (Hebrew) | |

| Name | Definition | Short forms/ Variations |
|------|-----------|------------------------|
| **Michael** | Who is like God (Hebrew) In Christian tradition, Michael is one of the archangels | *Mick, Mickey, Micky, Mike, Mikey / Miguel* |
| Michi | Pathway (Japanese) Also a girl's name | |
| **Mick** | Short for Cormick or Michael | *Mickey, Micky* |
| Miguel | [Mig-ell] Spanish form of Michael: who is like God | |
| **Mihir** | Sun (Sanskrit) | |
| Mike | Short for Michael | *Mikey* |
| **Mikhail** | [Mik-hile] Russian form of Michael: who is like God | *Mischa, Misha* |
| Milan | Meeting (Sanskrit) | |
| **Miles** | Soldier (Latin) | *Milo, Myles* |
| Miller | Originally a surname, meaning flour miller | |
| **Milo** | [My-low] See **Miles** | |
| Milton | Originally a surname, meaning mill farm. May be given in homage to 17th-century English poet John Milton | |
| **Miner** | Originally an English surname, meaning coal miner | |
| Mischa | [Mish-kah] Short for Mikhail | |
| **Misha** | [Mish-ah] Short for Mikhail | |
| Mitch | Short for Mitchell | |
| **Mitchell** | Medieval French form of Michael: who is like God | *Mitch* |
| Mohammed | Praiseworthy (Arabic) | *Mohammad, Muhammad, Muhammed* |
| **Mohan** | Enchanting (Sanskrit) Also another name for Lord Krishna | |
| Mohawk | A Native American tribe from Oregon, USA | |
| **Monroe** | See Munro | |
| Montague | Originally a French surname, meaning pointed hill | *Monty* |
| **Montgomery** | Originally a Norman surname, meaning Gomeric's hill | *Monty / Montgomerie* |
| Monty | Short for Egmont, Montague or Montgomery | |
| **Mordred** | In Arthurian legend, Mordred is a knight of the Round Table who betrays and kills King Arthur | |

| Name | Definition | Short forms/ Variations |
|------|------------|-------------------------|
| Morgan | Completion (Old Celtic) Also a girl's name | |
| Morley | Originally an English surname, meaning a moor by a wood | |
| Morris | See Maurice | Morrice |
| Morten | Norwegian and Danish form of Martin: taken from Mars, the Roman god of war | |
| Mortimer | Originally a Norman surname, meaning dead sea | |
| Morton | Originally an English surname, meaning town or village by a moor | |
| Morvryn | Sea king (Welsh) | |
| Moses | Born (Egyptian) | |
| Mostyn | Originally a Welsh surname, meaning field of the fortress | |
| Mudil | Moonlight (Sanskrit) | |
| Muhammad | Praiseworthy (Arabic) | Mohammad, Mohammed |
| Muir | Originally a Scottish surname, meaning moor | |
| Mukul | Soul (Sanskrit) | |
| Muneer | Shining (Arabic) | Munir |
| Mungo | My pet (Welsh) | |
| Munir | Bright, shining (Arabic) | |
| Munro | Originally an Irish surname, meaning mouth of the River Roe | Monroe |
| Murdo | Lord (Gaelic) | |
| Murdoch | Sailor (Gaelic) | Murdo / Murtoch |
| Murgatroyd | Originally a surname, meaning Margaret's clearing | |
| Murphy | Hound of the sea (Irish) | |
| Murray | Originally a surname; taken from the Moray region of Scotland | Moray |
| Mustafa | Chosen (Arabic) | Mustapha |
| Myron | Myrrh (Greek) | |

| Name | Definition | Short forms/ Variations |
|------|-----------|------------------------|
| **Nadim** | Companion (Arabic) | |
| Nadish | Lord of water (Sanskrit) | |
| **Nahum** | [Nay-hm] Source of comfort (Hebrew) | |
| Naim | Happy (Arabic) | |
| **Nalesh** | King of flowers (Sanskrit) | |
| Nalin | Born in water (Sanskrit) | |
| **Naphtali** | Wrestling (Hebrew) | |
| Napoleon | Lion of Naples (Italian) Sometimes given in homage to French emperor Napoleon Bonaparte | |
| **Narayan** | Son of man | |
| Narcissus | Sleep; numbness (Greek) The associations are not positive. In Greek myth, Narcissus was a handsome but vain youth who fell in love with his own reflection in a pond and wasted away while staring at it | |
| **Naresh** | Ruler of men (Sanskrit) | |
| Narun | Leader of mankind (Sanskrit) | |

| Name | Definition | Short forms/ Variations |
|---|---|---|
| **Naseem** | Breeze (Arabic) | *Nasim* |
| Nash | Cliff, headland (Old English) | |
| **Nasir** | Helper; protector (Arabic) | *Naseer* |
| Nat | Short for Nathan or Nathaniel | *Nattie, Natty / Nate* |
| **Nate** | Short for Nathan or Nathaniel | *Nat, Nattie, Natty* |
| Nathan | God has given (Hebrew) Protector (Sanskrit) | *Nat, Nate, Nattie, Natty / Nathen* |
| **Nathaniel** | God has given (Hebrew) | *Nat, Nate, Nattie, Natty / Nathanael* |
| Naughton | [Nor-ton] Originally a surname, meaning new town or village | |
| **Navarro** | Plains (Spanish) The name of a medieval Spanish kingdom | |
| Naveen | New (Sanskrit) | |
| **Nayan** | Chief (Sanskrit) | |
| Neal | See Neil | |
| **Ned** | Short for Edward or Edwin | |
| Neel | Mountain (Sanskrit) | |
| **Nehemiah** | Comforter (Hebrew) | |
| Neil | English form of Niall: champion | *Neal, Neill* |
| **Nelson** | Neil's son. Sometimes given in homage to Britain's greatest naval hero, Admiral Horatio Nelson, and sometimes to South African statesman Nelson Mandela | |
| Neo | New (Greek) | |
| **Nereo** | Taken from Nereus, a Greek sea god | |
| Nero | Short for Raniero | |
| **Nevan** | Saint, holy one (Irish) | |
| Neville | Originally an aristocratic French surname | *Nevil* |
| **Nevin** | Servant of the saint (Gaelic) | |
| Newton | Originally a surname, meaning new town or village. Sometimes given in homage to English scientist Sir Isaac Newton | |
| **Niall** | [Ny-al or Neel] Champion (Gaelic) | |
| Nicholas | Victorious people (Greek) | *Claus, Col, Klaus, Nic, Nick, Nicky, Nico / Colin, Nicolas, Niles* |

| Name | Definition | Short forms/ Variations |
|------|-----------|-------------------------|
| **Nick** | Short for Nicholas, Nico or Nicol | *Nic, Nicky* |
| Nico | Short for Nicholas | *Nic, Nick, Nicky / Niko* |
| **Nicol** | Short for Nicholas | *Nic, Nick, Nicky / Nichol* |
| Nigel | Black (Latin) | |
| **Nihal** | Content (Sanskrit) | |
| Nikhil | Complete (Sanskrit) | |
| **Nikita** | Unconquerable (Greek) Originally a boy's name, it's now more common for girls | |
| Nikolai | Russian form of Nicholas: victorious people | *Kolya, Nik* |
| **Niles** | See Nicholas | |
| Nimrod | In the Bible, Nimrod was Noah's great-grandson | |
| **Nirek** | Superior (Sanskrit) | |
| Nishith | Born at night (Sanskrit) | |
| **Nixon** | Nick's son. Former US president Richard Nixon resigned from office following the Watergate Scandal | |
| Noah | Comfort (Hebrew) In the Bible, God told Noah to build an ark to save his family from a great flood that would wipe out the rest of mankind | |
| **Noam** | Joy (Hebrew) | |
| Noel | Christmas (Old French) Sometimes given in homage to the debonair actor, playwright and composer Sir Noël Coward | *Nowell* |
| **Nolan** | Originally an Irish surname, meaning descendant of a nobleman | |
| Nolly | Pet form of Oliver | |
| **Noor** | Light (Arabic) Also a girl's name | |
| Norbert | Famous in the north (Old German) | *Bertie* |
| **Norman** | Norseman (Germanic) | *Norm* |
| Norris | Northerner (Old French) | |
| **Norton** | Originally an English surname, meaning northern town or village | |
| Norville | Northern town (French) | |
| **Nur** | Light (Arabic) Also a girl's name | |
| Nye | Short for Aneirin | |

| Name | Definition | Short forms/<br>Variations |
| --- | --- | --- |
| **Obadiah** | Servant of God (Hebrew) | |
| Oberon | See **Auberon** | *Bron* |
| **Octavio** | See Octavius | |
| Octavius | Eight (Latin) | *Octavian, Octavio* |
| **Odin** | In Old Norse myth, the god of war | |
| Odysseus | [Od-iss-yuss] The wandering hero in Homer's ancient Greek epic poem *The Odyssey* | *Ulysses* |
| **Ogden** | Originally an English surname, meaning valley of oak trees | |
| Oisin | [Oh-sheen] Strong (Irish) | |
| **Olaf** | Ancestor; descendant (Old Norse) | |
| Oleg | Prosperous, successful (Old Norse) | |
| **Oliver** | Olive tree (Latin) | *Nolly, Ollie, Olly-/ Olivier* |
| Olivier | French form of Oliver: olive tree | *Ollie, Olly* |
| **Ollie** | Short for Oliver or Olivier | *Olly* |
| Omar | Talkative (Hebrew) Long-lived (Arabic) | |

| Name | Definition | Short forms/ Variations |
|---|---|---|
| **Ophrah** | Fawn (Hebrew) Also a girl's name | |
| Oran | Dark-haired (Irish Gaelic) | |
| **Orestes** | [Or-rest-eez] Mountain (Greek) In Greek myth, Orestes and his sister Electra avenge their father's murder by their mother and her lover | |
| Orfeo | Italian form of Orpheus | |
| **Orion** | In Greek myth, Orion was a great hunter who was turned into a constellation | |
| Orlando | Italian form of Roland: fame; land | |
| **Ormond** | Mountain of bears (Old English) | |
| Orpheus | In Greek myth, the musician Orpheus descended into the Underworld to find his dead wife | *Orfeo* |
| **Orson** | Bear cub (French) May have gained in popularity thanks to the American actor and film director Orson Welles | |
| Orville | Gold town (French) | |
| **Osamu** | Ruler (Japanese) | |
| Osbert | God-bright (Old English) | |
| **Osborn** | Warrior god (Old Norse) | *Os, Ossie, Ossy, Oz, Ozzie, Ozzy / Osborne* |
| Oscar | Friendly deer (Irish) Sometimes given in homage to 19th-century writer Oscar Wilde | *Os, Ossie, Ossy, Oz, Ozzie, Ozzy / Oskar* |
| **Osgood** | Goth god (Old Norse) | |
| Osheen | English form of Oisin: strong | |
| **Osmond** | God's protection (Old English) | *Os, Ossie, Ossy, Oz, Ozzie, Ozzy / Osmund* |
| Osric | Divine rule (Teutonic) | *Os, Ossie, Ossy, Oz, Ozzie, Ozzy, Rick / Osrec* |
| **Ossian** | Stag (Scottish Gaelic) | *Os, Ossie, Ossy, Oz, Ozzie, Ozzy* |
| Ossie | Short for Osborn, Oscar, Osmond, Osric, Ossian, Oswald or Oswin | *Os, Oz / Ossy, Ozzie, Ozzy* |
| **Oswald** | God rules (Old English) | *Os, Ossie, Ossy, Oz, Ozzie, Ozzy* |

| Name | Definition | Short forms/Variations |
|------|-----------|------------------------|
| Oswin | God's friend (Old English) | Os, Ossie, Ossy, Oz, Ozzie, Ozzy |
| Othello | Wealth (Germanic) The associations are not positive. In Shakespeare's tragedy *Othello*, the main character is a 'noble Moor' who wrongly suspects his wife of being unfaithful and murders her. When he discovers his mistake, he commits suicide | |
| Otis | Originally a surname. Sometimes given in homage to the American soul singer Otis Redding | |
| Otto | Wealth (Germanic) | |
| Ottokar | Ottokar was a 13th-century king of Bohemia | |
| Owain | Born of the god Esos (Celtic) | Owen |
| Owen | See **Owain** | |
| Oz | Short for Osborn, Oscar, Osmond, Osric, Ossian, Oswald or Oswin | |
| Ozzie | Short for Osborn, Oscar, Osmond, Osric, Ossian, Oswald or Oswin | Oz / Ossie, Ossy, Ozzy |

| Name | Definition | Short forms/Variations |
|------|-----------|----------------------|
| **Pablo** | Spanish form of Paul: small | |
| Paco | Spanish pet form of Francisco | |
| **Paddy** | Short for Patrick | |
| Paderau | Rosary (Welsh) Also a girl's name | |
| **Padma** | Lotus (Sanskrit) The lotus chakra (one of the body's centres of spiritual energy) symbolises the link between the human and the divine. Also a girl's name | |
| Padmesh | King of the lotus (Sanskrit) Also another name for Lord Vishnu | |
| **Padraig** | Irish form of Patrick: patrician | *Padraic* |
| Padrig | Welsh form of Patrick: patrician | |
| **Page** | Originally a surname, meaning a page, a servant to a knight or lord. Also a girl's name | |
| Palin | Protect (Sanskrit) | |
| **Palmer** | Originally a surname, meaning pilgrim | |
| Panav | Prince (Sanskrit) | |
| **Paolo** | [Pow-lo] Italian form of Paul: small | |

| Name | Definition | Short forms/ Variations |
|---|---|---|
| Paresh | Supreme spirit (Sanskrit) Also another name for Lord Brahma | |
| Parker | Originally a surname, meaning gamekeeper. Also a girl's name | |
| Parminder | The greatest god (Sikh) Also a girl's name | |
| Parry | Son of Harry (Welsh) | |
| Parvesh | Lord of celebration (Sanskrit) | |
| Pascal | Easter (Old English) | Pascoe |
| Pascoe | Medieval form of Pascal: Easter | |
| Pasha | To pass over (Greek) Born at Easter. Also a girl's name | |
| Pastor | Priest (English) | |
| Pat | Short for Patrice or Patrick | |
| Patrice | Medieval French form of Patrick: patrician, belonging to the Roman nobility. Also a girl's name | Pat |
| Patrick | Patrician, belonging to the Roman nobility (Latin) St Patrick is the patron saint of Ireland | Paddy, Pat / Padraig, Padrig |
| Patterson | Originally an English surname, meaning son of Peter | |
| Paul | Small (Latin) St Paul is generally thought of as co-founder of the Christian Church. Originally called Saul, he was converted to Christianity on the road to Damascus | Paulo |
| Paulo | [Pow-lo] Spanish form of Paul: small | |
| Pavan | Holy (Sanskrit) | |
| Pavel | Czech and Russian form of Paul: small | |
| Pax | Peace (Latin) | |
| Paxton | Originally a surname | Pax |
| Payton | Originally an English surname, meaning soldiers' town. Also a girl's name | Peyton |
| Pearson | Originally a surname, meaning son of Piers | |
| Pedro | Spanish form of Peter: rock | |
| Pelham | Originally a surname | |
| Penn | Originally an English surname, meaning hill. In the US, it's sometimes given in homage to William Penn, founder of Pennsylvania | |
| Pepe | [Pepp-ay] Pet form of José | |

| Name | Definition | Short forms/ Variations |
|------|-----------|------------------------|
| **Percival** | In Arthurian legend, Percival is one of the knights of the Round Table | *Perceval* |
| Percy | Originally an aristocratic English surname. Sometimes given in homage to the Romantic poet Percy Bysshe Shelley | |
| **Peregrine** | Stranger (Latin) | *Perry* |
| Pericles | [Per-ee-kleez] Far-famed (Greek) In William Shakespeare's play of the same name, Pericles is Prince of Tyre | |
| **Perrin** | Pet form of Pierre: rock | |
| Perry | Originally an English surname, meaning pear tree | |
| **Peter** | Rock (Greek) St Peter is generally thought of as founder of the Christian Church | *Pete / Piers* |
| Petroc | Petroc was a 6th-century Welsh saint whose body is buried in Bodmin, Cornwall | |
| **Peyton** | See **Payton** | |
| Philemon | Loving and friendly (Greek) | *Phil* |
| **Philip** | Lover of horses (Greek) | *Phil, Pip / Phillip* |
| Philippe | French form of Philip: lover of horses | |
| **Phineas** | [Fin-ee-ass] Oracle (Hebrew) | |
| Phinian | [Fin-ee-an] See Finian | *Finnian, Phinean, Phinnian* |
| **Pierce** | See **Piers** | *Pearce* |
| Pierre | French form of Peter: rock | *Perrin* |
| **Piers** | [Peerz] See **Peter** | |
| Pip | Short for Philip | |
| **Piran** | Piran was a 6th-century Cornish saint – the patron saint of miners | |
| Pitt | Originally a surname | |
| **Placido** | [Pla-see-doh] Placid, untroubled (Latin) May have gained in popularity thanks to opera singer Placido Domingo | |
| Plato | [Play-toh] Broad-shouldered (Greek) May be given in homage to Plato, the Ancient Greek philosopher | |
| **Pompey** | Man from Pompeii | |

| Name | Definition | Short forms/ Variations |
| --- | --- | --- |
| Pontius | [Pon-shuss] Fifth (Latin) In the Bible, the judge Pontius Pilate hands over Jesus to be crucified | |
| Porter | Originally an English surname, meaning gatekeeper | |
| Pradeep | Light (Sanskrit) | |
| Pranay | Love (Sanskrit) | |
| Prem | Love (Sanskrit) | |
| Prentice | Apprentice (English) | |
| Presley | [Prez-lee] Originally a surname, meaning priest's meadow. May be given in homage to American musician Elvis Presley | *Priestley* |
| Price | Originally a surname, meaning Rhys's son | |
| Priestley | See Presley | |
| Primo | First (Latin) | |
| Prince | Prince (English) | *Prinze* |
| Prit | Love (Sanskrit) | |
| Pritesh | Lord of love (Sanskrit) | |
| Prospero | According to your wishes (Latin) Prospero is a magician in Shakespeare's *The Tempest* | |
| Pugh | [Pew] Son of Hugh (Welsh) | |

| Name | Definition | Short forms/ Variations |
|------|-----------|------------------------|
| **Quan** | Spring of water (Chinese) | |
| Quentin | Fifth (Latin) | *Quincy, Quintin, Quinton, Quintus* |
| **Quigley** | Originally a surname | |
| Quincy | See **Quentin** | *Quincey* |
| **Quinlan** | Originally an Irish surname, meaning beautiful shape | |
| Quinn | Originally an Irish surname, meaning descendant of Conn. Also a girl's name | |
| **Quintus** | See **Quentin** | |

| Name | Definition | Short forms/ Variations |
|------|-----------|------------------------|
| Rabbie | Scottish form of Robbie, short for Robert | Rab |
| Rad | Thunder (Arabic) | |
| Radford | Originally an English surname, meaning reedy ford | |
| Radley | Originally an English surname, meaning reedy meadow | |
| Rafe | Medieval form of Ralph: wolf counsel | |
| Rafferty | Originally an Irish surname, meaning descendant of Rohartach. Also a girl's name | Rafe, Raff |
| Rafiq | Kind, gentle (Arabic) | |
| Rahman | Kind, merciful (Arabic) | Rehman |
| Rahul | Capable (Sanskrit) | |
| Rainier | See **Rayner** | Raniero |
| Raj | Kind (Sanskrit) | |
| Raja | Hope (Arabic) | |
| Rajat | Silver (Sanskrit) | |
| Rajendra | Mighty king (Sanskrit) | |

| Name | Definition | Short forms/ Variations |
| --- | --- | --- |
| Rakesh | Lord of the full moon (Sanskrit) Also another name for Lord Shiva | |
| Raleigh | [Rah-lee or Ray-lee] Originally a surname, meaning clearing with roe deer. Sometimes given in homage to English writer, poet and explorer Sir Walter Raleigh, who introduced two of the great mainstays of modern British culture: potatoes and tobacco | |
| Ralph | [Ralf or Raif] Wolf counsel (Germanic) | Rafe, Ralf |
| Ralston | Originally a surname | |
| Raman | Loved (Sanskrit) | |
| Rambo | John J Rambo is a Vietnam war veteran played by Sylvester Stallone in the series of *Rambo* films | |
| Ramesh | The preserver (Sanskrit) Also another name for Lord Vishnu | |
| Ramon | [Ra-mone] Spanish form of Raymond: wise protection | Ramone |
| Ramone | See **Ramon** | |
| Ramsay | Originally a Scottish and English surname, meaning wild garlic island | Ramsey |
| Randal | Wolf shield (Old English) | Ranulph |
| Randolf | Raven; wolf (Old Norse) | Randy / Randolph |
| Randy | Short for Randolf | |
| Ranger | Originally a French surname, meaning forest guardian | |
| Rani | [Rah-nee] To gaze (Arabic) Song (Hebrew) | |
| Raniero | Italian form of Rayner: advice; army | Nero |
| Ranulf | Wolf advice (Scandinavian) | Ranulph |
| Raoul | French form of Ralph: wolf counsel | |
| Raphael | God heals (Hebrew) In Christian tradition, one of the archangels | Rafe, Raff / Rafael |
| Rashad | Good sense (Arabic) | |
| Rasputin | Grigori Rasputin was a Russian mystic, popularly known as 'the mad monk'. He was assassinated by a group of noblemen in 1916, as it was thought he had too much influence over Tsar Nicholas II and his wife, the Empress Alexandra | |

| Name | Definition | Short forms/ Variations |
| --- | --- | --- |
| **Ratan** | Precious stone (Sanskrit) | |
| Ravi | Sun (Sanskrit) | |
| **Ray** | Short for Raymond or Rayner | |
| Raymond | Wise protection (Old French) May have increased in popularity thanks to crime writer Raymond Chandler | *Ray* |
| **Rayner** | Advice; army (Germanic) | *Ray / Rainer* |
| Reagan | [Ray-gn or Ree-gn] Originally a Gaelic surname, meaning queen | |
| **Rearden** | Poet king (Irish) | *Riordan* |
| Redford | Originally an English surname, meaning reedy ford. May be given in homage to American actor, director and producer Robert Redford | |
| **Redmond** | Counsel protection (Teutonic) | |
| Reece | [Rees] English form of Rhys: ardour | *Rees* |
| **Regent** | Governor (English) | |
| Reggie | Short for Reginald | *Reg* |
| **Reginald** | Power force (Old English) | *Reg, Reggie* |
| Regis | [Ree-jis] Kingly (Latin) | |
| **Reid** | Originally an English surname, meaning red or ruddy | |
| Reilly | [Ry-lee] Originally an Irish surname, meaning courageous | |
| **Reinhard** | See **Reynard** | |
| Remington | Originally an English surname, meaning raven town or village | |
| **Remo** | Italian form of Remus: one of the founders of Rome, according to Roman legend | |
| Remus | According to Roman legend, Remus and his brother Romulus founded Rome | |
| **Remy** | Oarsman (Latin) | |
| Renato | Reborn (Latin) | |
| **Renaud** | French form of Reynard | |
| René | [R'nay] Reborn (Latin) | |
| **Reuben** | Behold, a son (Hebrew) | *Ruben* |
| Rex | King (Latin) May have gained in popularity thanks to *My Fair Lady* actor Rex Harrison | |

| Name | Definition | Short forms/Variations |
|------|-----------|------------------------|
| **Reynard** | Brave advice (Germanic) The name is often associated with medieval tales about Reynard the Fox | *Reinhard, Renaud* |
| Reynold | Ruler's decision (Germanic) | |
| **Rhett** | Originally a Dutch surname, meaning advice. It may have gained in popularity thanks to the character of charmer Rhett Butler in Margaret Mitchell's 1936 novel *Gone with the Wind* | |
| Rhodri | Ruler (Welsh) | |
| **Rhys** | [Rees] Ardour (Welsh) | *Reece, Rees* |
| Rian | King (Irish) | |
| **Riccardo** | Italian or Spanish form of Richard: strong and powerful | *Ricardo* |
| Richard | Strong and powerful (Germanic) | *Dick, Dickon, Rich, Richie, Rick, Rickie, Ricky / Riccardo* |
| **Richie** | Short for Richard. Also a girl's name | *Rich* |
| Rick | Short for Almerick or Richard | *Rickie, Ricky* |
| **Ridley** | Originally an English surname, meaning reeds in a wood | |
| Rigby | Originally an English surname, meaning ruler's valley | |
| **Riley** | Originally a surname, meaning rye clearing. Also a girl's name | *Ryley* |
| Ringo | May have increased in popularity thanks to *Beatles'* drummer Ringo Starr (born Richard Starkey) | |
| **Riordan** | Royal poet (Gaelic) | |
| Rip | *Rip Van Winkle* is a 19th-century short story by American author Washington Irving, in which the main character falls asleep for twenty years | |
| **Ripley** | Originally an English surname. Also a girl's name | |
| Rishi | Ray of light (Sanskrit) | |
| **Roald** | Famous ruler (Norwegian) May have gained in popularity thanks to children's author Roald Dahl | |
| Robbie | Short for Robert | *Rob / Rabbie, Robby* |

| Name | Definition | Short forms/ Variations |
|------|-----------|------------------------|
| **Robert** | Bright, shining fame (Germanic) | *Bob, Bobby, Rob, Robbie, Robby / Roberto* |
| Roberto | [Rob-air-toe] Italian or Spanish form of Robert: bright, shining fame | |
| **Robson** | Originally an English surname, meaning son of Robert | |
| Rocco | Rest (Germanic) | *Rocky* |
| **Roch** | [Rosh] French form of Rocco: rest | |
| Rocket | Spaceship (English). May also mean travels quickly | |
| **Rockwell** | Originally an English surname, meaning rocky spring | |
| Rocky | Short for Rocco | |
| **Roddy** | Short for Roderick or Rodney | *Rod / Roddie* |
| Rodeo | [Roe-day-oh] Round-up (French) Usually connected with the event where cowboys compete to ride wild horses or round up cattle | |
| **Roderick** | Famous rule (Old German) | *Rod, Roddie, Roddy / Roderic* |
| Rodney | Originally a surname | *Rod, Roddie, Roddy* |
| **Rodolfo** | Spanish form of Rudolf: famous wolf | |
| Rodrigo | Fame and power (Visigothic) | *Rodriguez* |
| **Rodriguez** | See Rodrigo | |
| Roger | Illustrious warrior (Old German) | |
| **Rohan** | Originally an aristocratic French surname | |

| Name | Definition | Short forms/ Variations |
|------|-----------|-------------------------|
| Roland | Fame; land (Germanic) | Roly / Rowland |
| Rolf | Famous wolf (Germanic) | Rollo, Rolph, Rudolf |
| Rollins | Originally a surname | |
| Rollo | Latin form of Rolf | |
| Roly | Short for Roland | |
| Roman | Roman (Latin) | Romano |
| Romeo | Pilgrim to Rome (Latin) The tragic lover in Shakespeare's *Romeo and Juliet*. Used by footballer David Beckham for his second son. | |
| Romney | Originally a Welsh surname, meaning winding river | |
| Romulo | Italian form of Romulus: according to legend, one of the founders of Rome | |
| Romulus | According to legend, one of the founders of Rome | |
| Ron | Short for Ronald | |
| Ronald | Scottish form of Reynold: ruler's decision. May have gained in popularity thanks to Ron (Ronald) Weasley, Harry's best friend in JK Rowling's Harry Potter novels | Ron, Ronnie, Ronny / Ranald |
| Ronan | Little seal (Irish) In Celtic legend, a seal is trapped on land in human form. She marries a mortal and has children, but eventually goes back to the sea – although she can always be seen swimming close by, keeping an eye on her family | |
| Ronit | Song (Sanskrit) | |
| Ronnie | Short for Ronald. Also a girl's name | Ron / Ronny |
| Rooney | Red-haired (Irish Gaelic) May be given in homage to the American actor Mickey Rooney or, more recently, the English footballer Wayne Rooney | |
| Roosevelt | Originally a Dutch surname, meaning wild rose. In the US, it's sometimes given in homage to former presidents Theodore Roosevelt or Franklin Delano Roosevelt | |
| Rory | Red king (Irish Gaelic) | Rorie |
| Roscoe | Originally a surname, meaning roe deer wood | |

| Name | Definition | Short forms/ Variations |
| --- | --- | --- |
| **Roshan** | Shining (Persian) Famous (Urdu) Also a girl's name | |
| Ross | Originally a Scottish surname, meaning headland | |
| **Roswell** | Originally an English surname, meaning rose spring | |
| Roth | Red (Old German) | |
| **Rover** | Wanderer, traveller (Middle English) | |
| Roy | Red (Gaelic) King (Old French) | |
| **Royal** | Royal (English) | |
| Royce | Originally a surname, meaning son of the king (Old French) Also linked to Rolls-Royce, the luxury cars | |
| **Ruben** | See **Reuben** | |
| Rudi | Short for Rudolf | *Rudy* |
| **Rudolf** | See **Rolf** | *Rudi, Rudy / Rodolf, Rodolfo, Rodolph, Rodolphe, Rudolph* |
| Rudy | See **Rudi** | |
| **Rudyard** | May be given in homage to English writer Rudyard Kipling, author of 19th-century children's novel *The Jungle Book*. He was named after Rudyard Lake in Staffordshire | |
| Rufus | Red or ruddy (Latin) | |
| **Rune** | A letter cut in stone (Old Norse) | |
| Rupert | German form of Robert: bright, shining fame | |
| **Rupesh** | Lord of beauty (Sanskrit) | |
| Rupinder | God of beauty (Sikh) Also a girl's name | |
| **Russ** | Short for Russell | |
| Russell | Originally a French surname, meaning little red one | *Russ* |
| **Rutherford** | Originally an English surname, meaning cattle crossing | |
| Rutledge | Originally an Old Norse surname, meaning red ledge | |
| **Ryan** | Little king (Irish) | *Rian* |
| Ryder | Originally a surname, meaning horse rider. Also a girl's name | *Rider* |

S

boys' names

| Name | Definition | Short forms/Variations |
|------|-----------|------------------------|
| **Sabir** | Patient (Arabic) | |
| Sabre | [Say-br] Sword (English) | *Saber* |
| **Saburo** | Third son (Japanese) | |
| Sacha | [Sash-uh] Short for Alexander. Also a girl's name | *Sasha* |
| **Sachin** | Affectionate (Sanskrit) Also another name for Lord Shiva | |
| Sadhi | Perfect (Sanskrit) | |
| **Sadler** | Originally an English surname, meaning saddler | |
| Saeed | [Sigh-eed] Holy (Arabic) | |
| **Safa** | Purity; sincerity (Arabic) Also a girl's name | |
| Sagar | Sea (Sanskrit) | |
| **Said** | Happy, lucky (Arabic) | |
| Sal | Short for Salvador or Salvatore | |
| **Salah** | Goodness (Arabic) | |
| Salim | Safe (Arabic) | |

| Name | Definition | Short forms/ Variations |
|------|-----------|------------------------|
| **Salvador** | Saviour (Latin) May be given in homage to the Spanish surrealist artist Salvador Dali | *Sal* |
| Salvatore | [Sal-vah-tor-ay] Italian form of Salvador: saviour | *Sal* |
| **Sam** | Short for Sami, Samir, Samson or Samuel | *Sammy / Sammy* |
| Sami | Sublime (Arabic) | *Sam* |
| **Samir** | Companion (Sanskrit) | *Sam / Sameer* |
| Sammy | See **Sam** | |
| **Samson** | Sun (Hebrew) In the Bible, Samson is a Jewish champion whose strength lies in his hair. His mistress, Delilah, finds out his secret, cuts his hair and betrays him to the Philistines. He is captured but God gives him a final bout of strength to pull down the Philistines' temple, killing himself and everyone in it | *Sam / Sampson* |
| Samuel | Asked of God (Hebrew) | *Sam, Sammy* |
| **Sancho** | [San-sho] Holy (Latin) | |
| Sandeep | Glowing (Sanskrit) | |
| **Sanders** | Short for Alexander | *Sandy / Saunders* |
| Sandy | Short for Alexander | |
| **Sanford** | Originally an English surname, meaning sandy ford | |
| Sanjay | Victorious (Sanskrit) | |
| **Santiago** | St James (Spanish) | |
| Santos | Saints (Spanish) | |
| **Sasha** | Short for Alexander | |
| Satchel | Bag (English) The jazz trumpeter and vocalist Louis Armstrong had the nickname 'Satchmo', for satchel-mouth. | |
| **Satoshi** | Quick-witted (Japanese) | |
| Saul | Asked for (Hebrew) | |
| **Savy** | Short for Xavier | |
| Saxon | A German people who invaded England (then Britannia) in the 5th century | |
| **Scanlon** | Trapper (Irish Gaelic) | |
| Scott | Scottish | *Scottie* |

| Name | Definition | Short forms/ Variations |
|------|-----------|-------------------------|
| **Scully** | Town crier (Irish Gaelic) May have increased in popularity thanks to Dana Scully, the sceptical FBI agent played by Gillian Anderson in American TV drama *The X-Files.* Also a girl's name | |
| Seamus | [Shay-mus] Modern Irish form of James: supplanter | *Seamas, Shamus* |
| **Sean** | [Shorn] Irish form of John: God is gracious | *Shane, Shaun, Shawn* |
| Seb | Short for Sebastian | |
| **Sebastian** | Venerable (Greek) | *Bastie, Basty, Seb* |
| Sekani | A Native Canadian people living in British Columbia. The name means 'dwellers on the rocks' | |
| **Selig** | Blessed; happy (Yiddish) | *Zelig* |
| Selwyn | Savage (Old French) | |
| **Septimus** | Seventh (Latin) | |
| Seraphim | An order of angels (Hebrew) | *Serafim* |
| **Sergei** | [Ser-gay] See **Sergio** | *Sergej* |
| Sergio | [Sur-jee-oh] Originally a Roman family name | |
| **Seth** | God has appointed (Hebrew) | |
| Seumas | [Shay-mus] Scottish form of James: supplanter | *Seamus* |
| **Seun** | Son (African) | |
| Seung | Winning (Korean) | |
| **Seven** | The number seven (English). Often thought to be a lucky number | |
| Seymour | Originally an aristocratic French surname | |
| **Shadrach** | [Shad-rak or Shay-drak] Command of Aku, the Babylonian god of the moon (Babylonian) | |
| Shafiq | Compassionate (Arabic) | |
| **Shakil** | Handsome (Arabic) | |
| Shakir | Thankful (Arabic) | |
| **Shamus** | English form of Seumas: supplanter | |
| Shan | Mountain (Chinese) Also a girl's name | |
| **Shane** | See **Sean** | |
| Sharif | Honourable (Arabic) | *Shareef* |
| **Shaun** | See **Sean** | |

| Name | Definition | Short forms/ Variations |
|---|---|---|
| Shaw | Originally an English surname, meaning copse | |
| **Shawn** | English form of Sean: God is gracious | |
| Shay | See **Shea** | |
| **Shea** | [Shay] Originally an Irish surname. Also a girl's name | *Shae, Shay* |
| Sheehan | Small and peaceful (Irish Gaelic) | |
| **Sheen** | Originally an Irish surname, meaning peaceful | |
| Shelby | Originally an English surname. Also a girl's name | |
| **Sheldon** | Originally an English surname | |
| Shem | Name (Hebrew) In the Bible, Shem was one of Noah's three sons | |
| **Sher** | Hope (Persian) | |
| Sheridan | Originally an Irish surname, meaning to seek. Also a girl's name | |
| **Sherlock** | Bright hair (Old English) May have increased in popularity thanks to Sir Arthur Conan Doyle's fictional detective, Sherlock Holmes | |
| Sherman | Originally a surname. May have gained in popularity thanks to 19th-century American civil war general William Tecumseh Sherman | |

| Name | Definition | Short forms/ Variations |
|---|---|---|
| **Shiloh** | [Shy-lo] He who is to be sent (Hebrew) In the Bible, this may refer to the Messiah. Occasionally used for girls | |
| Shiro | [Shee-ro] Fourth son (Japanese) | |
| **Sholto** | Fruitful (Gaelic) | |
| Sidney | Originally an aristocratic surname, meaning wide meadow. It gained in popularity thanks to Sydney Carton, the hero of Charles Dickens's 19th-century novel *A Tale of Two Cities*. Also a girl's name | *Sid, Syd* / *Sydney* |
| **Siegfried** | [Zeek-freet] Peace through victory (Germanic) Siegfried is a heroic character in Germanic legend | |
| Sigmund | [Zeeg-munt] Protector of victory (Germanic) Sometimes given in homage to the father of psychoanalysis, Sigmund Freud | |
| **Sigourney** | Conqueror (Scandinavian) Also a girl's name | |
| Silas | Wood (Latin) | |
| **Silvano** | Wood (Latin) | *Silvan, Sylvan* / *Silvanus, Sylvano, Sylvanus* |
| Silvester | Of the woods (Latin) | *Sly* / *Sylvester* |
| **Sim** | Short for Simcha or Simeon | |
| Simcha | Joy (Hebrew) Also a girl's name | *Sim* |
| **Simeon** | Hearkening (Hebrew) | *Sim* / *Simon* |
| Simon | English form of Simeon: hearkening | *Si* |
| **Simpson** | Originally an English surname, meaning Simon's son | |
| Sinai | [Sine-ay-eye] From Mount Sinai. In the Bible, this is the place where God gave Moses the Ten Commandments. Also a girl's name | |
| **Sinbad** | In the Middle Eastern epic *Arabian Nights*, Sinbad is a witty and ingenious sailor who has many adventures during his voyages | *Sindbad* |
| Sinclair | Originally a Norman/Scottish surname; taken from a place called Saint-Clair in La Manche, northern France | |
| **Sion** | Welsh form of John: God is gracious | |
| Skipper | Ship's captain (Middle Dutch) | *Skip* |

| Name | Definition | Short forms/ Variations |
|------|-----------|------------------------|
| **Skylar** | Scholar (Dutch) | |
| Slade | Originally an English surname, meaning valley | |
| **Slater** | Originally a surname, meaning somone who fixed slate roof tiles | |
| Sly | Short for Silvester or Sylvester | |
| **Smith** | Originally an English surname, meaning blacksmith | |
| Sohan | Handsome (Sanskrit) | |
| **Sol** | Sun (Latin) Also a girl's name | |
| Solomon | Peace (Hebrew) In the Bible, King Solomon was renowned for his wisdom | *Sol* |
| **Sonny** | Affectionate form of son (American) | |
| Sorley | Originally a Scottish and Irish surname, meaning summer wanderer | |
| **Spencer** | Originally a surname, meaning dispenser of supplies. May have gained in popularity thanks to American actor Spencer Tracy | |
| Spike | Usually given because of a baby's spiky hair! The name has become more popular thanks to band leader Spike Jones, comedian Spike Milligan and film director Spike Lee | *Spiker* |
| **Spiker** | See Spike | |
| Spyridon | Spirit (Latin) | *Spiro, Spyro* |
| **Spyro** | [Spigh-ro] Short for Spyridon | *Spiro* |
| St John | [Sin-jn] Devotee of St John | |
| **Stacey** | Short for Eustace. Now more common as a girl's name | *Stacy* |
| Stan | Short for Stanislas or Stanley | |
| **Stanislas** | Government's glory (Slavonic) | *Stan / Stanislaus, Stanislav* |
| Stanley | Originally a surname, meaning stone wood | *Stan* |
| **Stavros** | Cross (Greek) | |
| Steele | Steel (Old English) | |
| **Stefan** | Dutch, German, Polish and Scandinavian form of Stephen: crown | *Stef* |
| Stefano | Italian form of Stephen: crown | *Stef* |
| **Steffan** | Welsh form of Stephen: crown | *Stef* |

| Name | Definition | Short forms/Variations |
|---|---|---|
| Steinbeck | Originally a German surname, meaning stony brook. May be given in homage to American writer John Steinbeck, author of *The Grapes of Wrath* | |
| **Stephanos** | Greek form of Stephen: crown | |
| Stephen | Crown (Greek) | *Steve, Stevie / Étienne, Stefan, Stefano, Steffan, Steven* |
| **Sterling** | Originally an English surname, meaning little star | *Stirling* |
| Steve | Short for Stephen or Steven | |
| **Steven** | See **Stephen** | *Steve, Stevie* |
| Stevie | Short for Stephen or Steven. Also a girl's name | |
| **Stewart** | See **Stuart** | *Stu* |
| Stig | Wanderer (Old Norse) | |
| **Sting** | May have increased in popularity thanks to English rock musician Sting (born Gordon Matthew Thomas Sumner), whose stage name was apparently inspired by a black and yellow striped sweater that made him look like a bee | |
| Stockard | Originally an English surname, meaning tree stump. Also a girl's name | |
| **Stu** | Short for Stewart or Stuart | |
| Stuart | Originally a Scottish surname, meaning steward | *Stu / Stewart* |
| **Sudeep** | Bright, radiant (Sanskrit) | |
| Sullivan | Originally an Irish surname, meaning dark eyes | |
| **Sultan** | King; leader (Arabic) | |
| Suman | Wise and cheerful (Sanskrit) | |
| **Suresh** | Ruler of the gods (Sanskrit) | |
| Sven | Boy (Swedish) | |
| **Sweeney** | Little hero (Irish Gaelic) | |
| Sydney | See **Sidney** | |
| **Sylvan** | Of the woods (Latin) | |
| Sylvester | See **Silvester** | |

boys' names | S

| Name | Definition | Short forms/Variations |
|------|-----------|------------------------|
| Tad | Short for Thaddeus | *Thaddy* |
| **Tadhg** | [Tyg] Poet or philosopher (Irish) | *Tadhgh, Teague* |
| Taff | See **Taffy** | |
| **Taffy** | Short for Dafydd | *Taff* |
| Tahir | Virtuous (Arabic) | |
| **Taj** | Crown; jewel (Arabic) | |
| Talbot | Originally an aristocratic surname | |
| **Tanay** | Son (Sanskrit) | |
| Tancred | Thought counsel (Old German) | |
| **Tanner** | Originally an English surname, meaning someone who treated animal skins to make leather | |
| Tanvir | Illuminating (Arabic) Also a girl's name | |
| **Tao** | Great waves (Chinese) | |
| Taran | Heaven; thunder (Sanskrit) Also another name for Lord Vishnu | |
| **Tariq** | A morning star (Arabic) | |
| Tarquin | The family name of a line of Roman kings | |

| Name | Definition | Short forms/ Variations |
|---|---|---|
| **Tarun** | Youth (Sanskrit) | |
| Tate | Originally an English surname, meaning cheerful. Also a girl's name | |
| **Tatum** | Originally an English surname, meaning Tate's homestead. Also a girl's name | |
| Tavish | Heaven; lively (Sanskrit) | |
| **Tay** | The name of a river in the Scottish Highlands – the largest river in the UK | |
| Taylor | Originally a surname, meaning tailor. Also a girl's name | *Tayler* |
| **Teague** | [Teeg] English form of Tadhg: poet or philosopher. Also a girl's name | *Teigue* |
| Ted | See **Teddy** | |
| **Teddy** | Short for Edward, Edwin or Theodore | *Ted / Teddie, Teddy* |
| Tegan | [Tee-g'n] See **Teague** | |
| **Tej** | Light (Sanskrit) | |
| Templar | The Knights Templar was a medieval Christian order of warrior monks | |
| **Temple** | See Templar | |
| Templeton | Originally an English surname, meaning town or village with a temple | |
| **Tennyson** | Originally a surname, meaning son of Tenny (a medieval form of Dennis) May be given in homage to 19th-century English poet Alfred Lord Tennyson | |
| Terence | Instigator (Irish) | *Terry / Terrence* |
| **Terry** | Short for Terence | |
| Tex | Someone from Texas | |
| **Thad** | Short for Thaddeus | |
| Thaddeus | Gift of God (Greek) | *Tad, Thad, Thaddy / Thaddaeus* |
| **Thane** | Servant (Old English) In Scotland, it's the title of a clan chief | |
| Theo | Short for Theobald, Theodore or Theophilus | |
| **Theobald** | Brave people (Germanic) | *Theo / Tybalt* |
| Theodore | Gift from God (Greek) | *Ted, Teddie, Teddy, Theo / Theodoros, Tudor* |

| Name | Definition | Short forms/ Variations |
|------|-----------|------------------------|
| **Theodoros** | See Theodore | |
| Theophilus | Loved by God (Greek) | *Theo* |
| **Thomas** | Twin (Aramaic) | *Thom, Tom, Tommie, Tommy / Tomas* |
| Thompson | Originally an English surname, meaning son of Tom | *Thomson* |
| **Thor** | Norse god of thunder | |
| Thorold | Thor's rule (Teutonic) | *Thor / Thorald* |
| **Thurstan** | Thor's stone (Anglo Saxon) | |
| Tiernan | See **Tierney** | |
| **Tierney** | Originally an Irish surname, meaning kingly. Also a girl's name | *Tiernan* |
| Tim | Short for Timothy | *Timmie, Timmy* |
| **Timon** | [Ty-mon] Honour, esteem (Greek) In Shakespeare's *Timon of Athens*, Timon is a rich man with many false friends. He ends up hating them all | |
| Timothy | Honour God (Greek) | *Tim, Timmie, Timmy* |
| **Tirian** | Gentle (Welsh) | *Tirion* |
| Titan | In Greek legend, the Titans are a race of powerful gods | |
| **Tito** | [Tee-toe] Italian or Spanish form of Titus. In the Bible, Titus was a disciple of St Paul | |
| Titus | [Tigh-tuss] In the Bible, Titus was a disciple of St Paul | *Tito* |
| **Tobias** | [Toe-by-ass] God is good (Hebrew) | *Toby / Tobin* |
| Tobin | [Toe-bin] See **Tobias** | |

| Name | Definition | Short forms/<br>Variations |
|------|------------|---------------------------|
| **Toby** | Short for Tobias | |
| Todd | Originally an English surname, meaning fox | |
| **Tolly** | Short for Bartholomew | |
| Tom | Short for Thomas | *Tommie, Tommy /*<br>*Thom* |
| **Tomas** | [Toh-mash] Swedish form of Thomas: twin | |
| Tomek | Polish pet form of Thomas: twin | |
| **Tony** | Short for Anthony or Antoine | |
| Tor | Taken from Thor, the Norse god of thunder | *Tore* |
| **Torcan** | Wild boar (Irish) | |
| Torkel | See **Torquil** | |
| **Tormod** | Thor's courage (Old Norse) | |
| Torq | Short for Torquil | |
| **Torquil** | Thor's cauldron (Old Norse) | *Torq / Torkel* |
| Torsten | Thor's stone (Danish and Swedish) | |
| **Toru** | Wayfarer (Japanese) | |
| Torvald | Thor is ruler (Old Norse) | |
| **Toyah** | A small town in Texas. Also a girl's name | |
| Tracy | Originally a surname. Traditionally a boy's name, but now almost exclusively used for girls | |
| **Travis** | Originally a surname, meaning toll keeper | |
| Trevelyan | Originally a Cornish surname, meaning Elian's homestead | |
| **Trevor** | Originally a Welsh surname, meaning large settlement | *Trefor* |
| Trey | Three (Latin) | |
| **Trip** | Traveller (English) | *Tripp* |
| Tristan | Sad (Latin) The legend of lovers Tristan and Isolde was a popular medieval romance. Tristan died of battle wounds and Isolde died of grief | *Tris / Tristram* |
| **Tristram** | See Tristan | *Drystan* |
| Truman | Originally a surname, meaning trusted man. It may have gained in popularity thanks to Truman Capote, American author of *Breakfast at Tiffany's*, or former American president Harry S Truman | |

| Name | Definition | Short forms/Variations |
|------|-----------|------------------------|
| **Tuathal** | Ruler of a tribe (Irish) | |
| Tucker | Originally an English surname, meaning garment maker | |
| **Tudor** | Welsh form of Theodore: gift from God | |
| Turag | Thought; swift mover (Sanskrit) | |
| **Turner** | Originally an English surname, meaning wood turner | |
| Tushar | Dew (Sanskrit) | |
| **Twain** | Two (Old English) May have gained in popularity thanks to American writer Mark Twain (born Samuel Langhorne Clemens), author of *Adventures of Huckleberry Finn*. The pen name 'Mark Twain' came from an expression used on Mississippi steamboats, meaning the depth of the water measured two fathoms | |
| Tybalt | [Tib-ahlt] See **Theobald** | |
| **Tyler** | Originally a surname, meaning roof tiler. In the US, it may be given in homage to former president John Tyler. Also a girl's name. | *Ty* |
| Tyr | In Old Norse myth, Tyr was god of war and justice | |
| **Tyrrell** | Originally a surname, possibly meaning stubborn | *Tirrell* |
| Tyson | Firebrand (Old French) | |

| Name | Definition | Short forms/ Variations |
|------|------------|--------------------------|
| **Uday** | Sunrise; prosperity (Sanskrit) | |
| Uland | Noble country (Germanic) | |
| **Ulf** | Wolf (Old Norse) | |
| Ulick | Mind reward (Gaelic) | |
| **Ulric** | [Ull-rik] Wolf power (Old English) | *Ulrich, Ulrick* |
| Ulysses | [Yu-la-seez] Latin form of Odysseus. In the US, it may be given in homage to 19th-century president Ulysses S Grant | |
| **Urban** | City dweller (Latin) | |
| Uri | [Yur-ee] Light (Hebrew) | |
| **Uriah** | [Yur-eye-ah] God is my light (Hebrew) | |
| Uriel | God is my light (Hebrew) | |
| **Urquhart** | [Ur-kut] Originally a Scottish surname, meaning at the woodside | |
| Usher | Door keeper (Old French) | |
| **Utpal** | Blue lotus (Sanskrit) | |

| Name | Definition | Short forms/ Variations |
|------|-----------|------------------------|
| Vada | Rose (Hebrew) Also a girl's name | |
| Val | Short for Valentine, Valerian or Valerius | |
| Valentine | Healthy; strong (Latin) The feast of St Valentine is celebrated on 14 February, which coincided with a pagan fertility festival – hence the modern St Valentine's Day | Val / Valentin, Valentino |
| Valerian | See Valerius | Val |
| Valerius | Healthy, strong (Latin) | Val / Valerian |
| Vanna | Golden (Khmer) Also a girl's name | |
| Vansh | Son (Sanskrit) | |
| Vanya | Pet form of Ivan. Occasionally used for girls | |
| Varad | God of fire (Sanskrit) | |
| Varin | Gifts (Sanskrit) | |
| Vaughan | [Vorn] Originally a Welsh surname, meaning small | Vaughn |
| Veer | Hero (Sanskrit) | |
| Vere | [Veer] Originally an aristocratic French surname | |

| Name | Definition | Short forms/ Variations |
|------|-----------|------------------------|
| **Vernon** | Originally an aristocratic French surname, meaning place of alders | |
| Vic | Short for Victor | |
| **Victor** | Conqueror (Latin) | *Vic / Vittorio* |
| Vidal | [Vee-dal] Life (Hebrew) Lively (Latin) | |
| **Viggo** | War (Old Danish) | |
| Vijay | Victory (Sanskrit) | |
| **Vik** | Short for Vikram | |
| Vikram | Brave (Sanskrit) | *Vik* |
| **Vin** | Short for Vincent | |
| Vince | Short for Vincent | |
| **Vincent** | To conquer (Latin) Sometimes given in homage to 19th-century painter Vincent Van Gogh | *Vin, Vince, Vinny / Vincenzo* |
| Vincenzo | [Vin-chen-zo] Italian form of Vincent: to conquer | |
| **Vinesh** | [Vin-esh] Religious (Sanskrit) | |
| Vinny | Short for Vincent | |
| **Virgil** | May be given in homage to the ancient Roman poet, writer of the epic *Aeneid* | |
| Vitale | [Vit-ah-lay] Italian form of Vitalis: full of life, vital | |
| **Vitalis** | [Vit-ah-lis] Full of life, vital (Latin) | *Vitale* |
| Vittorio | Italian form of Victor: conqueror | |
| **Viv** | Short for Vivian | |
| Vivek | Intellect (Sanskrit) | |
| **Vivian** | Alive (Latin) | *Viv* |
| Vlad | Short for Vladimir | |
| **Vladimir** | Great ruler (Slavonic) | *Vlad* |

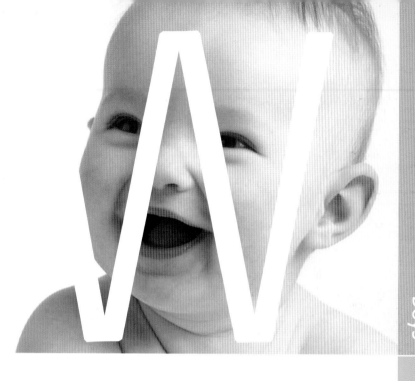

| Name | Definition | Short forms/ Variations |
|------|-----------|------------------------|
| **Wade** | Originally an English surname, meaning ford | |
| Wagner | Originally a German surname, meaning wagon builder. May be given in homage to 19th-century German composer Richard Wagner | |
| **Walden** | Wooded valley (Old English) | |
| Waldo | Rule (Germanic) | |
| **Walker** | Originally an English surname, meaning traveller | |
| Wallace | Originally a surname, meaning foreign. Sometimes given in homage to the Scottish patriot Sir William Wallace, depicted in the 1995 film *Braveheart* | *Wallis* |
| **Walsh** | Welsh (Old English) | |
| Walt | Short for Walter | |
| **Walter** | Folk ruler (Old German) Sometimes given in homage to 19th-century American poet Walt (Walter) Whitman | *Walt, Wat* |
| Walton | Originally an English surname, meaning walled town or village | |
| **Ward** | Originally a surname, meaning watchman | |

| Name | Definition | Short forms/ Variations |
|------|-----------|-------------------------|
| Warner | Originally a Norman surname, meaning a man who watched out for ships as they approached the harbour | |
| Warren | Originally a French surname. It may have increased in popularity thanks to *Bonnie and Clyde* actor Warren Beatty | |
| Washington | Originally a surname. Usually given in homage to George Washington, the first US president | |
| Wasim | Handsome (Arabic) | |
| Wat | Short for Walter | |
| Waverley | Originally an English surname, meaning wood or meadow with aspen trees | |
| Wayne | Originally a surname, meaning carter. Its popularity may be thanks to American actor John Wayne | |
| Webster | Originally a surname, meaning weaver | |
| Weldon | Originally a surname, meaning hill with a spring | |
| Wenceslas | Greater glory (Slavic) | |
| Wendell | Wandering man (Old German) | |
| Wensley | Originally a surname, meaning clearing sacred to the Germanic god Woden | |
| Wesley | Originally an English surname, meaning west wood. Sometimes given in homage to the founder of the Methodist Church, John Wesley, and his brother, the preacher Charles Wesley | *Wes* |
| Weston | Originally a surname, meaning west town or village | *West* |
| Whistler | Originally a surname. May be given in homage to the American-born artist James Abbott McNeill Whistler | |
| Whitney | Originally an English surname, meaning white island. Also a girl's name | |
| Whittaker | Originally an English surname, meaning white field | *Whitaker* |
| Wilberforce | Originally a surname, meaning Wilbur's ditch | |
| Wilbur | Desire; fortress (Old English) | |
| Wilder | Originally a German surname, meaning wild, untamed | |

| Name | Definition | Short forms/ Variations |
|------|-----------|------------------------|
| Wilfred | Desiring peace (Old English) May have gained in popularity thanks to the WW1 poet Wilfred Owen | *Fred, Freddie, Wilf / Wilfrid* |
| Wilhelm | German form of William: protector | |
| Will | Short for Willard, William, Willis or Willoughby | |
| Willard | Desire; bravery (Old English) | *Will* |
| William | Protector (Germanic) | *Bill, Billy, Liam, Will / Wilhelm, Willis* |
| Willis | See William | *Will* |
| Willoughby | [Will-uh-bee] Originally an English surname, meaning a settlement by a willow tree | *Will* |
| Wilmer | Willing warrior (Teutonic) | |
| Wilson | Will's son. In the US, it's sometimes given in homage to president Woodrow Wilson | |
| Wilton | Originally an English surname, meaning well town or village | |
| Winslow | Originally an English surname, meaning friend's hill | |
| Winston | Joy; stone (Old English) Sometimes given in homage to Britain's WW2 prime minister Sir Winston Churchill | *Win* |
| Winthrop | Originally an English surname, meaning friend's village | |
| Wolfgang | Travelling wolf (Germanic) May be given in homage to 18th-century Austrian composer Wolfgang Amadeus Mozart | |
| Wolfram | Wolf and raven (Germanic) | |

boys'

W

names

| Name | Definition | Short forms/ Variations |
|------|-----------|------------------------|
| **Woodrow** | Originally a surname, meaning row of houses by a wood. In the US, it's sometimes given in homage to president Woodrow Wilson | *Woody* |
| Woodward | Originally an English surname, meaning warden of the wood | |
| **Woody** | Short for Edward or Woodrow. May be given in homage to American folk singer Woody Guthrie or American actor and film director Woody Allen | |
| Wordsworth | Originally an English surname. May be given in homage to English Romantic poet William Wordsworth | |
| **Worth** | Originally an English surname, meaning fenced farm | |
| Wyatt | Originally an English surname, meaning brave in war | |
| **Wyndham** | Originally a surname, meaning Wyman's homestead | |
| Wystan | Battle stone (Old English) | |

| Name | Definition | Short forms/ Variations |
|------|-----------|-------------------------|
| **Xander** | [Zan-der or Zarn-der] Short for Alexander | |
| Xanthus | [Zan-thus] Golden-haired (Greek) | |
| **Xavier** | [Zav-ee-ay] From Javier in Navarre, northern Spain | *Savy / Javier* |
| Xenos | [Zee-nos] Stranger (Greek) | |
| **Xerxes** | [Zurk-sees] Ruler over heroes (Greek) | |

| Name | Definition | Short forms/ Variations |
|------|-----------|-------------------------|
| Yael | See Jael | |
| **Yale** | Originally a Welsh surname, meaning fertile upland. | |
| Yates | Originally an English surname, meaning gates or gatekeeper | *Yeats* |
| **Yeats** | See Yates. May be given in homage to the Irish poet and dramatist William Butler Yeats | |
| Yehudi | Jew (Hebrew) May have gained in popularity thanks to violinist Yehudi Menuhin | |
| **Yevgeni** | Russian form of Eugene: well-born, noble | |
| Yi | Result (Chinese) | |
| **Yosef** | Hebrew form of Joseph: God shall add | |
| Yoshi | Good (Japanese) Also a girl's name | |
| **Yoshito** | Good man; lucky man (Japanese) | |
| Yule | Winter solstice (Old English) | |
| **Yuri** | Russian form of George: farmer | |
| Yusuf | Arabic form of Joseph: God shall add | *Yousif* |
| **Yuvraj** | Young king (Sanskrit) | |
| Yves | [Eeves] Yew (Germanic) | *Ivo, Yvain* |

| Name | Definition | Short forms/ Variations |
|------|-----------|-------------------------|
| Zach | Short for Isaac, Zacharias, Zachary or Zechariah | Zac, Zack, Zak |
| Zacharias | See **Zechariah** | Zach, Zack, Zak / Zachariah, Zachary |
| Zachary | [Zak-ar-ee] See **Zechariah** | Zach, Zack, Zak, Zooey / Zachariah, Zacharias |
| Zadok | [Zay-dok] Righteous (Hebrew) | |
| Zahir | Shining, radiant (Arabic) | |
| Zaki | Virtuous (Arabic) | |
| Zakir | Someone who thinks of God constantly (Arabic) | |
| Zane | Originally a surname | |
| Zappa | Originally a surname. May have gained in popularity thanks to American rock musician Frank Zappa | |
| Zayd | Growth (Arabic) | |
| Zayn | Good looks; grace (Arabic) | |
| Zeb | Short for Zebadiah, Zebedee or Zebulun | |

| Name | Definition | Short forms/ Variations |
|------|------------|-------------------------|
| Zebadiah | Gift of Jehovah (Hebrew) | *Zeb / Zebedee, Zebediah* |
| **Zebedee** | See Zebadiah | *Zeb* |
| Zebulun | To live (Hebrew) | *Zeb / Zebulon* |
| **Zechariah** | God has remembered (Hebrew) | *Zach, Zack, Zak / Zachariah, Zacharias, Zachary* |
| Zed | Short for Zedekiah | |
| **Zedekiah** | Justice of Yahweh (God) (Hebrew) | *Zed* |
| Zeev | Wolf (Hebrew) | |
| **Zeke** | Short for Ezekiel | |
| Zelig | See **Selig** | |
| **Zen** | A form of Buddhism | |
| Zeno | Taken from Zeus, in Greek legend, king of the gods | |
| **Zeph** | Short for Zephaniah | |
| Zephaniah | Hidden by God (Hebrew) | *Zeph* |
| **Zeus** | [Z'yoos] In Greek legend, Zeus was king of the gods | |
| Zhi | Ambition; wisdom (Chinese) Also a girl's name | |
| **Zhivago** | [Jhiv-ah-go] Life (Russian) May be given in homage to the idealistic hero of Boris Pasternak's 1957 novel *Doctor Zhivago* | |
| Zia | [Zee-uh] Splendour; light (Arabic) Also a girl's name | *Ziya* |
| **Zian** | Self peace (Chinese) | |
| Ziggy | To get rid of anger (Polish) The name may have increased in popularity thanks to musician David Bowie's 1970s alter ego Ziggy Stardust | |
| **Zion** | The name used to refer to a Jewish homeland and to heaven | |
| Zooey | Invented by novelist JD Salinger for Franny's brother in his cult 1961 book *Franny and Zooey*. In the book, it's short for Zachary. Also a girl's name | |
| **Zorba** | Live each day (Greek) | |